Life with Heroin

Life with Heroin

Voices from the Inner City

edited by

Bill Hanson
Mary Washington College

George Beschner
National Institute on Drug Abuse

James M. Walters
Citizens Crime Commission
of Delaware Valley

Elliott Bovelle
University of the District of Columbia

Lexington Books
D.C. Heath and Company/Lexington, Massachusetts/Toronto

Library of Congress Cataloging in Publication Data

Main entry under title:

Life with Heroin.

Bibliography: p.
1. Heroin habit—United States—Addresses, essays, lectures. 2. Afro-Americans—Drug use—Addresses, essays, lectures. 3. Narcotic addicts—United States—Addresses, essays, lectures. I. Hanson, William (William B.)
HV5822.H4H465 1985   306′.1   84-40722
ISBN 0-669-09933-3 (alk. paper)
ISBN 0-669-10303-9 (pbk.: alk. paper)

47,566

Second printing, October 1985
Published simultaneously in Canada
Printed in the United States of America on acid-free paper
International Standard Book Number: 0-669-09933-3 Casebound
International Standard Book Number: 0-669-10303-9 Paperbound
Library of Congress Catalog Card Number: 84-40722

Contents

Acknowledgments

The writing of this book was truly a collective effort. From the original idea for the heroin lifestyle study, through the collection, recording, coding, and analysis of data, to the planning and writing of the book itself, a large and diverse group of people participated. We are deeply grateful to the heroin users who agreed to be interviewed and who talked so freely about the intimate details and harsh conditions of their lives. Likewise, we are also greatly indebted to the indigenous interviewers who made the street contacts with current heroin users, screened them, and did the interviewing. Howard Elkins, Fred Graves, Allan Rhoades, Forrest Trotter, and Napoleon Turner were invaluable as "contact men" and sensitive, skilled interviewers. They also made important contributions to the development and authenticity of the interview schedule as well as to the selection of topics for analysis and writing. We are also grateful to the many experts in the drug abuse field who provided substantial advice throughout the project and whose commentary, analysis, and reviews played an important role in the development of the final product: Barry Brown, Harvey Feldman, John French, Alfred Friedman, Gerry Mandel, Ed Preble, Frank Tims, and Dan Waldorf. We would like to thank the drug researchers and/or drug clinic administrators who so willingly aided us in recruiting interviewers, establishing a network of field supervision, and coordinating our field and data-recording operations: Marsha Baumgardner, Christopher D'Amanda, Bill DeMarle, Caroline Katz, Lynn Kotranski, Carver Leach, David Nurco, Edward Senay, Yoav Santo, Father Ben Taylor, and John Watters. Additionally, grateful appreciation is extended to Kerry Treasure, Norma Wegner, and Margaret Blasinsky, who provided valuable editorial assistance on portions of the manuscript during its preparation. The book could not have been done without the ongoing editorial assistance and retyping of manuscript drafts by Debbie Brown.

1
Introduction

Bill Hanson

I'm talking about I'm trying to get out there and get something for me. Like a nice little piece of property where I could have me a nice little home that I could come to, you understand. My lady here and a couple of kids. I don't have to have a brand new car, you understand? Something that I can have me a place to keep me warm, I don't have to be cold, things like that. I don't want a whole lot, I just want . . . something, ya know. See, I been in the ghetto all my life. I been hustlin' all my life, and I can't put my hand on anything and say it's mine. I don't know if you can understand that, and I don't know if anyone else can understand. But to put your hand on the door of your house and come in and there's nobody livin' here but you and your family; and you open the door and know this is yours, it's a hell of a feelin'. You don't get a chance to get that, man. So, you get disgusted and discouraged and it's like there's nowhere to turn. (Dave, age 35, Philadelphia)

This book is about inner-city Black male heroin users. It relies on the users' own words to describe lives that revolve around the use of heroin—lifestyles in which a "jones" (heroin habit) is a constant companion. Most of these men have been shooting heroin daily for many years. Many have lived at the edge of survival and many have been arrested and served time in prison. All use heroin regularly and are active in street life, and most have never received or wanted any form of drug treatment. It is this "treatment-free" lifestyle that this book will describe and explain from the viewpoint of those men who live it hour by hour, day by day.

These men shared their lives by participating in the Heroin Lifestyle Study (HLS). In-depth interviews were conducted with 124 men in ghettos of Chicago, New York, Washington, D.C., and Philadelphia. The interviews, which were conducted by former heroin addicts, reveal a wide range of skills and adaptive strategies that enable the HLS men to survive and be a part of the daily routine of their neighborhoods. As they vividly report, this is not easy; the heroin lifestyle is demanding and full of complicated and contradictory emotions. These stories reveal men who, while mostly poor, are proud of their ability to control their lives and to obtain heroin regularly even in today's hard economic times. At the same time, they express remorse and self-blame for being "hooked," anger at and attraction to "straight" society, and frustration in their attempts to better their lives. Yet most have dreams and are hopeful about the future. While we update and question some previous knowledge regarding Black inner-city male heroin users, we seek to avoid replacing old stereotypes with new ones. Rather, the challenge of this book is reflected in our two interrelated goals: first, to accurately pass on the rich, descriptive firsthand accounts of the daily lives of Black heroin users who have not been in treatment; and second, to search for and analyze emergent patterns which reveal the complex social and psychological mosaic that comprises the contemporary Black inner-city heroin lifestyle.

In accomplishing these goals we have focused on similarities across cities rather than attempting a city-by-city comparison. Indeed, some differences do exist by city on selected social and demographic variables. However, the similarity of patterns in all four cities is striking, as revealed by the open-ended questions on the broader areas discussed in this book such as typical daily activities, types of hustlers, shooting heroin, the heroin high, language, self-esteem and attitudes toward treatment.[1]

It is clear from recent research (Gay 1972; Waldorf 1973; Waldorf and Biernacki 1979, 1981; Zinberg 1982) that a large number of people (Black and White) use heroin either on an experimental or regular basis, yet control their use and have never been in treatment. It has been estimated by Nightingale (Zinberg 1982) that there may be as many as 300,000 to 400,000 opiate addicts not in treatment and that the majority have never been in treatment. Instead, users learn to manage their habits. The purpose of the Heroin Lifestyle Study was to gain a better understanding of the life of inner-city Black male regular heroin users who have never been in drug treatment. Questions include the following: How do they typically spend their days? How do they perceive their own world and the social world around them? How and with whom do they socialize? From whom do they obtain money and win peer respect? Why did they start using heroin and how much do they actually use on a regular basis? How does shooting heroin and being "high" make them feel? Why do they continue to use heroin? How do they manage their "hustling" and "copping" (buying) activities and to what degree do they strive to regulate their heroin use? How do they remain treatment free? What are their attitudes about treatment?

Analysis of answers to these kinds of questions fills a gap in the research literature. Much of the current knowledge about heroin abuse comes from studies of users in treatment or prison. As a result, little is known about the daily lives of heroin users who are surviving in their communities but who have not sought treatment. Increased knowledge of this nontreatment population should contribute to a fuller and more accurate perception of the current inner-city Black male heroin lifestyle. This, in turn, will have important implications for formulating social policy during the next decade and will contribute to a more accurate public image of individual inner-city untreated Black male heroin users.

These two goals become clearer when viewed in the context of the emergence of the heroin problem in this country and the response to it. In the remainder of the chapter we outline past research on Black heroin users, discuss the rationale for our research approach, and conclude with an overview of the book.

Recent History of Heroin Abuse in the United States

Illegal drug use has been occurring for decades. It was not until the 1950s and 1960s, however, that it received widespread public attention. The 1960s were marked by the rise of the counterculture with its antiestablishment perspective symbolized by long hair, rock music, sexual freedom, and drugs. The counterculture image of heroin and heroin users was widely popularized in the media and in books such as Williams Burroughs *Junkie* (1953). This image became firmly implanted in the public mind during the mid-1960s, when assassinations, antiwar protests, and social unrest began to surface. Many observers began to link these uncomfortable social trends and rising crime and delinquency rates with illegal drug use.

Although abuse of specific drugs by many subpopulation groups (for example, marijuana by teenagers, sedatives by the middle-class and middle-aged, and heroin use among returning Vietnam veterans) was on the rise in the 1960s, use of heroin by poor Black inner-city dwellers received the greatest attention, in terms of its assumed association with crime. This assumption, made for perhaps racist and cultural reasons, was fostered by the marked increase in the number of Blacks residing within the central cities of metropolitan areas between 1950 and 1960. By 1966, the twelve largest northern cities contained over two-thirds of the Black population outside the South and almost one-third of the total U.S. Black population (Report of the National Advisory Commission on Civil Disorders, 1968).

Already crowded with poor, unskilled people looking for a better life, these central cities proved inhospitable. Many of the minority newcomers became victims of unemployment, poverty, and racial discrimination, and developed a sense of futility. Is it surprising that they sometimes coped with this situation by turning to drugs? We know, for instance, that heroin use became widespread among Black teenagers during the 1950s (Chein et al. 1964). By the late 1960s and early 1970s, Waldorf (1973) observed that:

Heroin is seemingly everywhere in Black and Puerto Rican ghettos and young people are aware of it from an early age. They know of heroin and addicts through close scrutiny—they see the endless trade of money for white powder; they see the user nodding on the front stoop; they watch him "get off" in the communal bathroom down the hall; they see his theft of the family TV set. It is a wonder, not that so many ghetto dwellers become users and addicts, but that the majority somehow, someway, resist this powerful drug that offers relief from the oppressive environment.

In addition, studies in the 1960s (Abrams et al. 1968; Ball and Chambers 1970) claimed that Blacks were disproportionately involved in illicit drug abuse, and the public continued to identify heroin addiction as a Black problem related to the poor inner-city neighborhoods where Blacks congregated. Dumont (1972) noted that, "like everything else that emerges from the ranks of an underclass, heroin addiction was perceived with rage and terror by middle America." The connection between illicit drug use and crime became one of the major issues in Richard Nixon's successful "law and order" presidential campaign of 1968. By February of 1970, the Nixon administration had publicly launched a two-pronged approach to reduce the supply of heroin and to establish an ambitious treatment system to reduce the demand for heroin.

A national opinion poll in 1971 reported that the public viewed drug addiction as the third most serious social problem facing the country (Nelkin 1973). This increased public concern and the federal drug-abuse policy of the early 1970s resulted in a rapid increase in the number of treatment facilities. By 1980, there were more than 3,000 federally funded drug-treatment programs in the United States capable of serving some 207,946 clients in a one-year period (National Institute on Drug Abuse 1981). Establishment of this treatment system appeared to be motivated in large part by the public's feeling that drug use—especially heroin use—was responsible for the increase in crime and for making the inner core of large cities violent and unsafe. As Jaffe (1979) notes, "the outpouring of concern for treatment did not stem from profound public empathy for the heroin addict, but rather from the belief that heroin addicts committed crimes and created other addicts."

Thus, in the 1960s and 1970s, the majority of treatment facilities for heroin addicts were established in and around inner-city communities. As a result, blacks constituted a disproportionate number of all heroin addicts in treatment facilities throughout the 1970s. According to data from the National Institute on Drug Abuse, by 1978 nearly half (44 percent) of all admissions to treatment centers were from minority groups; and Blacks (43.6 percent) and Hispanics (20 percent) comprised nearly two-thirds (63.6 percent) of all treatment admissions with heroin as the primary drug of use. In 1980, Blacks constituted 46 percent of clients in treatment who reported heroin as the primary drug of abuse (National Institute on Drug Abuse 1981).

Whether or not these and other facts suggest that minority people of color are more likely than Whites to develop serious drug (especially heroin) problems, Espada (1979) has made clear the disproportionate impact of substance misuse on minority individuals and communities. Yet, despite public awareness and federal and state programs, no large body of research or understanding has emerged about the relationship between social and ethnic variables and drug use and abuse.

Black Heroin Users and Past Research

In the past, the majority of drug studies were carried out on heroin users who were in treatment or in prison either at the time of the study or who had been previously.[2] Such studies did not focus on the social relationships and roles of addicts outside of treatment settings. A primary goal of these studies was to assess the role of racial and ethnic variables on the effectiveness of treatment. This assessment has typically taken place without consideration of the larger lifestyle context of the addicts and without information from addicts who have never been in treatment.

Some recent surveys have involved interviews with drug users in community settings who were not in treatment (for example, Brunswick 1977, 1979) and with adolescents and senior high school students (for example, Paton and Kandel 1978; Dembo et al. 1979, 1980). These studies have generally focused on correlating drug use patterns with selected social and psychological variables. Although useful knowledge has been gained from these and other studies, their intent was not to interview or observe respondents in their natural surroundings. Similarly, the investigators were not concerned with the dynamics of heroin use or with reporting drug users' own views of their social worlds as is typical of ethnographic approaches.

However, a small number of researchers using ethnographic and participant observation methods (see appendix) have studied various types of drug users, including heroin users, in their natural surroundings. Among the earliest of these were Lindesmith's study, *Opiate Addiction* (1947) and Becker's work (1953) on marijuana smokers. Since then, several classical ethnographic studies have focused on low-income urban heroin users. These studies, beginning with the publication of Finestone's "Cats, Kicks, and Color" (1957) through Preble and Casey's article "Taking Care of Business" (1969), have helped to present a view of heroin users from their own perspective: that is, an ethnographic view from the "inside" showing the meaning the heroin habit holds for the users themselves.[3]

The samples in these studies taken as a whole have included a large number of Black males, generally from inner city communities rather than from treatment agencies. Often, however, other ethnic groups and females were included as well, so that the focus was not exclusively on Black males. The studies also made no attempt to differentiate between users who had been in treatment and those who had not. Finally, none of these studies simultaneously sampled different urban areas; therefore, they lack the cross-regional perspective of the HLS. Of course, these earlier studies provided many insights as well as a new empirical and theoretical view of chronic low-income inner-city heroin users. Equally important, they stimulated an interest in ethnographic approaches which gave rise to a number of important studies in the 1970s. As with the earlier "classics" the findings from these more recent studies continued to point to the importance of understanding the meaning users attach to heroin use and to different aspects of their lifestyles.[4] They have helped change the focus of researchers and treatment personnel from an emphasis on the pathological traits of heroin users to a more holistic approach incorporating the insiders view and stressing the significance of larger social and cultural contexts.

Even these studies, however, have been somewhat narrowly focused. Many continued to use samples from a treatment population (or did not distinguish between users who had been in treatment and those who had not)[5] and samples containing respondents of mixed ethnicity. Although this permits useful ethnic comparisons to be made, it makes it more difficult to obtain an in-depth view of any one ethnic group and provides no information on treatment-free users.

Finally, although studies completed in the 1970s and early 1980s were undertaken with an understanding and appreciation of the knowledge gained from early ethnographic studies, they did not consistently employ research techniques which permitted respondents to "tell it like it is" from their own perspective. Consequently, little systematic knowledge has emerged regarding the relationship between the social contexts within which inner-city Black drug users live, their own view of their social worlds, and their drug use. This, and the fact that heroin abuse has a disproportionate effect on Black individuals in ghetto communities, led us to focus the Heroin Lifestyle Study on those inner-city Black males who, for the most part, are long-time, serious heroin users, yet are still active in their communities and have never received drug treatment. It was decided to limit the study to one ethnic group since resources were limited and it was not possible to obtain a large or random sample. It was felt that if the study proved successful, it would lead to subsequent research focusing on women and other ethnic populations. In this sense, the HLS study is exploratory. Further, the use of an all-Black-male sample is not based on the misleading stereotype view that links Blacks to drugs and crime. Indeed, a major goal of this study is to ignore this stereotype and to portray inner-city Black heroin users from a holistic perspective, documenting their own views and feelings as human beings who regularly use heroin, rather than to see them in the more simplistic view as "just addicts." The study was designed so that the investigators would be in a position to provide from the inside more accurate images of inner-city Black men who use heroin regularly, yet do not seek treatment.

Using an ethnographic framework, and collecting data simultaneously in four large U.S. cities, we hoped to improve upon the existing knowledge about Black male inner-city heroin users. We wanted to learn from the perspectives of these men what it is like to be a regular heroin user in large urban ghettos in the 1980s. We wanted to know what it is like to hustle, cop, and shoot heroin daily. We wanted to understand how such men are able to avoid drug treatment and to what degree they are able to control their heroin use. We also wanted to learn about the meaning and importance of their social worlds to them and the importance of these worlds as they relate to the larger cultural and political context of their drug use.

A Modified Ethnographic Research Approach

Since the dramatic heroin epidemic of the 1960s and early 1970s, federal, state, and private agencies have been investigating ways to learn more about drug abuse and illegal drug activity. In the mid-1970s, the federal government established two different but complementary monitoring systems to learn more about drug users and the source and quantity of illicit drugs:

> The Client-Oriented Data Acquisition Process (CODAP) which was used from 1975 to 1981, to collect information about clients entering federally funded drug treatment programs.[6]

> The Drug Abuse Warning Network (DAWN) which was designed to collect information about drug use from hospital emergency-room visits and medical examiners' records.

Although both data systems provide valuable information, both have shortcomings. A major limitation of these data systems is that they include information only about drug users who require medical treatment. Yet, as noted earlier, perhaps as many as 300,000 to 400,000 heroin users may not be coming into treatment. Thus, information is not being obtained on a large number of users. The only way to obtain data on this population is to go to them.

The ethnographic approach used in the drug abuse field evolved from this line of thinking. An approach was needed whereby researchers could be in frequent contact with what is "goin' down" in the streets among users, touters, buyers, and dealers, in their neighborhoods and in other areas of the city "where the action is." Utilizing ethnographic techniques, researchers can maintain contact with and study heroin users in their "natural habitat," rather than as clients in drug-treatment centers.

Drug ethnographers have used varied approaches in their work. However, their goals have been basically the same, namely, to discover and understand how users view themselves, and how they interpret their cultural milieu and social activities.

Government support and acceptance of ethnography as a valid research approach has been slow but is growing steadily. In 1978, an ethnographic team was established to study phencyclidine (PCP) use. It was determined that ethnographers in four different cities, using an established protocol and coordinated by a single director, could quickly collect useful data amenable to cross-site analyses (Feldman et al. 1979). Although not entirely trouble free (Agar 1979), this collaborative ethnographic approach provided a model upon which the Heroin Lifestyle Study could be based. Its approach allowed us to make contact with users in their communities simultaneously in four major cities and, using the same interview guide, to gather data systematically. Interviews were conducted by indigenous former long-term heroin users who made the street contacts themselves. Their activities were coordinated and monitored at one central location by the study directors.

Research Design and Techniques

The editors of this book, with the help of former heroin addicts, designed the overall research plan, developed and tested the Heroin Lifestyle Study Interview Schedule, and coordinated the data collection and analysis and the writing phases of the project.[7] Three of the study coordinators, all sociologists, trained the interviewers. A field supervisor was selected in each of the four cities to supervise the interviewers and monitor the incoming data for completeness and accuracy. The "street level" interviewing team consisted of Black former heroin users who were intimately familiar with the local drug scene in their respective cities. Through their familiarity with the study areas, the indigenous interviewers contacted potential respondents (many times through "contact men"), screened them with regard to the eligibility requirements for the study, and interviewed them. Each of the respondents was paid twenty dollars for the interview.

The plan was to interview inner-city Black male heroin users who had never been in treatment and who had injected heroin at least once a day for at least eight days during the two weeks prior to the interview. In fact, most men interviewed injected heroin at least once a day. The sample was to be divided into three equal age groups (15–19, 20–27, 28–35) and was to include twenty-five to thirty males from each city from at least two separate social networks and "copping corners." Most sample selection criteria were met, but we were unable to locate enough young (ages 15–19) heroin users and, as a result, only 14 percent of the HLS men fell into this age range. Thus, ours is a purposive sample of Black heroin users who have never invested themselves in drug treatment and who represent a variety of age groups, social networks, and experiences.[8]

Interviews lasted two and a half to three hours and were usually conducted on the respondent's "turf" (parked cars, restaurants, playgrounds, apartments, or occasionally in the interviewer's apartment or even the user's residence). Interviewers first collected basic social and demographic information (birth, marital status, educational level, present living arrangements, patterns of drug use, and so on) and then progressed to about two hours of guided open-ended questions which were tape recorded. The interviewers were trained to encourage free-flowing conversation, suggesting as few words or ideas as possible to the respondents.

It is mainly in this regard that ours is a modified ethnographic approach. We have strictly held to the goal of ethnographic research in gaining the insiders view without imposing categorical answers or even a theoretical perspective on the questions and answers. However, we have not, as is traditional in ethnographic work, engaged in participant observation by living in the respondents neighborhoods or by observing their daily round of activities.

After collecting, transcribing, and coding the data, a team of experts (both former heroin users and nonusers, both White and Black men) analyzed the data and prepared material for the book. Writers were chosen for content areas appropriate to their areas of experience and expertise. (The raw data were made available to them and the editors worked with each on developing their chapters.) In addition, each of the editors was involved in researching and writing chapters. The result is a rich, sensitive view of the inside of the social world of the contemporary untreated inner-city Black male regular heroin user.

Organization of the Book

This book is organized in terms of the two major goals of the research. Part I describes the modal Black inner-city community and the typical daily activities in which the HLS men say they are involved, and the hustling, copping, and taking of heroin. In the context of this rich cultural description and analysis, part II focuses more on exploring the HLS men's views about themselves, their relationships to the Black and White straight communities, and their attitudes about treatment. The book ends with a summary of patterns evident in the preceding chapters and with comments on the implications of these for the public image of Black heroin users, and for social policy and future research.

The first chapter in part I provides a context for the book. In this chapter, "The Scene," George Beschner and William Brower present the physical and social conditions of the Black inner-city urban communities where HLS respondents live and were interviewed. This chapter, based on personal observations and written and oral reports from the interviewers, focuses on the daily dynamics of the ghetto marketplace. The human feeling of this description is enhanced by opinions and insights quoted from HLS respondents' comments about their communities.

It is within this community setting that the daily activities of the heroin user take place. The second chapter, "Taking Care of Business," turns to a discussion of aspects of the everyday life of HLS men as seen through their collective descriptions. It begins with an hour-by-hour description of what HLS respondents say they do in a typical day from morning until night. James M. Walters, the author, has identified processes and events in HLS men's typical days, assessing the difference between the lives of the HLS men and those of nonusers. Further, Walters' discussion raises questions about the accuracy of the public image of the inner-city heroin user as "a sick predator enslaved by a chemical horror . . . for which he robs the aged and burglarizes the just."

These two related themes—the degree of difference between the ordinary lives of users and of nonusers, and the public stereotype of Black heroin users—echo throughout the next two chapters. In "Hustling: Supporting a Heroin Habit," Allen Fields and James M. Walters discuss hustlers and their role in the ghetto community and economy by identifying the range of hustling activities and the different social types of hustlers that exist in the inner city. In addition, the authors use their typology of hustlers to question the assumed relationship between heroin use and crime. Once again, this analysis tends to challenge the popular unidimensional image of heroin users and their typical hustles. Further, it questions current thinking regarding the role of economics in determining heroin use and the relationship between heroin use and crime.

After users hustle up enough "scratch" to "score some dope," they of course ingest it, usually by injecting it in a vein. In "Life with Heroin: Voices of Experience," George Beschner and Elliott Bovelle focus on the experiences of HLS men while high on heroin. The authors take us through the heroin experience, beginning with the initiation phase, on through the initial occasion of injecting, the feeling of fear, the rush, the sick feeling, the ultimate first time high, and the user's best and worst experiences while using heroin. Also included are discussions of the effects of heroin on sex and the importance of social relationships and economic realities to the HLS men. This chapter challenges popular thinking about how much heroin many users actually take, how many times a day they shoot up, and what a heroin high is really like for regular users. Combined with the chapters about the typical day and about hustling, this provides an important new in-depth picture of the lifestyle of contemporary inner-city Black heroin users who have never been in treatment.

While part I pertains largely to lifestyle activities within the boundaries of the inner city, part II broadens the picture to include activities and attitudes regarding user's relationships to the larger straight society, their self-image and feelings of control over their lives, and their ideas and actions pertaining to drug treatment. For instance, the first chapter, "Brickin' It and Going to the Pan: Vernacular in the Black Inner-City Heroin Lifestyle," by Austin Iglehart takes a quite different look at the HLS men. By examining their language and speech patterns, Iglehart shows how the language of heroin users is an adaptation of Black English. He analyzes the functions of language as information exchange in the inner city. One of his conclusions is that, although the speaking patterns and language of heroin users function as a self-protective mechanism, they also serve to connect Black heroin users with Blacks in the straight inner-city world.

The next chapter, "Not the Cause, Nor the Cure—Self-Image and Control Among Black Male Heroin Users," by Richard Morris examines the HLS men's perception of their self-image and the relationship of the heroin lifestyle to the larger straight society. He begins by showing how the use of heroin and the heroin lifestyle itself produce contradictory feelings, of reward and empowerment on the one hand, and distress, enslavement, and threat on the other. These feelings contribute to the formulation of users' self-image and feelings of control over their lives. Morris shows how these contradictory feelings are related to the HLS men's involvement in two different social worlds—the "street world" and the "straight world." He ends by pointing out how detailed knowledge of users' feelings about their self-image and self-control and of their connections with both social worlds could have implications for treatment.

The last chapter in part II, chapter 8, picks up the treatment theme more directly. George Beschner and James M. Walters begin with the views of HLS men about methadone-maintenance treatment, then compare them with the results of research on the same questions. They include data on what these untreated users say would influence them to enter and stay in treatment.

Finally, Elliott Bovelle and Andress Taylor conclude by summarizing and drawing together the major patterns explored in the preceding chapters. Their discussion asks us to consider the possibility that the type of heroin user and the attendant lifestyle described in this book is, or is becoming, the predominant type in inner cities in the United States. With this in mind the authors raise some implications of the study findings for the public image of inner-city heroin users and their lifestyles, for the prevention and treatment of heroin use, and for future research.

In summary, this book reflects the way the HLS men think and talk about their day-to-day activities and their lives. The editors have sought to have each author do his research and analysis thoroughly, yet to write in a style sensitive to the tone and feeling conveyed by the HLS men. With this in mind, the authors have tried to develop chapters which will appeal to a broad lay public, as well as to drug-treatment professionals and academic and research-oriented audiences. Our data base takes us well beyond autobiographical or single person accounts (for example, Cain 1970; Miles and Harrell 1972), yet retains in large measure the rich, colorful personal descriptions and feelings of the HLS men. This book is, then, an attempt to use social-science research to attain a sound basis for understanding contemporary inner-city Black male heroin users and their lifestyles from their own perspective.

Notes

1. In a similar vein we have not focused on differences by age, education, economic status or other typical social variables. In some cases our N's (e.g., teenagers, education, economic status, etc.) in each city were too small for meaningful comparisons. Also, as noted earlier, as we examined the responses to the open-ended questions, it became clear that, generally, among the broad areas in which we were interested, there were far more similarities than differences across cities. Thus, our efforts centered on assembling a view as seen by the HLS men, emphasizing commonalities in all four locations.

2. For examples see Hunt and Odoroff 1962; Vaillant 1966; Dale and Dale 1973; Iiyama 1976; Joe et al. 1977; Creative Socio-Medics 1977; Reed 1978; Edwards 1978–1979; Linn and Shane 1979; Cohen 1980; Craig 1980a, 1980b; Penk et al. 1980).

3. The key studies referred to here are: Finestones' (1957) interviews with over 50 young Black male heroin users in Chicago, from which he derived an ideal social type of heroin user: the "cat" whose life was composed of the "hustle" and the "kick"; Sutter's (1966) informal interviews in Oakland, California, of 140 addicts and nonaddicts, and his portrayal of the "righteous dope fiend" as one who prefers heroin and who ranks himself above people who use other drugs; Fiddle's (1967) interviews with adolescent addicts (mixed ethnicity) in New York City who were both in and outside treatment, in which he described six different characteristic lifestyles of addicts and pointed out that the addicts' cool style was actually a myth created by the addict subculture to insulate addicts from the realities of conventional society; Feldman's (1968) observations of young Black, Mexican-American, Puerto Rican, and white heroin users in a slum neighborhood in New York City, in which he examined the role of ideology in supporting and meeting the challenges of heroin addiction; and Preble and Casey's study (1969) of 150 Irish, Italian, Black and Puerto Rican informants from New York City, which led them to conclude that using heroin was not an "escape," but rather provided users with the motivation to construct a meaningful life. For a review of these and some recent studies see Catton and Shain (1976), and Waldorf (1980).

4. Lifestyle oriented studies in the 1970s looked at: "the street addict role" (Stephens and Levine 1971; Stephens and Slatin 1974); the demographic and social-structural aspects of a heroin copping community (Hughes et al. 1971); the central events in the everyday lives of addicts (Agar 1973); users' perceptions of heroin and

the importance of "connections" (Gould 1974); the process of becoming a street addict (Stephens and McBride 1976); the values of the street addict subculture (Stephens, Levine and Ross 1976); the copping and consumer behavior of street addicts (Stephens and Smith 1976); hustling and social status among addicts (Smith and Stephens 1976; Biernacki 1979); the family environments and characteristics of heroin addicts (Penk et al. 1979; Crawford et al. 1980); the relationship between lifestyle types and entrance into and progress in drug treatment (Nurco 1981a, 1980b); addicts natural recovery from heroin use (Waldorf and Biernacki 1979, 1981) and "nonaddictive" or "controlled" opiate use (Zinberg 1982).

5. Possible exceptions to this include Waldorf and Biernacki (1979) which is a review of the literature on "natural recovery" from heroin addiction and their study (Waldorf and Biernacki 1981) in which they interviewed 50 untreated former addicts and 84 treated ones to study the process of natural recovery. Some of their interviewees were of course not current, but rather former untreated users. Zinberg (1982) has identified "nonaddictive" or "controlled" opiate users. Thus, he has interviewed untreated current users. Zinberg is one of the few researchers who has attempted to carefully explain the role and importance of "social setting variables" in influencing opiate use.

6. This data system was discontinued at the end of 1981.

7. For a more detailed account and critique of the HLS research design and methods see the appendix, "Heroin Lifestyle Study Methodology."

8. Eighty percent of the sample reported having never received treatment of any kind for drug abuse; of the 20 percent who mentioned receiving some sort of treatment, about 15 percent had undergone short detoxification treatment or had made drug-related emergency room visits only. Based on the short and emergency nature of these respondents' contacts with treatment facilities and on other information and check questions we feel these men had not invested themselves in treatment programs. Some selected basic parameters of our sample are as follows. Thirteen percent are married and 64 percent have never been married. At the time of the interview 12 percent were living with their wives, 36 percent with close relatives and 26 percent alone. The average reported educational level completed by the men is approximately 11 years with 52 percent not completing high school. About 62 percent said that their economic status is very poor or poor, with the remaining saying it is about average. Approximately 29 percent of the HLS men are usually employed in legitimate work. For those not employed at the time of the interview it had been an average of about 2½ years since they had worked either part or full time. The average age by which the men first tried heroin is about 16 years. The majority (63 percent) reported having snorted it and 35 percent shot it the first time. The average age by which these men began to shoot heroin is about 17 years.

These data are based on the structured questions and an N of 134 respondents. Due to some incomplete responses on the longer open-ended questions only 124 interviews were usable: 52 from Chicago, 29 from New York, 21 from Philadelphia, and 22 from Washington, D.C. ($N = 124$).

References

Abrams, Arnold; Gagron, John H.; and Levin, Joseph J. 1968. Psychological aspects of addiction. *American Journal of Public Health* 58(11):2142.

Agar, Michael H. 1973. *Ripping and Running: A Formal Ethnography of Heroin Addicts.* New York: Seminar Press.

Agar, Michael H. 1979. Study methodology. In *Angel Dust: An Ethnographic Study of PCP Users*, eds. Harvey W. Feldman, Michael Agar, and George Beschner, 19–28. Lexington, Massachusetts: Lexington Books.

Ball, J.C., and Chambers, C.D. 1970. *The Epidemiology of Opiate Addiction in the United States.* Springfield, Illinois: Charles C. Thomas.

Becker, Howard S. 1953. Becoming a marijuana user. *American Journal of Sociology* 59:235–242.

Biernacki, Patrick. 1979. Junkie work, hustles, and social status among heroin addicts. *Journal of Drug Issues*, Fall: 535–551.

Brunswick, A.F. 1977. Health and drug behavior: A study of urban black adolescents. *Addictive Diseases* 3(2):215–233.

Brunswick, A.F. 1979. Black youths and drug-use behavior. In *Youth Drug Abuse*, eds. George M. Beschner and Alfred S. Friedman, 443–490. Lexington, Massachusetts: D.C. Heath.

Burroughs, William. *Junkie.* 1953. New York: Ace Books.

Cain, George. 1970. *Blueschild Baby.* New York: McGraw Hill.

Catton, Katherine, and Shain, Martin. 1976. Heroin users in the community: A review of the drug use and lifestyles of addicts and users not in treatment. *Addictive Diseases* 2(3):421–440.

Chein, I.; Gerard, D.L.; Lee, R.S.; and Rosenfeld, E. 1964. *The Road to H: Narcotics Delinquency and Social Policy.* New York: Basic Books.

Cohen, Gary H.; Gary, Richard E.; Evans, Andrew; and Wilchinsky, Mark. 1980. Treatment of heroin addicts: Is the client-therapist relationship important? *International Journal of the Addictions* 15(2):207–214.

Craig, Robert J. 1980a. Characteristics of inner-city heroin addicts applying for treatment in a Veteran Administration Hospital drug program (Chicago). *International Journal of the Addictions* 15(2):409–418.

Craig, Robert J. 1980b. Effectiveness of low dose methadone maintenance for the treatment of inner-city heroin addicts. *International Journal of the Addictions* 15(5):701–710.

Crawford, Gail; Washington, Melvin; and Senay, Edward. 1980. Socio-familial characteristics of black male heroin addicts and their non-addicted friends. *Drug and Alcohol Dependence* 6:383–390.

Creative Socio-Medics. 1977. *Drug Treatment Outcome Among Minorities.* Report prepared for the National Institute on Drug Abuse, Rockville, Maryland.

Dale, Robert, and Dale, Farley-Ross. 1973. The use of methadone in a representative group of heroin addicts. *International Journal of the Addictions* 8(2):293–308.

Dembo, R.; Burgos, W.; Des Jarlceis, D.; and Schmeidler, J. 1979. Ethnicity and drug use among urban high school youths. *International Journal of the Addictions* 14(4):557–568.

Dembo, Richard; Schmeidler, James; and Burgos, William. 1980. Life-style and drug involvement among youths in an inner-city junior high school. *International Journal of the Addictions* 15(2):171–188.

Dumont, Matthew. 1972. The politics of drugs. *Social Policy* 3(2):32–35.

Edwards, Elizabeth D. 1978–1979. Arrest and conviction histories, before, during and after participation in a substance abuse treatment program. *Drug Forum* 7(3 and 4):259–264.

Espada, Frank. 1979. The drug abuse industry and the "minority" communities: Time for change. In *Handbook on Drug Abuse*, eds. Robert L. Dupont, Avram Goldstein and John O'Donnel, 293–300. Rockville, Maryland: National Institute on Drug Abuse.

Feldman, H. 1968. Ideological supports to becoming and remaining a heroin addict. *Journal of Health and Social Behavior* 9:131–139.

Feldman, Harvey W.; Agar, Michael H.; and Beschner, George M. 1979. *Angel Dust: An Ethnographic Study of PCP Users*. Lexington, Massachusetts: Lexington Books.

Fiddle, Seymour. 1967. *Portraits from a Shooting Gallery*. New York: Harper and Row.

Fiddle, Seymour. 1980. Catting: A synoptic view of addicts living outside conventional shelters. *International Journal of the Addictions* 15(1):39–45.

Finestone, H. 1957. Cats, kicks, and color. *Social Problems* 5(1):3–13.

Gay, G.; Smith, D.; and Sheppard, C. 1972. *Yesterday's Flower Child is Today's Junkie: The Changing Pattern of Heroin Addiction*. New York: Insight Publishing.

Gould, L.C.; Walker, A.L.; Crane, L.E.; and Lidz, C.W. 1974. *Connections: Notes from the Heroin World*. New Haven, Connecticut: Yale University Press.

Hughes, P.H.; Crawford, G.A.; Barker, N.W.; Schumann, S.; and Jaffe, J.H. 1971. The social structure of a heroin copping community. *American Journal of Psychiatry* 125(5):551–558.

Hunt, G.H., and Odoroff, Maurice E. 1962. Follow-up study of narcotic drug addicts after hospitalization. *Public Health Reports* 77(1):41–54.

Iiyama, Patti; Nishi, Sitsuko Matsunaga; and Johnson, Bruce D. 1976. *Drug Use and Abuse Among U.S. Minorities: An Annotated Bibliography*. New York: Praeger.

Jaffe, Jerome. 1979. The swinging pendulum: The treatment of drug users in America. In *Handbook on Drug Abuse*, eds. Robert Dupont, Avram Goldstein, and John O'Donnell. Rockville, Maryland: National Institute on Drug Abuse.

Joe, G.W.; Singh, B.K.; Finklea, D.; Hudeburg, R.; and Sells, S.B. 1977. *Community Factors, Racial Composition of Treatment Programs and Outcomes*. Services Research Report. Rockville, Maryland: National Institute on Drug Abuse.

Lindesmith, Alfred, R. 1947. *Opiate Addict*. Evanston, Illinois: Principia Press.

Linn, Margaret W., and Shane, Rachel. 1979. Cultural factors and attrition in drug abuse treatment. *International Journal of the Addictions* 14(2):259–280.

Miles, Floyd, and Harrel, Irene. 1972. *Black Tracks: Nineteen Years on the Mainline*. Plainfield, New Jersey: Logos International.

National Institute on Drug Abuse. 1981. *Statistical Series E: Data from the Client Oriented Data Acquisition Process*. Rockville, Maryland: National Institute on Drug Abuse, DHHS Pub. No. (ADM) 81–1143.

Nelkin, Dorothy. 1973. *Methadone Maintenance: A Technological Fix*. New York: George Braziller.

Nurco, David N.; Cisin, Ira H.; and Balter, Mitchell B. 1981a. Addict careers: I. A new typology. *International Journal of the Addictions* 16(8):1305–1325.

Nurco, David N.; Cisin, Ira H.; and Balter, Mitchell B. 1981b. Addict careers: II. The first ten years. *International Journal of the Addictions* 16(7):1327–1356.

Paton, Stephanie M., and Kandel, Denise B. 1978. Psychological factors and adolescent illicit drug use: Ethnicity and sex differences. *Adolescence* 13(50):187–200.

Penk, W.; Robinowitz, R.; Kidd, R.; and Nisle, A. 1979. Perceived family environments among ethnic groups of compulsive heroin users. *Addictive Behaviors* 4:297–309.

Penk, W.E.; Robinowitz, R.; Woodward, W.A.; and Hess, J.L. 1980. MMPI factor scale differences among heroin addicts differing in race and admission states. *International Journal of the Addictions* 15(3):329–337.

Preble, E., and Casey, J. 1969. Taking care of business: The heroin user's life on the streets. *International Journal of the Addictions* 4(1):1–24.

Reed, Thomas. 1978. Outcome research on treatment and on the drug abuser: An exploration. *International Journal of the Addictions* 13(1):149–171.

Report of the National Advisory Commission on Civil Disorders. 1968. Washington, D.C.: Government Printing Office.

Smith, R.B., and Stephens, Richard C. 1976. Drug use and "hustling." *Criminology* 14(2):155–166.

Stephens, Richard C., and Levine, Stephen. 1971. The street addict role. Implications for treatment. *Psychiatry* 34(4):351–357.

Stephens, Richard C.; Levine, Stephen; and Ross, W. 1976. Street addict values: A factor analytic study. *Journal of Social Psychology* 99(2):273–281.

Stephens, Richard C., and McBride, Duane C. 1976. Becoming a street addict. *Human Organization: Journal of the Society for Applied Anthropology* 35(1):85–93.

Stephens, Richard C., and Slatin, Gerald. 1974. The street addict role: Toward the definition of a type. *Drug Forum* 3(4):375–389.

Stephens, Richard C., and Smith R.B. 1976. Copping and caveat emptor: The street addict as consumer. *Addictive Diseases: An International Journal* 2(4):585–600.

Sutter, Alan G. 1966. The world of the righteous dope fiend. *Issues in Criminology* 2(2):177–222.

Vaillant, George E. 1966. A twelve-year follow-up of New York narcotic addicts. *Archives of General Psychiatry* 15:599–608.

Waldorf, Dan. 1973. *Careers in Dope.* Englewood Cliffs, New Jersey: Prentice-Hall.

Waldorf, Dan, and Biernacki, Patrick. 1979. Natural recovery from heroin addiction: A review of the incidence literature. *Journal of Drug Issues* 9(2):281–289.

Waldorf, Dan. 1980. In *Ethnography: A Research Tool for Policymakers in the Drug and Alcohol Fields*, 21–35, eds. Carl Akins and George Beschner. Rockville, Maryland: National Institute on Drug Abuse.

Waldorf, D., and Biernacki, P. 1981. The natural recovery from opiate addiction: Some preliminary findings. *Journal of Drug Issues* 11(1):61–74.

Zinberg, Norman E. 1982. Nonaddictive opiate use. In *Criminal Justice and Drugs: The Unresolved Connection*, 5–21, eds., James C. Weissman, and Robert L. Dupont. Port Washington, New York: Kennikat Press.

Part I

2
The Scene

George M. Beschner
William Brower

It's like a jungle sometimes, it makes me wonder how I keep from going under. Broken glass everywhere, people pissing on the stairs, you know they just don't care, I can't take the smell, can't take the noise, got no money to move out, I guess I got no choice. Rats in the front room, roaches in the back, junkies in the alley with a baseball bat. I tried to get away, but I couldn't get far, 'cause a man with a tow truck would possess my car. Don't push me 'cause I'm close to the edge. I'm trying not to lose my head. It's like a jungle sometimes, it makes me wonder how I keep from going under. . . .

> from "The Message" by Grandmaster Flash and the Furious Five

"The Message" is no deranged soliloquy by a clever commercial musician. It is an angry and disturbingly insightful cry by a real young Black man. At the height of its popularity teens, Black and White, could be seen faultlessly "lip-synching" this fifteen-minute contemporary *Odyssey,* so in tune were they with its message.

"The Message" describes the social situation and pain across the tracks, in the crowded city corners from which many Black Americans can find no exit. Frustrated and unfulfilled in a land of plenty, many inner-city Blacks find opportunity beyond their reach.

That Black inner-city youth in particular relate to this message is no surprise, since the world it describes is the one most encounter en route to play, to school, to church. For many young Blacks, this is the only world they know. And many will go over that "edge" into an abyss of desperation made bearable to them only by alcohol and drugs.

Listen to the message of Nathan, a 28-year-old Black heroin user from Washington, D.C.:

A Black man has no control over what goes down in this world. Not in America. There's no heroin where the White boys hang out at. They don't let it up in their neighborhood. They send it down to where the poor Black boys hang out at. You get better education where the money is, where the white is you get better education. There's better jobs; there's better houses; better places to buy your groceries; you get more for your money. If you got that kind of paper to put you in that position, you get the better things in life. But if you don't have that paper, buddy, and you're Black, you ain't got nothing. Who controls those types of things, the White man. The Jew boys, the Italian boys, them are the ones that got control; who sit in Congress and stuff like that; they make the laws, and any time a Black man get involved in anything like that, into makin' some money and it happen to be dealin' with drugs, those are the ones who do thirty, forty, fifty years; and the White man that was at the top of it, he don't get nothin', ya know. If he go to jail, if he just happen to accidentally go to jail, they send him to a resort area. They put us into those concentration camps called the United States Penal System. That's what they do to us, they put us in them concentration camps, but they don't do that to those White boys, they put them in the nice spots. They call them white collar criminals. Now ain't that something? When I ain't high, I think about it. When I don't have access to these things. No Black man could have brought that kind of shit [heroin] into this country, they just don't allow that, they don't allow that. They ain't gonna let nobody, other than those Anglo-Saxon males make that kinda money. They ain't gonna let us make that kinda money.

There was a time in my life when I wasn't usin' any drugs, when I tried to have the middle-class American dream. Have yourself a little piece of property, send your kids to a nice school. The "All-American Dream." I had those dreams too. You want to be community orientated; go to a nice church; do things in your community; make sure the schools are really giving your kids a good education; dress nicely; eat good foods; do things; just the things that Whities take for normal.

I've got those dreams. But that's all it has been is dreams and visions because you can never reach the type of success that they can. A chicken in every pot. I'd like to have that. Come home to a nice meal. Drive me a nice automobile. Dress yourself nicely. These are all creature comforts, you know. Your kids say, "Well, dad, I need this and the other." The things that they take for granted is so much for us. They don't have to go to the grocery store with a pocket full of food stamps, or to the clothin' store to buy the secondhand pair of shoes. They don't have to buy the lower line. If I was in Africa where I was supposed to be I might be chuckin' spears and huntin' buffalo and stuff like that. The only dreams that I have is the dreams that have been instilled upon me by this society. So I don't know any other dreams, that's the only dreams that I know. In Africa I'd look like an asshole drivin' an Eldorado or a Sedan de Ville. The only dreams that we've ever known is stuff that's been instilled upon us from generation to generation. We understood that if your hair was slick and shit, if you was a light complexion, you could do a little bit more. They done that. They breeded us to make up special color niggers. The lighter your complexion, the more you were able to obtain. Dream? What kind of dreams can a Black man have in this country? They control those things. Some of us are able to deal and accept that and those are the ones that don't have to use drugs. Politics is run just like everything else in this country. Those with money get what they want and those without don't get shit. They take the leftovers. Money runs this whole thing and we just happen to be the unfortunate group not to have enough money. We have the numbers, but we don't have the money to influence anything. So whatever happens, happens, and we have to accept it. But the main thing is, what are we doin' to control the importation of heroin into this country; the people who are makin' the big money off of this; what are we doin' to the people in this country. Those are the big questions. And, we are avoidin' those issues. We're only fuckin' with the small man. We messin' with the low man on the totem pole. When the shit rolls downhill, you don't start at the bottom of the hill to get to the big shit. You have to go to the top of the hill. That's where the decisions are made. You go to the top and you start choppin' heads at that end where the shit is better. There would not be no drug problem if there was no drugs in this country. What are we gonna do to the people who is bringin' the drugs into this country? That's where you start. Don't start with me or Joe Blow. Me and Joe Blow between the both of us we ain't got twenty dollars, we can't even cop a quarter. We got to go out and steal money to get some. Don't start with us. Why give me thirty or forty years just for usin' some? You get the man that gets the money from me usin', get him. Do somethin' to him. And, that's when we'll all be better. Until we decide that we gonna do that it's just gonna be a vicious circle, we'll always have methadone maintenance clinics, you'll always have those ten-day, thirty-day detox shit. You know, our economy can't afford it. Those niggers are usin' methadone and dope too. You substitutin' one drug for another. I think this is in the eyes of most Black men, that you don't trust the government. A couple of hundred years ago, our people believed in that forty acre and a mule shit. How many of us got forty acres and how many of us got a mule? If you're a Black man in the ghetto you can't believe that kind of shit, Jack. You might as well believe that Sunday is every day. That every day is Mother's Day. It just don't happen.

6:00 A.M.

Some call it "the marketplace," but early in the morning it's just another dirty neglected strip on the other side of the tracks, a fitting backdrop to newspaper postmortems and television specials on the aftermath of ghetto riots. Some buildings are boarded, others stripped of all fixtures, with most windows broken. Signs of neglect and decay are everywhere—empty beer cans, broken wine bottles, uncollected trash, a dead cat on the curb.

There is little to suggest that this was once a thriving business district, the hub of Black social life. A once famous theater where Blacks found comfortable entertainment before desegregation is now shuttered, plastered over with weatherbeaten advertisements for entertainment that takes place somewhere else and for politicians who rarely set foot here.

Most businesses have moved or just plain failed. Gone are the family-owned restaurants noted for spicy home-cooked soul cuisine. In their place are fast-food franchises, specializing in tasteless "all-American" food. Gone are retail and service stores run by local Black businessmen. In their place are all-night, all-purpose quick-stop shops run by recent immigrants from Asia and Latin America. Gone, and replaced by nothing, are soul music stores, stores selling religious and mystical paraphernalia, and mom-and-pop corner stores that were a hub of the community.

And then there is the burgeoning illicit drug business. Aptly named "the markeplace," this neighborhood is a ready source for all types of drugs: marijuana, cocaine, dilaudid, quaaludes, amphetamines, barbiturates, Valium, and the heavyweight champion of the drug world—king heroin, smack, dope, dogie ("doo-gee"). Every major city—Washington, D.C., Chicago, New York, Philadelphia—has a marketplace; without drug trafficking and the copping corners where it takes place, some Black neighborhoods would be virtual ghost towns.

8:00 A.M.

The sparse early morning human activity suggests little of what transpired here yesterday and last night. Straight working people with nine-to-five jobs cluster at bus stops. Kids run, skip, and play on their way to school. Alcoholics, winos, and bag people, with nowhere else to go, lie curled in doorways, sprawled on corrugated carton mattresses. The main sounds are traffic noises—impatient horns, squeaky brakes, untuned engines—as people pass quickly through the marketplace:

> We are like monkeys in the zoo. You can go into certain areas where there are a lot of people using public modes of transportation, like the bus, cab, are always passing through. You can see them sittin' on the bus staring at us, for the most part. Some of them show signs of pity; some of them show signs of anger; some of them show signs of hate: "I hate them dope fiends." Another might say, "Look, look, look at that man hoverin' over the trash cans, he's funny;" and some others might say, "That's a shame," they're sympathetic, they sympathize. It's somethin' that, for the most part, they can't understand because they're not a part of it. (Joe, age 24, Washington, D.C.)

10:00 A.M.

The texture and tenor of the marketplace begins to change. Winos and dope fiends asleep in the street begin to stir, pooling their few coins, in anticipation of liquor stores being opened. Nonworking straight folks wearing masks of despair and resignation, excess weight, and weathered clothing emerge from their meager dwellings and move through the streets on errands—buying groceries, paying final bill notices, lugging dirty clothes to the laundromat, attending a school conference on a "disruptive" child.

The curbside drug emporium gears up for business, consumers and entrepreneurs arriving in waves:

Starting around ten o'clock the first waves start coming through. They're looking for hustling partners. They're looking for copping partners, somebody they can put their money in with to get some dope. They seeking information—what went on last night, what's going on today, who's hot, what police are working. Who's gonna get busted and who is snitching. (Rio, age 19, Chicago)

Clusters of straights at bus stops are replaced by users and sellers, mostly men busily setting agendas for the day. The ones with enough money are looking for the dope man, especially the man with the best dope:

I go to different neighborhoods to cop. Most of the dudes that know me, old timers or whatever, that have been around for a few minutes, I got respect for them. Cause I don't be bullshittin', I be straight up and be about my business. You run upon different dudes in different days. Certain neighborhoods you run upon the same dudes. By me floatin' around different neighborhoods where the stuff is decent I find the best stuff around. When I see the man we are cool, man, that's the thing. They recognize me and I recognize them. I know what they about. That's the key to finding good dope man, we take care of our business and we step on. (Chico, age 34, Chicago)

The ones without enough money are looking for copping partners to pool money so that they can purchase some "tragic magic" (heroin):

My associates usually stop by in the morning and we get down together. I know them from the neighborhood, gettin' high every day with somebody you get tight with them. By you gettin' high, they come by and ask you "what's happenin', man, what's happenin' out here." Ya know, they want to know what you doin'. Sometimes you have no money and they say "well come with me, man, let's go boostin'." Sometimes, one of the dudes will have a quarter and say, "hey, man, let's get down on this." So I get it off with him. He might not exactly give me a half, but it's usually enough to get me by. (Slim, age 38, New York)

Even the strung-out beggars and "vultures," craving in their glazed eyes, are out trying to find a free fix. An especially sick and desperate man bends over and liquid gushes from his mouth; he straightens up quickly, wipes his mouth with his arm, and moves into the circle of activity as if failing to notice that things have gone awry:

My complexion is duller, I have a dull hollow look. I don't seem to be as lively as other people. My dress is shabbier and it's getting shabbier and shabbier. I've had most of my teeth pulled. I've tried to keep them in good shape because I've seen how they poison an addict's system by not taking care of them. Heroin is something I have to take every day. When I don't get it I feel horrible. My hands are swollen, my arms are swollen, my character, I become very impulsive. I get very angry over nonsense. You get in that drug slouch. You're so used to shooting heroin that you're nodding when you're not nodding. Your face is bent that way. And if you're used to walking on a slouch when you're nodding, you're gonna walk that way when you ain't high. I was never born to be swollen like this. I wasn't born to limp, I wasn't born for my bowels to lock for me. I don't eat regular no more. You have that feeling about your swollen body, you don't want to really introduce yourself to somebody new because you're feeling that you're gonna be rejected. I have to be around where I can get my shot of dope or I'm gonna be sick. I have no self-confidence now. Self-esteem is something of the past. It's just a basic feeling of worthlessness. (Butch, age 28, New York)

The marketplace is the information network for members of the street drug culture. Here they gather intelligence about who's been busted, who's hot, who has the best drugs, who's overdosed or hospitalized, who's been seen talking with the police (possibly snitching), and most of all, what, if anything, is expected from the "Romans" (police)?

We talk about how the Romans go today. Are the Romans tough today? Or haven't they been out here too much lately? Or who they busted the day before? Or who they goin' to bust today? (Jay, age 35, New York)

There is a constant flow of people, some who cop "bam" (phenmetrazine hydrochloride, a central nervous system stimulant used alone and in combination with other drugs, including heroin) and keep moving, and others going about their "work," hustles they hope will provide enough money to cop later in the day. The only stationary figures are small scale dealers and their vendors—the touters, who actively and openly advertise various products, and the "jugglers," who act as middlemen. Lurking inconspicuously in the background are the vultures, awaiting a chance to raid a dealer's stash or exploit another opportunity for free drugs.

12:00 Noon

By noon these streets are full, full of addicts, full of thieves and people who earn their living by doing dope. You got number writers. You got information people, guys who make their hustle selling information. They stay on the corner all day and count the drugs. They know where the fences are and who needs what. When the boosters come through they'll take you down anywhere and you come back with scratch. (Albert, age 21, Washington, D.C.)

At lunchtime the pace of drug trafficking accelerates. Foolish, fearless, or well-known customers stroll through. Those who indulge in drugs while holding down daily jobs roam the marketplace to make lunchtime purchases. Because of the increase in street activity, noon is also the safest time for suburbanites, mostly Whites who use or push drugs, to make their buys.

The curbside drug service is in full swing. Cars cruise through the marketplace slowly, their occupants scrutinizing touters and jugglers for a familiar face, someone from whom they have bought before. By dealing with someone they know they stand less chance of getting burned with an inferior drug or getting busted by a "narc" imposter.

The Whites, and most everyone else, keep their car windows rolled up and the doors locked as they cruise. Touters and dealers use an elaborate finger signal to describe their wares: one finger for bam, two fingers for ludes, three for reefer, four for caine, a full house for the big boy. Some look like frantically signalling third base coaches, others like flamboyant traffic cops. Exchanges are made through barely cracked windows, exits are made rapidly.

Hawkers speak their peculiar language, calling cocaine "pepsi-cola," "caine," "nose candy," "girl," and describing diluted coke as "stepped on" and pure coke "for your brother." Marijuana brands are distinguished by their place of origin "lum" (columbian), "gold" (acapulco), "green" (Chicago); synthetic marijuana is hawked by potency: "wack attack" (most potent), and "monster," "lovely," and "dust."

The most colorful language is reserved for the "big boy." Dealers vie for trade names implying that their dope is the most potent. Terms suggesting a super high—"747" or "ET"—are common, as are terms suggesting purity strong enough to cause overdoses—"black tape" or "black death." It's mostly marketing and gamesmanship a la Madison Avenue because most marketplace dope is about the same, two to five percent pure.

The street drug subculture and its unique social hierarchy are evident. "Dope fiends" and "vultures," hopelessly strung out and worn out by their habits, are the dregs of the street, shabbily dressed and unkempt, their eyes filled with craving and desperation. Drug users with hustles and cons take care to look presentable. They know the dirt-ball junkie look is a dead giveaway, so they try to look casual, like the average working person:

> Being a drug addict is different than being a downright junkie. Man, you have to keep yourself halfway clean. You can't walk too tough and steal. If you're a thief you cannot be dirty. You can't afford to attract yourself, 'cause I'm going in department stores and stealing—clothing, good perfume and furs and shit like that. You can't walk in there lookin' like you ain't got no money. And Black too. Shit, no. (Ben, age 27, Philadelphia)

Those with position in the drug trafficking hierarchy are stylishly dressed. Freshly pressed designer jeans take the place of worn overalls and loose fitting trousers. NBA-style leather sneakers grace their feet. The most telling status symbol is jewelry—gold and diamond rings, bracelets, and necklaces. More than just a status symbol, jewelry is also convertible into money or drugs, a hedge against difficult times.

The underground economy is also in full swing. Substances like quinine and lactose (used to cut drugs) and syringes are readily available, as are "hot" designer clothes, audio equipment, cameras, televisions, and weapons. Merchandise is being sold out of paper bags, tote bags, backpacks, large suitcases, and car trunks:

> I was the one who had the goods but I didn't like it because I never get what I want from what I be selling. I always feel like I'm being ripped off. I had a really nice watch, an Omega. I thought I could get at least fifty dollars off of it. But when we went around to different places to sell it they wouldn't go high. They acted like they didn't want it anyway. Five, ten dollars, man. The guys were laughing at me. They'd say, "Man, I got too many watches." In the bar the straight guys would crack jokes. They were getting their kicks out of me. It kinda hurt my pride. Heard one of them say, "Here comes a junkie." I say, "Man, I got this here Omega watch." One guy says, "I don't want no watch; what about that coat you got on?" Another guy says, "Why don't you sell me your shoes?" They know a junkie will sell anything. I still have a little bit of pride left so it still hurts. So, you learn to swallow your pride. (Quinn, age 27, Philadelphia)

This illegal activity goes on underneath the eyes and ears of "big brother." The area is frequently scanned by videotape cameras and omnidirectional microphones that are in plain view atop telephone poles. Several blocks away a plainly marked police tractor-trailer packed with sophisticated equipment is manned by police specialists who monitor marketplace activity. The police and the drug undergound engage in a war of attrition in which the police alternate between conventional warfare and counterinsurgency tactics:

> There is more violence, more police and more sophisticated equipment. In the old days a foot patrolman could not be in constant contact with his supervisor. They had a big old command center downtown. Now they work out of campers and use TV cameras to find out what the niggers are up to. The whole thing is calibrated to the police officer. It seems to me that all that new equipment adds to the challenge. (Black Charlie, age 30, Chicago)

Periodically police make a show of force, appearing suddenly in platoon formation, setting up blockades at both ends of the marketplace, detaining and frisking everyone in the area, and busting as many people as possible. Sometimes the fire department participates, hosing down the area to flood out and destroy drug stashes hastily secreted along curbs, in tree stumps, trash cans, car bumpers, and elsewhere.

Marketplace dwellers have a sixth sense and generally disperse before police make their moves. The drug traffic moves a block or two away, and business goes on as usual. People busted during the day will be on the street again that night. If the police action is particularly severe, trafficking action retreats to one-way, dead-end streets and alleys where police cannot maneuver in great numbers without being observed and evaded. Such actions create a solidarity in the subculture, integrating the drug trafficking more deeply into community life.

When police zero in on a particular dealer, they employ a type of counter-insurgency tactic popularized by television. Referred to as "cowboy cops," they are mean and sometimes brutal, running roughshod over anybody or anything in their way. Unlike uniformed police, the cowboy cops are camouflaged as alcoholics or derelicts, as repairmen or mailmen, making it difficult to see them coming; street people rarely know when they will "jump out."

As in guerilla warfare, drug counterinsurgency work attacks the psychological security of the "insurgent" as well as physically crippling him:

> We know cops by sight and by action, the kind that are in the take, what they do and don't do. They call one cop Brute Force because he's so cruel. Like one day he jumped out of the car and rammed me up against a wall. Tried to bust me for selling dope but he knew goddam well I wasn't nothing but a thief and a dope fiend. He jammed me, he really jammed me. It's gotten to the point where dope fiends talk about killing him and shit like that. It could happen. One of them crazy motherfuckers will try to take him out—what better way to go out. (Red, age 36, New York)

Of course, not every arrest is dramatic. Some are merely terrifying, others humiliating, and still others downright vicious and dangerous even to ordinary citizens caught in the crossfire. Some involve high-speed car chases and gun battles, others undercover arrests. In these situations police are generally nervous and battle-weary; tempers are short; mistakes are made; hostility grows. Community reactions are ambivalent. They range from curiosity to anger at the police, the accosted, or both. On the one hand, residents view drug trafficking as an economic and social plague and want it eradicated. On the other hand, since the heroin users, touters, and dealers sometimes are their loved ones—husbands, brothers, daughters, sons, and other relatives—there are some attempts to protect heroin users from the police.

3:00 P.M.

This is a quiet time of day for the heroin crowd. Most heroin users have found refuge. Those not "kicking back" indoors are doing casual things. Most have scored:

> We go out, smoke reefer and go to the movies or somethin', just slip-slide. Either that or I'm just layin' back and takin' it easy, and bullshittin' around the house, smokin' a little marijuana, listening to the music . . . (Buck, age 29, Washington, D.C.)

Some stay home and take care of business:

> People come by my house, right? I mean, I don't have no shootin' gallery, but some of my associates come by and, ya know, I let them use my gimmicks, I let them use my works. Sometimes they pay me, sometimes they give me drugs, ya know, depends, ya know. That's how I mostly spend afternoons. (Slim, age 38, New York)

The few users left on the corner are "clean;" they have used the drugs copped earlier and are now rapping, talkin' shit," letting their opiate-influenced thoughts unwind:

> We all a bunch of dreamers, you know. We all see ourselves in Rolls Royces, owning planes and pullin' off a big crime . . . I mean, in your nods, you fantasize. (Ron, age 27, Chicago)

Younger men who have not yet made the heroin commitment are on the corner lot playing basketball, waiting their turn or just watching. Some are standing in front of the pool hall patiently waiting for a dealer, hoping for a little extra dope or to pay for drugs fronted to them earlier. Others hang around the pool halls and the record store, listening to the music.

By late afternoon, working people are returning to the area. The schools are out and day jobs are ending. Once again the straights and members of the drug subculture engage in an uneasy coexistence. Hawkers try to solicit some straights; a few pleasantries are exchanged by people of long acquaintance. Some homecomers stop for small talk, others openly express resentment toward the street people and move quickly through the neighborhood. School children stake out sidewalk turf for their games. As the afternoon wears on, curbside traffic resumes as a new wave of buyers move through the marketplace. They are mostly working people, Black and White, who score after their nine-to-five jobs.

After 6:00 P.M.

As evening descends, the marketplace becomes the setting for a variety of activities. For some inhabitants this includes relaxing, visiting with friends and relatives, and partying. Others, especially working men, return home, eat quickly, change, and rush out to catch the action. After their daily relaxer, heroin users usually snack and return to the marketplace to finish their business, take part in the evening rituals, and get ready for the next day. Business is brisk at the local carryout stands. The suburbanites are gone from the scene.

Skimpily and tightly clad hookers can be seen on the sidewalk. Some stand near the curb, aggressively soliciting business from the cars cruising by. Others linger in doorways, waiting for regular customers or just biding time before turning another trick. Drivers peer through their car windows, looking for particular women, a particular type of woman, or sizing up the situation before making their choices. "Chili" pimps (who live off earnings of prostitutes with little involvement in their business) are keeping watch over their women, making sure they swing into action.

New arrivals are continuously coming on the scene. Quick deals are being made with men in double-parked cars. Occasionally, one of the "big men" rolls through in a huge limo. Although he doesn't control much of the corner's traffic, and he never stops there, his presence is felt, especially by those heroin users who dream of escaping their "hand to arm" existences. The marketplace is soon bustling with throngs of people who cluster along the main street. Vultures, beggars, junkies, and nighttime hustlers are competing for time and attention. This is the most dangerous time of the day, when scores between competing drug trade factions are settled. Money is at stake for those who control or want to control drugs in the marketplace.

Most of the men are actively involved in conversations—negotiating, bartering, bargaining, transacting, selling, and occasionally arguing. Violence is not unusual. They are all serious, with no buffoonery, joking, or laughing. There is only determination and businesslike behavior. Everyone seems to have a purpose for being there. To outsiders, the atmosphere is tense and forbidding.

Heads are instinctively bobbing up and down, as different men take turns checking for newcomers, potential customers, and intruders. They are always on the alert for police. There is a sense of intrigue and danger as they bargain, negotiate, and try to make deals.

A wide variety of outfits is being worn. Some men are slickly decked out in three-piece suits and sport jackets; many are wearing old worn jeans and T-shirts. Several men are carrying nylon shoulder bags. As people interact, jewelry, watches, and various garments change hands, and wads of bills are flashed. For some, nighttime at the marketplace presents an opportunity to make a last minute deal. For others, it is a chance to interact with peers in what is, to many of them, a provocative and captivating environment.

3

"Taking Care of Business" Updated: A Fresh Look at the Daily Routine of the Heroin User*

James M. Walters

Introduction: The Dope Fiend Myth

> The human race is consuming every year many thousands of tons of . . . narcotic drugs . . . addicts . . . consider getting their drug supply as the supreme consideration, in many cases as a matter of life and death.
>
> The motive and urge that constantly drive the traffic on are the enormous profits . . . so great because the poor addict, under the awful depression and torture of withdrawal symptoms, . . . when the drug begins to subside (every) few hours, . . . feels he must have the drug no matter what the cost or the consequences, whether he has to spend his last dollar, whether he has to steal to get the money, whether he has to rob or even commit murder . . . The heroin addict will more quickly commit crime, with no sense of regret or responsibility for it . . . Heroin is the worst evil of them all.

It was 1925 when Richmond Pearson Hobson, ardent Prohibitionist and Spanish-American War hero, wrote that in his eight-page pamphlet, *The Perils of Narcotics*. His broadside articulated what was to become the decades-enduring arch-image of the addict as "dope fiend."

Since that time the public has viewed the drug addict or user as a sick predator enslaved by a chemical horror. His days are alleged stupors interrupted only—and all too often—by a maniacal need for another fix, for which he robs the aged and burglarizes the just.

No one, of course, could totally deny this image. All myths grow around some kernel of truth. Drug addicts do lie, cheat, and steal to get money. But so do nonaddicts. And just as nonaddicts have legitimate jobs, so do addicts. The Heroin Lifestyle Study (HLS) was designed to develop a more accurate perspective on the heroin user and his lifestyle.[1]

---

*No phrase better captures the essence of the user's typical day than does Ed Preble's "Taking Care of Business," first published in 1969. I use this phrase in his honor, and I dedicate this chapter to his memory.

The Heroin Routine: Theme and Variations

What emerged from the thousands of pages of interviews with 124 respondent heroin users in The Heroin Lifestyle Study is more than a glimpse into lives mysterious to most people. Though unique, as all lives are, these show common themes across cities and age groups. All HLS respondents are committed, daily users of heroin who spend most of their time in pursuit of the money and personal connections they need to maintain their daily habits. Along with their heroin use, many of these men (44.6 percent) report using an assortment of other drugs in the course of a typical day. Often this includes alcohol, both hard liquor and wine; most also regularly use marijuana, a commodity that is easily available to addicts in ghetto communities.

In order to support their lifestyle, heroin users engage in hustling, begging, borrowing, stealing, pushing, and taking whatever legitimate jobs that may come their way. Even those who hold legitimate full-time jobs frequently must find different ways to augment their drug money. While the cost of heroin varies from day to day, the average daily cost is not in the hundreds of dollars as often reported, but is less than twenty-five. And even that average is affected by the few extremely heavy users. According to the most frequently reported value, the cost of daily use is about twenty dollars. Supporting a habit of this cost hardly demands a crime spree, but for the unemployed in the ghetto it does require dedication, discipline, and relationships with fellow users. In fact, the habits could be well within the budgets of almost one third of these men (29.5 percent) who are usually legitimately employed. These distinctions are not trivial, because they go to the heart of the dope fiend myth that supports the expenditure of almost $125 million per year for methadone treatment alone.

In many respects, these men lead quite ordinary lives, sometimes not unlike those of nonaddicts. Probably the best capsule portrait of the heroin life was given by a 27-year-old user from Chicago. Hollywood sums up his routine by saying, "I hustle (Hollywood is a pickpocket) during the day so that in the nighttime I can relax when I get my drugs . . . that's how I do it . . . it is like a job." In the broadest terms Hollywood's summary is a fair description of the user's typical routine. Like most of us, they go about their business during the day and pursue their private pleasures in the evenings. Hustling, "like a job," not only provides income, it also supplies an organizing principle to the heroin user's life. It sets his pace, enlivens his day. It even broadens his network and provides opportunities for socializing.

Still, users and hustlers do move about in a world on the margin of society, at the edge of legality and social convention. Theirs is a world of bars and brothels, hustling for dollars, and getting high. But it is a world, too, of passing time listening to music, watching television, or socializing with the boys; a world, even, of working, running errands, and spending time with

with family. Despite the pressure to "hit the streets" and hustle, for example, Ace, a 34-year-old Philadelphian, feeds his pet birds each morning and gives his mother her morning eye drops. "Then I take her to the clinic for an appointment which is approximately two hours . . . that's a regular routine."

Getting the Day Started

Most of these men (80 percent) begin to plan their day while washing and dressing in the morning. The legitimately employed users organize their lives primarily by the dictates of the job. Since many are laborers, working from 7:00 A.M. to 3:00 P.M., their day demands disciplined rising. Anthony, 30, a user who works as a mailman in Washington, D.C., gets up at five o'clock, dresses and eats, and is out of his house by six. Ski, 27, a Philadelphian who calls himself an early riser, described his typical morning routine.

> I got up as usual, you know I'm an early riser; it was between seven-thirty and eight, and well, I had to shave. I usually shave every day or every other day . . . I put my radio on. I get news seven to eight; I try to keep up with the current events of the day, 'cause, you know, that helps me spend my day. I don't usually eat breakfast. My biggest thing is coffee, and I have a cup of coffee and try to rationalize out things. You know, sort of decide what kind of pants I'm gonna put on with these shoes, so I won't mess my outfit up. It ain't up to par nohow, but I try to dress the best I can under the circumstances.

Ski's account of his morning routine shows a marked similarity to the following account from Chicago. Zulu, 33, a thief and minor dealer, notes that:

> By me doin' time I have a tendency of wakin' up early. I woke up by the time my daughter's gone to school, and that's about eight-thirty. Then, if anything has to be done around the house, like takin' the garbage out or moppin' I do that first, then I take care of myself . . . my hygiene, washin' up . . . I was brought up where, you know, clothes makes the man. You don't have to be super-clean, but be presentable. I eat a large breakfast, take me a multiple vitamin, and drink some protein. That way I don't have to worry about no dinner or nothin' like that.

The Wake-Up Shot

Ski, Zulu and other respondents describe a morning that could be almost anyone's—except that theirs begins with a "wake-up fix." Although many non-addicts would be hard pressed to see each day's routines as vital, the heroin user is reminded of essentials from the moment he awakens, lips parched, cotton-mouthed, wanting heroin. Some need a shot of heroin not for its "rush," its euphoria, but, as Solo, 26, a New Yorker says, "just to get straight so I can wake up like a normal human being . . . I could walk, you know, and do my thing." Because this need is ever present, Solo and a very few other respondents plan ahead for it and try to have a wake-up fix (or "get-up fix") left over from the previous day's supply. This account from Icepick, a 35-year-old Washington, D.C. federal employee, is typical.

(I) sat on the side of the bed as always, lit a cigarette and smoked that. Got up, went in the bathroom, brushed my teeth, showered up. Sat on the side of the bed, lit another cigarette up and proceeded to put my shot in the pan [a small vessel, for example, a bottlecap, used to cook the heroin mixed with water]. I always try to take my stuff home, to have somethin' when I wake up the next mornin'. I was by myself with the exception of my wife; she doesn't like it, but she puts up with it. When I come out of the bathroom [where Icepick shoots up], that's her cue to move out, and she goes downstairs and makes coffee before I go to work.

Slim, 38, a building superintendent in New York, describes a similar morning:

Well, I went into the bathroom 'cause, you know I don't do nothin' in front of her. She aware of what I'm doin' [but] I didn't do anything in front of her, you know. Came out, oh, she was cookin' . . .

Slim's and Icepick's days begin with a central ritual in their lives, an act repeated at least daily by almost every one of America's more than 500,000 heroin users and addicts. Each mixes his heroin with some water and brings the solution to a slight boil; a match flame is enough to do the job. He finds a "rope" (vein) for his injection—a good vein, one near the surface and not collapsed or scarred over. After he finds that day's vein, Icepick or Slim puts a tourniquet (a belt or a tie, for example) on the limb and slaps at the vein to bring it up. While the vein is swelling up, he draws the heroin solution carefully into his syringe, making sure he gets it all, and then taps the tube to eliminate air bubbles. By now the vein is ready and he eases in the needle in the direction of the blood flow—towards his heart.

Since most users feel that it is important to get an even mixture and maintain control over the injection, Icepick and Slim probably "boot" the shot (putting a little pressure on the syringe's squeezer-ball before injecting). In that way they can avoid shooting any of the heroin into the bloodstream immediately upon entering the vein. Instead, they release the pressure on the needle so that a fraction of their blood is sucked up into the tube. Then, in a series of quick squeezes/releases they mix the "gravy" (blood and heroin) and shoot in only as much as needed for the effect wanted. For Icepick and Slim, "getting the edge off" will be all they want for now, for the morning, because there is a day's work to be done. Heroin's rush and languorous stupor will come another time, later in the evening perhaps, when they will have the time to shoot for the pleasure of it.

In one sense Icepick and Slim are exceptional men. Few HLS men seem to have their foresight, or perhaps their desire, to save enough heroin for the wake-up shot that all would, nonetheless, cherish. So for most users, the morning begins with reefer, rye, or "ripple" before the day's imperative—to get a hustle under way and finance that day's high. Ike, a 35-year-old Philadelphian whose aggressive hustling days are over, sums up the feelings and routines of most HLS respondents:

> I get up an' it starts out pretty rough . . . If you come out the house with five or ten dollars, man, you can get things workin'. When you come out broke, you ain't gonna get nothing all day long. You come out of the house first thing in the morning with ten dollars . . . borrow that . . . you can work with somethin' . . . people might say, "look, we tryin' to down a check" or whatever, you can [get in on it].

Hitting the Street

Ike and most other hustler-users have to hit the streets as soon as possible. They head down to the corners or to local bars which are beginning to fill up with other junkies, assorted hustlers, the off-work, the out-of-work and the never-worked. Through casual greetings and exchanges of "what's happening," these men share the important news of the day: what is the up-to-date information about cops, arrests and deaths; who's got some bread; who has a lead to a good connection; who has a hot idea for a hustle—critically important, casual social exchange that will recur throughout the day. By ten o'clock most of these men will have teamed up with a regular associate, a "walking partner" as they are frequently called. Together they will begin a race against the clock, earning enough money in the morning to cop a day's worth of heroin in the afternoon. The remaining men (10 percent perhaps), mostly loners and "old-heads" (burned-out dope fiends), must get by as best they can. Perhaps they will beg for some money from their families or panhandle. Perhaps, like Ike, they will earn a bag of heroin or two in exchange for being the middleman in a hustle or drug deal. Or perhaps they will pass the day with a bottle of Tokay.

Hustling: The Daily Grind

These heroin users are patient, flexible and versatile hustlers, ready to steal, deal, or run a con. The addict must always be prepared to take advantage of opportunities chance sends his way, as Sluggo, 22, from Chicago attests:

> I can steal, hustle, borrow, and any kind of way possible that I can get the money I need to get a hold of it [heroin]. I don't go out stickin' up or nothin' like that. I ain't never done anything like that or taking it from other *people.* On the days when I don't have it, I borrow it; if I don't do that I just sit up and do without. [Italics added]

A variety of hustles, from stealing and robbery to drug sales and cons, are available to these users to take care of business. At one time or another, in fact, most users employ all of them. On any given day, chance factors—the partner he meets, or the appearance of an easy mark—lead a user to choose one or another. They must always be prepared to take advantage of whatever opportunities come their way.

Most heroin users identify a main hustle that they do best, and for almost half of them (49 percent) that means thefts, robberies, and con games. But it is virtually impossible to rely on only one or two methods of raising money for the daily fix. One thing is clear, however. As Sluggo suggested, there is an overwhelming preference for getting money by the most available, non-violent, least risky way. The users know from experience that risks and danger increase in confrontations with others.

Each day, user-hustlers and their walking partners most likely will leave the corner with "boosting" (shoplifting) or petty larcenies on their minds. Shorty, 18, a New Yorker, is a shoplifter who echoes the heroin user's preference for avoiding violence:

> I don't stick-up, I don't snatch ladies' pocketbooks, man. My mother brought me up to know better than that. . . . We have what we call a "boostin' crew." There are three girls and four of us, and we look out for each other in stores. We go boostin', stealin' meat and coffee and things like that, mainly just runnin' back and forth to the stores.

Of course, not all thieves avoid violence; there is a fraction of these users who commit burglaries (10 percent) and stick-ups (18 percent). For some the promise of a bigger take is the inducement to chance greater risks. Yet, some others, like James, a 22-year-old from Washington, D.C., seem driven by the high-risk adventure of those felonies:

> I like to stick-up. I like to take the risk. Besides, I figure that I can make my getaway. . . . You pick certain people . . . people that be comin' out of the bank, just cashin' their check or something.

But a career of robbery is not so easy and even James' bravado wears thin as he recalls another holdup:

Me and my partner, we need dope. We hadn't did too much hustlin'. . . so we went out and . . . try to raise this store. The guy got a pistol from somewhere and he just started firin' . . . he came so close to my head, I heard bells a week later. . . . It shouldn't've happened that way . . . just started shootin' . . . close range. . . . Got to be a better way.

As sobering as nearly getting shot might be, as worrisome as it may be to be caught by police, as real as those daily risks are, they are not the toughest challenges these hustlers face in their pursuit of fix money. Their real challenge is the daily grind of competition. So, by choice or by force, legitimate work is not foreign to them.

Most (61 percent) work legitimate jobs at least from time to time, and many of them (24 percent) count it as their main source of income. Their enterprise, in fact, seems almost boundless and no job seems beyond their dignity. Vick, 26, from Philadelphia, cleans houses for five or ten dollars. John, a 17-year-old New York student, runs errands. Michael, 21, from Washington, D.C., does freelance auto repair and wholesales syringes. Zulu prefers to help his father-in-law haul junk. "By workin' in his truck a half a day I can make me fifty dollars or so," he boasts. Driving through any poor Black neighborhoods, one can spot car after car, parked with trunks open, their drivers peddling everything from dresses to meat. Dave, a 35-year-old Philadelphia user, typifies this wholesale hustle:

Sometimes I go out . . . there's a wholesale house . . . I have about $200 to $300 and buy some coats and ladies' dresses, and go 'round the bars and sell 'em.

Some even try to pass off these goods as stolen because, as one slyly noted, "people are more likely to buy it when they feel they're gettin' a bargain."

Although users may feel a preference for legitimate work, the pressures to hustle are enormous. Not only is hustling a norm, as evidenced by the pressure to pass off legal merchandise as hot, but economic deprivation in urban ghettos robs people of opportunities and slowly eats away at the will to work. Dave, from Philadelphia, complains bitterly:

Last year I got into this program for dudes thirty to forty-five years to get jobs . . . I worked for about three months. They was supposed to send us to school. By sendin' us through school, [we] could pass through the jobs . . . So when we go to apply for the job the man cracked, "How much experience you got?" . . . You show your diplomas and stuff and he say, "Well, you ain't got enough experience. . . ." I went through all this an' here's this smart fella smackin' me in the face. It's a whole lot of disappointments, man.

So hustling for buy money becomes the workaday grind for heroin users, and on the whole they treat it like a job. Like most jobs, it loses its glamor. But unlike most regular jobs, it demands that the user be freshly inventive every day. It is not surprising that users regard it with a sense of pride and dignity, that they stand tall in "the hustler's limelight" as one said. Hustling is a daily test of purpose and resourcefulness, even of stamina, as Frank, 28, a Philadelphian boasts:

> You find that heroin users are more active than nonusers 'cause there's a lot of reasons why he has to be on the move. That's why I say you'd be surprised that a person who uses drugs is in better shape than the average person out there. 'Cause they constantly use, but still be runnin' from the police. Often times you have to walk downtown 'cause you don't have no transportation. You bundle yourself up against the weather. You got to withstand a lot of things.

After three or four hours of hustling and odd-jobbing and chance socializing, most of these users will have gotten together enough money for the day's supply of heroin. The majority of them need less than twenty-five dollars. The burglars and shoplifters will have fenced their goods or have sold their take on the corners or in bars. Some few will even have squeezed in a quick visit home. By midafternoon, it is time to head back to the copping corner to socialize a bit more, and connect for today's fix and the first satisfying high of the day.

Shooting Up and Socializing: The Afternoon Routine

The day's events thus far have been prologue to the next few hours. The odd-jobbing, the hustling, even for the many users (over 40 percent) who take pride and satisfaction from it, has been aimed at this afternoon's copping. Even this morning's wake-up fix, for the few who had one, was only an instrumental ritual that pales in comparison to upcoming pleasures, as Butch, a 28-year-old shoplifter from New York notes, ". . . the first shot never [gets] us high. It just [keeps] us from bein' sick." The next few hours will be a microcosm of the addict's life. His resources will be tested again as he makes a connection, scores some dope and finds a safe place to shoot up and "get off."

Copping

The first order of business, now, is to connect with a dealer to buy some heroin in the shortest possible time since, as Ski describes, "my nose is in disorder . . . my person is in disorder . . . I got to cop." Ski's and every addict's goal is to score the best deal on some quality stuff, stretching the few dollars they have to spend. In practice, this means one of two things: stretching the buck or stretching the bag. Either the user must deal directly with a dealer and bargain for a discount, or even get his heroin "on the eye" (on credit) if he can, regardless of whether he has money. Or he must opt for quality and potency in hopes of making a smaller amount go farther.

For most hustlers the morning's work was successful; they have cash to bargain with. Also, most are not desperately sick; they can afford the time to shop around for a dealer or connection they know personally and who has a good reputation. These are critically important to the heroin user or addict: first, because only a dealer will give discounts, much less credit; second, because the addict runs ever greater risks of being "ripped off" (robbed) or "burned" (cheated by being sold a short count) as he deals with unknown people. Zulu tries:

> . . . to see the same people I been dealin' over a period of time, so that way I know the quality of the drugs is not bullshit. . . . If you got quality merchandise . . . then your reputation gonna speak for itself. If you got good drugs, then the clientele gonna try to get to you.

Some, like Zulu, have their own personal connections and usually enough money to act independently. "Now and then I get high with somebody," he says, "but mostly I get high by myself." For many others a piece of the puzzle is missing: they lack either cash or a personal connection. At the end of a morning's hustling, they usually begin a circuit of familiar corners, hoping to team up to cop. Like Tap (a petty shoplifter in Philly), they will be waiting to meet addicts with cash but no connections. Even at 27, Tap is already beginning to be "tapped out"; his hustling resources are low, but he has extensive connections.

> You may want something, crank [speed] or heroin and you may want it in quantity. I'll go get it from people that I know, and I'll get it at less price . . . making something on the deal. I may do that two or three times. There's no certain price that you spend on dope. . . . At one time it was all one price, and if you didn't have it, you couldn't cop. It's different now. . . . A guy might be used to paying, say, seventy-five dollars for a bundle (twenty-five bags), and I may be able to give him [the dealer] fifty-five dollars because I know the dealer. So, you got twenty dollars for [your] own. Plus, [the buyer will] probably give me a few of the bags.

Others, unlike Tap, will not leave their profit to chance or good will. Milton, 20, from New York, runs customers and, when he can, "beats" them:

> I told him the quarter was fifty dollars but I got it for twenty. So, I made thirty for myself. Plus the people offered me half quarter . . .

Tap, Milton, and users like them are able to parlay their experience into sharing in another user's buy, to their mutual benefit. This is one form of the touting that has long been part of the heroin scene. More recently, another kind of cooperation among users is being seen—outright pooling of cash. The heroin economy is becoming more capitalistic, as Tap observed. Dealers are undercutting each other and discounting for bulk purchases. Sometimes the motivation for pooling is to wangle a volume discount. Ski describes how it works. He and his partner had just stolen eighty dollars worth of food stamps. They bought some dinner meat and got fifty dollars in cash, twenty-five apiece. If he were alone, with twenty-five dollars in buy money, Ski says:

> I can get a fifteen-dollar bag or two ten-dollar bags. But bein' him and I are together, we gonna get, like I say, two fifteen-dollar bags and a ten-dollar bag, too. *Apiece.*

By pooling their twenty-five dollars apiece, Ski and his partner are able to buy eighty dollars worth of heroin for fifty. Most often, however, the sharing is more penny ante. A few users, unsuccessful on the day, will chip in their individual five or ten dollars and cop just enough to stave off withdrawal for another day, as Tap, describes:

> It's a lot different from back in the days when . . . say everybody was all for themselves . . . like I say, if I've got somethin' I'm gonna say, "Hey, Al, me and you; we're gonna do this together." This way it keeps a lot of the pressure off and you always have something to get high with in some way. Both of us are gonna get over. That's the way it is . . . you just want to go get enough to maintain, you know, like keeping the edges off.

Sharing and borrowing are common practice among these men. The majority of HLS respondents (78 percent) have resorted to begging, borrowing, and sharing in some way at one time or another. It is not something to be proud of—only about 4 percent claim it as their main source of buy money. But the alternative is worse than the small humiliation of going in on "nickels and dimes": withdrawal. A user from Washington, D.C. described it:

> It's rough, man. You can't sleep. You be havin' wild dreams. Stomach be bent over with cramps . . . an' you get to sweating, your nose runnin'. You be jumpin', you be shakin'. You get high. You get calm.

For some, withdrawal may be in the cards today. A loner, perhaps, who could not make a connection. Some hustler whose day just went bad. An ill-fated "chump" who got ripped off or burned by an unscrupulous dealer. Or a user snitched on, and busted by the police while he was "holding" (in possession of) his day's fix. For them this day will be ugly. But for those other users, most probably, who did manage to hustle their way to copping a few bags, today is "easy street." They anticipate this kind of day with the almost devil-may-care attitude expressed by Ron, a 27-year-old respondent from Chicago:

> I'm ready to go to the pool room, kicking around, flash me a little money, get a bite to eat, kick around with the fellows, find out what they been doin', plannin'. . . . The day is still young, but I jus' stay laid back and take it easy. So, I jus' hang around watchin' everybody else scuffle 'cause I got mine. Now, I'm coasting, you know. Just coasting.

Solo, from New York, is in the same frame of mind after making a successful connection:

> Went to Murphy's and drank some alcohol, ya know. We went back and laid in my man's house, makin' some phone calls. . . . Now I'm ready. Now, I feel ready.

All they need do now is find a safe place to shoot up so that they can "get down."

Getting Off

Once these men have copped their day's supply, their immediate goal is to "fire" (shoot up) their stuff as soon as possible. They are eager to experience heroin: its rush, its nodding languor, its freedom from life's pain. This is the part of the day that makes the risks of hustling, the frustrations of copping and the price of dependency worthwhile, or as Zulu puts it, ". . . if you want to enjoy the pleasures life presents, you know, you got to deal with it." But this is also one of the riskiest parts of a user's day, because for probably the first time this day, he is holding.

Dope is frequently a priority law enforcement issue in most communities and heroin users often are, or at least see themselves as, victims of these sporadic crackdowns. But to a certain degree the junkie is always at the mercy of police. Known junkies are easy marks for the cop who feels pressured to "turn in more activity" to his or her sergeant. Sometimes it may be "necessary" to "farm out" (plant) evidence on a user, as John, 17, a student in New York complains: "They trap you for somethin' even though you ain't doin' it." But the street-wise cop rarely has to resort to such tactics because at this time of day many junkies are sitting ducks, in possession of heroin. These users may find themselves preyed upon even in the absence of "selective enforcement priorities." Precinct police with no intention of arresting the heroin user may confiscate his few bags as a harassment measure or to demonstrate dominance on the street. But most likely a cop will harass a junkie in this way in order to turn him into an informer. The strategy is to harass by confiscation but without arrest. Soon, the cop will try to make the user feel beholden by "cutting him a break" by not even confiscating. Then, he tries to "hook" the junkie, suggesting that he share information while holding the threat of future arrest over the "target's" head. Every street user is open to this manipulation; Bosco, 33, a stick-up man from New York, has been on the spot:

> The police boss me, right. They know who they got. . . . They will give someone my picture that been robbed. "Ain't that who robbed you?" Now, how a person who been robbed gonna' know who robbed him? They'll say, "That's him. That's him." They'll put it in the complaintiff's mind that I robbed him . . . I go to court [and] beat it. When they cut me loose they re-arrest me . . . get me framed . . . they want you be their snitch. Talk about, "Look here, I get you cut loose; give you up and send you right back to the dogs."

Their vulnerability to such harassment and enforcement techniques explains why junkies try to be in possession of heroin for as short a time as possible. In fact, many—perhaps most—junkies avoid even carrying their "works" (tourniquet, cooker cup, cotton, syringe) around with them. So, when the user cops, he is often faced with two pressing logistical problems: where is the nearest safe place to shoot up, and how to get a set of works, if he doesn't have one. In rare instances, a user will be able to shoot up at the dealer's place, but most dealers refuse to offer this premium. For one thing, they want to avoid lingering traffic; for another, dealers often disdain and mistrust their customers, as Little D, 26, a dealer and pimp from New York, admitted:

> I don't have no shootin' gallery . . . I don't believe in that and I don't like over ten people in the house, because I can't watch them. Not that peoples' stealing but gettin' dizzy and anything liable to happen. I don't want a nigger to come and tell me they' sorry for breakin' my television set. I ain't got no more television and they just say, "I'm sorry."

In practice the user usually has three choices for a place to get off. If he has his own works, or if he is with a friend who does, he will opt either for a car, a bar's bathroom or similar public but secure spots or, preferably, a "crib," that is, his own home or someone else's. The loner without works or junkies whose cribs are too far away will very likely go to a nearby gallery. There, for a fee of about two dollars, he can get a set of works and relax while he gets off. The gallery is an important institution at the copping corner, and most users have to take advantage of it at least occasionally. In fact, some, like Buck, 29, from D.C., even prefer it. He claims that his partner and he "usually go to a street house, ya' know. We go to those houses where you get high and socialize. Then, he goes his way and I go mine."

In spite of the ready availability of galleries near every copping area, most users, unlike Buck, do not prefer them as places to shoot up. To begin with, no user likes to part with the fee; two dollars looms larger when, after buying a few bags, you have only five or maybe ten dollars left for the day. In addition to cost, a gallery's hygiene is often miserable—dirty, broken down, with only one or two sets of works to be used by all of the customers. Not that users or addicts are models of personal hygiene, but none takes lightly the threat of hepatitis from a dirty syringe. That is the reason why Ron, from Chicago, and many others avoid galleries.

> I'm mostly alone when I shoot. Not in a gallery, because one guy tellin' you to take one outfit. I have to be careful of my hygiene; I had hep years ago, so I have to be very careful.

Also, there is the stigma of degradation that some feel about the gallery, as Ben, age 27, a Philadelphian, sums up:

> Galleries, ain't where it's at. We wasn't brought up like that. They be definitely hardcore junkies and they don't give a damn no more about how their appearance is or nothing like that. Ain't nobody want to give another two dollars. Their works, the shit all dirty, man. An' people be shootin' blood all over you.

Still, cost and physical conditions are not the only reasons why shooting galleries are not used by most users. Most who have been successful in their work and hustling so far today are now looking to "lay back and take it easy . . . kick around with the fellows," as Ron put it. Galleries are too often like flophouses, their transient clientele and sometimes squalid interiors not conducive to easy socializing. So most will opt for more hospitable surroundings. Some, like Ron, will head for a friendly bar or pool room. There they will secret themselves in the bathroom while they shoot up. Still others, most perhaps, will go to someone's crib, preferably their own or their partner's. There, safe from police, mellow from the sounds of jazz, and among such friends as they have, these men for the first time today can surrender themselves to the rush and enveloping comfort of heroin about which James, from Washington, D.C. rhapsodizes:

> [It] felt like there wasn't no end, it's like you are standing on air. During the rush, about the second hit I fell back. I was sitting on the couch and I went into a deep sweat, and I was just sweating. And I felt like I was about to snap, like the whole world was closing in one me. . . . I felt so good and I felt

so bad that I didn't know what to do. I just stayed there . . . decent music and a lot of females.

Living the High Life

It is a common myth that heroin users are forever chasing the "ultimate high," according to Mike, a 28-year-old addict from Washington, D.C., and a former chef for Congress. For some, in fact, the goal is nothing more than "getting straight," as Ace, 34, a burned-out junkie from Philadelphia, confessed:

> I don't get drunk, I don't get ossified. I just get normal . . . the term "high" is to describe the act of other people . . . I'm comin' back to normality when I get high. I live a rather drab existence, you know.

For a few others, the goal is to compensate for a sense of personal inadequacy, as Curly, a teenager from New York, admitted:

> I most enjoy shooting drugs so I can just keep people off my back. You know when I'm not high, I'm scared of people . . . I'm littler that they are, so whatever I do I got to do double hard, and when I'm high it doesn't bother me . . .

And for some, it is to compensate for the general inadequacy or pressures of life, as Anthony, the mailman from D.C., said:

> . . . it's an escape, you know. It pushes reality a thousand miles away. Regardless of what you're doin' when you're getting high, it's like pushing everything else out of your mind . . . the pain just goes away.

But such self-deprecation and lamentation for their lot in life were rare among HLS respondents. These heroin users more often see themselves as making the most of a hard-scrabble life in which, because of poverty and perhaps racism, they have been dealt a short hand. They approach daily life ready to capitalize on any opportunities that come their way. For these men this midafternoon high is the act which organizes and gives focus to their day. It is its own daily reward for their skill in "getting over" once again. And it is the context, the stage, for socializing among themselves.

After he emerges from the private world of the rush and the nod, the user, according to a respondent from Washington, D.C., can finally afford to relax in the company of:

> . . . my walk boys. We can rap about things like that where we can't with others, like family or somebody on your job . . . you can exaggerate with them on your job, [like] you ain't had no pussy in a week but you say, "yeah,

I been fuckin' every night." They don't know if you lie or you don't. But your walk boys, they be with you; they know what's goin' on.

These afternoon moments allow the users to share ideas for hustles and make plans to carry them out, as another HLS respondent described:

[We] talk about how we gonna get our next high. We talk about how to maneuver, trying to let [each other] know where we at. If we form up, [we] got to know where [every] one goes, because we form up together.

They share information about who has the best dope. As the afternoon whiles away, they share, too, their big time dreams. "When you see an airplane goin' overhead, you say: 'Damn. I wish that was me,'" says Solo, "'with a million bucks and goin' to Puerto Rico'." Ron, a Chicagoan, is more expansive, though with a pang of fatalism:

We all a bunch of dreamers, you know. We all see ourselves in Rolls Royces, owning planes and pullin' off a big crime . . . in your nods you fantasize . . . We talk about kicking, 'cause the dope gets worse. It depends. Sometimes we get some good dope and we say, man, now, we don't feel bad about this here. But, man, you're on your last twenty or thirty dollars and the dope ain't nothin' you sayin', "I don't need this motherfucker," you know. Yeah, I think about kickin'—till somebody comes up with good stuff.

So goes an afternoon for men who scored well earlier in the day. Some, however, who were less successful or whose habits are larger than routine hustling can support, could not afford such coasting. For them, this afternoon, there was only a brief time-out in their hectic-paced hustling. Tonight, if they are lucky, will be their time to "enjoy the pleasures life presents," as Zulu put it.

Reprise or Reprieve: The Evening Routine

With few exceptions—whores who work a night shift and the occasional legitimate day-worker who may still have to cop, for example—heroin users hustle during the day so that in the nighttime they can relax. The corners and bars, which during the day had been the domain largely of male addicts, hustlers, and deadbeats, now begin to fill up with a menagerie of street life—pimps and whores, workers and wives. It is time for the user to close out his day. Get a bite to eat. Socialize. Score some more drugs and maybe some sex.

By five o'clock or so, the typical user will have run his hustle, copped and fired, and finished the afternoon with a few dollars to spare, dollars to spend on the family perhaps, but more likely to spend on partying tonight. If he has a family, he probably will head home, now, to be with his children and eat with his "old lady" and kids. A few may even spend the evening at home, like Max, 24, from D.C., who often passes the evening with his elderly father. But most users, even if they have families, are not "family men." Icepick, of Washington, laments his not being a better father:

> My kids are part of me. When you look at kids, you know, like kids are helpless . . . like, when I look at my kids, I see myself because I'm helpless, too. . . . When you become addicted, usin' stuff . . . is as much a part of you as bein' a husband, a father, provider or whatever. It's an integral part of you.

Slim, from New York, feels the same conflicts but tries to defend himself by being colder:

> . . . a lot of conflict came in with my family 'cause I'm not workin'. The kids need this, you need that . . . I don't have it to give them, sometimes . . . I only have enough to take care of me and there's not even enough to do that.

So, after running a few errands, grabbing some supper and shooting, most of these men are ready to "shave and finish tidying myself up," as Ski said, and "change my clothes for evening attire," as Ron bragged.

Once this is done, it is time again to hit the streets, but not to run their hustles, though they might if opportunity knocked. Rather, the night is party time and these men will be looking for a party high and maybe some sex. If they cop again at all, it is as likely to be for cocaine and some reefer as it is for heroin, as Solo reports:

> We went out coppin' again because the high was comin' down. We got us some coke and some heroin. I say, "Fuck it. Let's do it right this time, man. Let's do it up right."

With a party high, a user will stroll down to a bar to mix with the neighborhood gang, drink some whiskey and wine, and maybe hook up with some women. Solo's night continued typically:

> We finally got in touch with some chicks about seven o'clock. We went to a bar, you know, and got high again with the bitches. They had money and we didn't let on that we had any money.

This illustrates again how users take advantage of every opportunity that comes their way. In similar circumstances, for example, Ron went to a bar where, as he tells it, he:

> met this little old dame . . . [she] was a little ill and like I say, I had this pile [supply of dope] at my crib. I could see she was a rookie . . . and I knew I

could take her to the crib and give her the drugs for sex, you know. Maybe even flip her, make a whore out of her. She had no business in . . . my world; she was meddling and I had more experience. I jus' decided to trip her off. Had a bottle of wine; had the reefer. We stayed together all that night.

Running a whore must have been attractive to Ron. Pimping is regarded by many HLS men as the best hustle of all, since the woman does all the work. (It is surprising that only about 4 percent of HLS users reported being involved in it.) But Ron, a shoplifter, does not have a pimp's aggressiveness. Besides, the allure of having sex with the girl overshadowed her commercial value.

The overwhelming majority of HLS men, like Ron, reported having an active sex life. Reports of intercourse several times a week was common. However, as James, from Washington, D.C., typifies, the physical and emotional gratification of sex can be overshadowed by the pleasure of heroin's high:

> I have two women . . . I split their time up, they get three days apiece out of the week. But I don't be nutting [ejaculating] every time. I be fucking man, and just don't nut [I] be so high . . . I mean sometime you get lame at the post, man. You can think about the fattest woman in the world, man. . . . Sometimes you be so hyped up, man, that you just keep fucking and fucking. They think you superman and you don't even nut. She doesn't know if you come or what. That's the whole feeling she's lookin' for.

Sex provides these users with yet another marker of success. As in other aspects of life, performance is what counts: "makin' it." Having a legitimate job says no more about a user's worth than does his hustling. His not experiencing the joys of sex says nothing about his ability to perform. His woman is satisfied with his virility and he is proud. Heroin fills the gaps.

Closing Out the Day

As the evening nears midnight, most HLS men can look back on a full, even rewarding day. Once again they have met the challenges of poverty and addiction. They have parlayed their wake-up dollars into enough money to satisfy their "jones" (habit) one more day. For one more day they have avoided being burned, busted, or spasmed by withdrawal. And along the way they have had adventures, high times and maybe even some loving. Some users, like Solo, Dap Daddy, or Lucky, for instance, might now go out one more time to cop for tomorrow's wake-up shot. Most will not. Most will ease on back to their cribs where, as Dave fondly describes:

> . . . you ain't got nobody beatin' on your door, botherin' ya. You just come in the house [and] relax . . . [you got] a little bit of cash, you got your drug with you and you're ready to go to bed. . . . you settle down . . . you take your drug before your meal, then you go to sleep. That's the enjoyable part of the day.

Solo's night ended in a similarly typical way:

> When I got back to the neighborhood I took [my wake-up] and went home. My wife had the TV on . . . it was a good flick. I nodded through most of it. Next thing I knew it was daybreak.

Epilogue

Daybreak and the dawn of another yesterday, another tomorrow. Just another day in the mosaic of every user's life. In an impoverished world with little to look forward to, these men have heroin to organize their mundane lives and reward them for another day survived. Lives measured not by stages or five-year plans. Lives where men find some small measure of justly felt pride and self-respect in their stamina and skills to make one-day plans, to manage one-day lives.

Note

1. The heroin lifestyle study (HLS) sought to gain a more informed perspective on the dynamics of heroin use and the lifestyles of heroin users. The interview schedule included a series of guided but open-ended questions which chronicled a heroin user's typical day. To prepare this chapter, all 124 interview transcripts were reviewed and reduced to summaries of typical day questions. The first was an aggregated count of responses to 29 questions covering such areas as: rising time; washing, bathing or showering; eating; joining a walking partner or associate; cost of a day's heroin supply; and sources of income. Second, possible significant variations were explored by two additional sortings of these data: the first by age level, the second by city of origin. Finally, 28 transcripts (7 per city) were chosen at random for a more detailed reading and review in an effort to capture more indepth material for this chapter.

4
Hustling: Supporting A Heroin Habit

Allen Fields
James M. Walters

I n the past, researchers have acknowledged the variety of activities of the
heroin lifestyle, but they have tended to emphasize the more dramatic
ways its users support their habit. Some researchers have portrayed the
user as a member of an elite world of drug dealers (Sutter 1966) who conspic-
uously displays his wealth (Stephens and Levine 1971) and whose primary
concern is with making his life a "gracious work of art" (Finestone 1964).
This has contributed to the view of the heroin user as a skilled supercriminal
who sustains himself primarily from one lucrative hustle. This perception is
far from true for the majority of HLS respondents.

Although some regular heroin users are successful specialists, the majority are hardly members of a world of elite hustlers. Those who are specialized
hustlers have usually developed their skills before they become drug dependent. Most of these inner-city heroin users have little money and often cannot
raise the twenty or twenty-five dollars needed for their daily fix. They may
specialize in one way of raising money, but these specialized hustles are only
one of a number of methods used to support heroin habits. The truth is that
today's heroin user and addict mostly scrounges around the streets in search
of any opportunity that might help him maintain his habit. To him survival
means that he must use a variety of ways to raise the money or obtain the
drugs he needs.

This chapter examines the different ways that the HLS men support their
heroin habits. The term "hustling" was introduced into the social sciences literature by Ned Polsky (1969) to characterize the activities of men who earned
a living by betting on pool and billiard games. In the drug literature the term
has been used to describe the unlawful activities that heroin addicts employ to
raise money for drugs (Finestone 1964; Preble and Casey 1969; Nash 1972;
Smith and Stephens 1976; Biernacki 1979). More recently Goldstein (1981)
defined hustling as a dynamic process in which an addict achieves success
(usually economic) through illegal activities that involve some degree of
scheming or conning. Although hustling frequently involves illegal behaviors,
many hustling activities are legal. Therefore, "hustling" is defined in this
chapter as unconventional activities that are designed to produce economic

and/or narcotic gain. By unconventional we mean that these activities are unorthodox when compared to the activities normally associated with a conventional nine-to-five job. Moreover, these activities may require the hustler to use guile, deceit, or coercion.

In order to raise money, the unemployed user must invest a significant part of each day planning, arranging, and participating in some hustling activity (Waldorf 1973; Goldstein 1981). Like everyone else, he must have enough money for basic needs—food, clothing, and rent. But the user's need for his fix is central to any understanding of the heroin lifestyle of the 1980s. But even when he has his fix, even when he relaxes and is not actively engaged in hustling, he is planning and thinking of ways to get money for his next meal, perhaps, and certainly for his next shot of heroin. This point is illustrated by Jimmy, 30, of Chicago, a long-term participant in "the life:"

> When you relax, you can think. Do you understand what I'm trying to say? If you can relax you can think of how to make some more money. At night when you get high, you can think of how to get some money for the next day.

Some researchers have described different roles in the drug business (Preble and Casey 1969) and the range of hustles available to the addict (Goldstein 1981). Others have limited their descriptions to specific groups of hustlers (Maurer 1949; Iceberg Slim 1969; Polksy 1969; Agar 1973). The most common approach is to view behavior from a social-problems perspective, focusing attention on problems the heroin user does or does not pose for society (Gould 1974; Chambers 1974; Voss and Stephens 1973; Helmer 1977). Despite these different approaches, the literature provides only a superficial view of hustling and the lifestyle of the heroin user. Past research has failed to address crucial questions such as: How much variety is employed by hustlers? How competent are they? What is the level of return from hustling? How does legitimate work figure into the overall hustling patterns? What are some of the specific processes involved in hustling activities? Do all hustling activities have a negative impact upon society? How might hustling benefit some neighborhoods?

Our ethnographic approach allowed us to broach these questions. Polsky (1969) refers to it as an "approach from within." This chapter describes and discusses the hustling activities of heroin addicts from the point of view of the men studied, using terms and concepts that the hustlers themselves provide. This approach has a number of advantages over other studies. Chief among these is that we do not view users' activities from a social-problems perspective. We look at problems that society, events, and people create for the user as he seeks to satisfy his needs through hustling. This approach not only helps the reader view hustling from the heroin user's perspective, it also provides a better understanding of the level of crime committed and illuminates other functions that hustling serves.[1]

In this chapter, therefore, we will describe varieties of hustling activities and examine their unique problems. We will also consider the implications of these lifestyles on the image of the heroin user and his criminality, and on public policy, especially toward crime and treatment.

The Diversity of Hustles

Few people have firsthand knowledge of the way heroin users hustle. Rather, they construct images of them from movies such as *The Hustler, Superfly,* and *The Mack.* For the more esoteric reader, there are descriptions of the hustling activities of urban nomads and ghetto residents (Spradley 1970; Valentine 1978), the elaborate games of the confidence man (Maurer 1949), pool hustlers (Polsky 1969), and biographic sketches of the successful pimp (Iceberg Slim 1969). Finally, news coverage of major drug raids and the arrests of high-level drug dealers also shapes the image of the addict hustler. The media generally project the false image of a person who is a skilled criminal, sustaining a drug lifestyle solely on the basis of some single, specialized, lucrative hustling method.

Analysis of the HLS data suggests a far different image for the addict hustler. Diversity, the need to be flexible, rather than specialization in hustling is a requisite for survival. HLS men know there are far too many risks associated with a life of hustling for them to restrict their activities to one method. Any one of a number of problems can frustrate efforts to "score" (raise money) or, as one man puts it, "knock you off your main thing." Further, and contrary to popular belief, legitimate work as a source of income is cited by more persons in our sample than any type of illegal activity. Well over half of all HLS men said that they obtained money for heroin at least occasionally by legitimate work. Borrowing, as another legal way to get money, is reported by about half (52 percent) of all HLS men. Only about a third (31 percent) of the HLS men said they stole regularly. About one quarter said they sometimes conned women (which could be legal as well as illegal), sold drugs, or shoplifted. Finally, robbery was reported by only about a fifth (18 percent) of the men and burglary by only a tenth (10 percent).

So, most of the HLS men are not consummate drug sellers, skilled thieves, or burglars but rather are unskilled opportunists who face each day as it arrives and do whatever they can to "get over." They seldom begin the day with any money or even a wake-up supply of heroin. Generally, the first thing they do is explore whatever opportunities present themselves. All tend to live their lives day to day. There is seldom the luxury of a day without hustling, or enough money or heroin for a long weekend or a week's vacation. From descriptions of the details of a typical day it is apparent that most of the HLS men scuffle for whatever money or heroin they can get. They engage in mundane hustling activities that offer them little self-satisfaction and only small amounts of heroin.

The role of legitimate work was illustrated by Zulu, 33, a hustler from Chicago:

> Whenever I can, I do legitimate work. I may help my father-in-law, ya know, he hauls junk. I may help my father-in-law work on his truck a half a day and I may make me fifty-five dollars. So, I don't have to do nothin' that day but ride around with him and pick up shit.

When asked about the different ways that he raises money for drugs, Mack, 24, from Philadelphia responded:

> My main hustle is to buy me a half ounce, roll up about 100 joints out of it and sell them. But I have to hustle day by day. I do errands every day for people in the building. They pay me a dollar or two dollars to go to the store for them, stuff like that too. That's how I make my little bit of money.

No job, no matter how menial, is beyond the dignity of the regular heroin users. In fact, many of the HLS men spoke about the advantages of the legitimate hustle. Several men said that they felt better when they were not "beating somebody" or ripping someone off.

Family and friendship networks are another source of support for HLS men. The money that families and lovers supply is especially crucial among hustlers who achieve little success from regular hustling activities. This point is illustrated by Leroy, a 32-year-old shoplifter who lives in Washington, D.C.:

> I started hustling about twelve o'clock. I had to wait all morning because twelve o'clock is the best time to go downtown. At twelve o'clock, things be moving, people be getting off for lunch and they be moving in the stores. It's the best time. But I didn't get anything. So, I went to see my mother to beg her for some money.

Borrowing and begging from relatives and lovers is a common practice among over half of HLS men. Acquiring money from family members often requires manipulation, as Black Charlie, a 30-year-old addict, confessed:

> Sometimes I have to obtain money to buy stuff through manipulating people, you know, manipulating members of my family. You know what I mean, being deceitful, tricking them.

HLS men rarely borrow money from friends and associates because it is a commodity that is always in short supply among heroin users. They are more likely to borrow an item that can be used to raise the money needed. Larry, 26, of Chicago, explains:

> I needed twenty dollars, right. So, I used this credit card, went and bought a few things, you know, two pair of pants and a shirt. It was a buddy's of mine. He lent it me. I don't know whose card it was, I don't know who he got it from. He lent it to me and I just got a few things to get over, to generate some money. I sold what I had bought, went back downtown and copped.

At other times, HLS men can arrange to get drugs on credit. Milt, a 20-year-old thief from New York City, points out:

> Usually I can get a half a quarter on credit. The people I go to know I'm a steady customer. I'm always havin' the women's sweaters to sell or jeans to sell. So, like they know I'm good for something. I either bring them some money or merchandise that they can wear, and they know I can go downtown to the department store and most generally I come off [succeed] the majority of the time.

However, only a few HLS men can regularly exercise this option, because of the low level of trust between those buying and selling. George, 23, from D.C., a distrusting hustler, explains how skepticism becomes the standard for dealer-user relationships:

> I don't trust too many people. I guess I got the attitude from selling stuff. Even my partners, I'm kinda shaky with them. I watch them very closely, 'cause I don't want them to try to beat me.

Finally, friendship networks provide a framework in which HLS men can share drugs when all other efforts fail. Tap, a 27-year-old chili pimp from Philadelphia, describes the importance of sharing drugs with associates:

> If I have something, I'm gonna say, "Hey Al, me and you we're going to do this [heroin] together. This is my day." This way it keeps a lot of pressure off and you always have something to get high with in some way. Even when none of us have no money, I know somebody out there will give me some [dope]. That's the way it is man. If I get it or you get it, both of us are going to be over.

Although it can be said that sharing drugs with associates may be a way of showing others how successful one is at hustling, sharing is done for a more utilitarian reason. Little D, a 26-year-old user from New York, explains:

If I ain't got it, you've got it. You usually be sharing your drugs to make your ends meet. It takes the pressure off you from having to hustle. If you don't have nothing you can call up somebody you usually share with. "What you got man?" You know, I take what they got. They're moral like that. If I share, if they got something, they gonna let me have some.

Three-fourths of the HLS men also steal, many only occasionally, as another means of raising money for drugs. Most of this stealing takes place in their immediate neighborhoods, involving thefts from small stores, relatives, and friends. Favorite targets are the many mom-and-pop stores in inner-city neighborhoods. These stores seldom have the security devices found in large department stores; thus, this type of store is a prime target for the hustler. For example, Bill, a 22-year-old burglar from Chicago, points out the importance of this alternative source of money:

My main thing, I burglarize, I deal with pipe. Ya know, if you steal copper and brass pipe out of buildings and get caught, that's burglary. That's what I mainly do. I go out and look for my friend and we go looking for buildings that we can get pipe out of and sell. Yeah, we get pipe out of buildings and take them to the junkman to sell. If we can't find no pipes and stuff, then we go boosting the stores. We go into the grocery stores around here and steal meat, coffee, cheese, and whatever we can get to make the money. Yeah, we mainly be running back and forth to the stores and looking for buildings that we can get pipe and stuff out of.

Main Hustles

Despite the wide range of hustles, heroin users generally favor an activity in which their knowledge, skills, and/or contacts make it easier for them to generate money. When asked "What is your main hustle?" about a third of these men said that it was stealing, which covers a variety of activities including shoplifting. Yet, very few HLS men reported burglary and fewer still said that picking pockets was their main hustle.

It is most interesting that legitimate work is cited as their main source of income by one out of every four HLS men. Of these, more than half (53 percent) said that they supported their habits exclusively with money earned from legal activities. As Ron, a 27-year-old government employee from Chicago, points out:

Contrary to what people think, there are a lot of dope fiends that work every day. Basically, uh, people have their conceptions that all junkies and drug addicts live through their diabolical wits, rippin' people off, which may be. But then there's those so-called isolated cases where people do work.

One major source of revenue for heroin users is the drug business itself (Goldstein 1981; Preble and Casey 1969). In fact, these users view drug-related activities as one of the better hustles (Waldorf 1973). Drug-related activities (primarily street-level dealing) as a common main hustle are mentioned by 19 percent of HLS respondents. Less frequently reported is "conning" (9 percent), generally requiring little sophistication, planning, or time. For example, several HLS men explained that they would buy heroin for someone at a reduced price and pocket the extra money. Others said that they simply kept the money given them by others to purchase drugs.

Conning women is another type of main hustle. An illustration of this was provided by Torre, 28, a heroin user from Washington, D.C.:

> I run this little con game on my woman. I got to be sick, I be dying. Really that's just to get that money, you know. Cause she'll say, "Oh baby," she talk that shit. I be faking myself. I run in the bathroom and stick my finger down my throat, run back in there and try to throw up in front of her. Get down on my knees and pretend I'm in the cramps and shit like that. She got one of them ways she can go to the bank, push one of them little buttons and that money shoot up. Money come out the wall for me anytime.

When asked about the way he raises money to buy heroin, Little D, a dealer and pimp, described his woman's activities:

> My woman hustles. She's a bona fide hustler; when she hustles, she hustles. Sometimes my woman go out and I don't have to do nothing. She give me money, yeah. She give me the money so I don't have to do nothing. I don't have to share it back with her. She goes out and gets money. I want you to know that that's the way [to get money for drugs] 'cause the money is given to me. I don't consider it to be like a pimp, but really that's what it is. You follow me? That's what it is. She makes good money, do you understand where I'm coming from? It is my money, you know.

Unlike the classic pimp, a chili pimp, like Little D, seldom helps a prostitute get tricks and rarely assists her with her trade. Most often, he maintains a distance from her work, keeping his hands in other hustling activities. Although he may engage in other forms of hustling, his woman provides most of the money he needs to support his habit. Consequently, the chili pimp is more likely to "pimp off" rather than "pimp for" his woman. What influence he has on her is usually the result of his being her lover, boyfriend, or in some cases, husband.

The Social Typology of Hustlers

To characterize the different types of hustles, we performed a content analysis of the open-ended questions and descriptive materials corresponding with the hustling patterns. We found that HLS men could be assigned to different categories of hustles based on the following criteria: (1) the degree of skill, planning or sophistication required in hustling (Waldorf 1973; Biernacki 1979); (2) the target that is selected for hustling (Gould 1974; Goldstein 1981); and (3) the method of hustling (Chambers 1974; Preble and Casey 1969; Agar 1973). Using these criteria, we identified the following types: (1) the opportunistic hustler, (2) the legitimate hustler, (3) the skilled hustler and (4) the dope hustler.

The Opportunistic Hustler

Expediency governs the behavior of many hustlers. Hustlers must seize any opportunity that comes along to acquire money and/or drugs (Biernacki 1979). No opportunity, legitimate or illegitimate, that promises a quick and easy financial reward will be passed up. The opportunistic hustler tends to be a generalist who lets expediency, rather than other factors such as skill or contacts, dictate the hustling activity he engages in. As a result, he devotes little or no time to planning hustles and takes them as they come. Since little skill or sophistication is required for most of these activities, it is important to be alert and in the right place at the right time.

A majority of these users steal at least at some time to support their habits. But burglary, picking pockets, and shoplifting tend to require a greater amount of skill, planning, and sophistication than other kinds of nonspecific thievery. Further, men who engage in these activities tend to select specific targets while those who engage in nonspecific kinds of stealing select their targets haphazardly or at random. That is, of the latter group almost any opportunity that holds out the possibility of financial or narcotic gain is a likely target for their hustling.

The opportunistic hustler is the jack-of-all-trades. His hustling activities cover a range of hustles. For example, Gut, an 18-year-old heroin user from Philly, talks about a few of the many activities in which the opportunistic hustler engages:

> Yesterday morning, I got up about eight. Got downtown by nine. I wanted to see this guy about some money he owed me. I got thirty-five dollars and left downtown about ten-thirty. I left downtown and went up on 67th and St. Lawrence, you know. The money that I had, I was going to buy me a bag of dope. I ran into this guy I know. We hooked up and got a fifty-dollar bag. Once we got the edges off and nobody was sick, then we scheme on how we gonna get our next fix. So, we went boosting, got a couple of leather coats, brought them back and sold them. He dropped me off, I guess about two o'clock. So, I go around to the dope house. I'm gonna snatch some dope from the dope man when he ain't looking. Instead of doing that, I go around to my guy's house and bag up three twenty-dollar bags of foot powder, right.

I tell the guys that we gone around to the dope house and the man gonna let us check the package in the hall to see if we like the weight on it and we gonna switch. So, we go around there, he give me the three bags, we check them and we switch. We went and took off and I laid up for a while. Went back up on the corner and ran into this girl I knew. She had about twenty-five dollars. So, I took her and beat her out of her twenty-five dollars and bought me a bag of dope. I waited for some new people to come and cop, beat 'em out of their money so I could cop again.

Therefore, on any given day, the opportunistic hustler like Gut is searching for people who owe him money, hooking up with others and combining money to buy drugs, boosting and conning people out of their money and/or dope. At other times, he is a thief, a burglar's lookout or a chili pimp.

The opportunistic hustler, with little time for personal grooming, generally hits the streets and begins hustling before the skilled hustler starts. There are several reasons for starting early. For example, Ron, a 30-year-old opportunistic hustler from Chicago, states:

I woke about seven. I woke up just tasting drugs, and I started to think of how I was going to get money for my fix. I just had a funny taste in my mouth like I wanted to chew something. I know I needed some drugs. I was just feeling drowsy, like I wasn't alive, you know. So, therefore, I put on my clothes and hit the streets. I just got out immediately. I didn't even comb my hair.

By starting early, he is in a position to exploit situations as they become available. For example, he might position himself in areas where early morning deliveries are made in order to catch truck drivers who fail to lock their trucks while making deliveries. Opportunities are presented when merchandise is delivered before a store opens. If one situation does not yield results, the opportunistic hustler has ample time to seek other possibilities. Ron made this point:

I "hit the streets" about seven-thirty. I seen Jake and all these fellows and we kicked it around for a while. We were watching the truckdrivers making deliveries, hoping for a slip, somebody make a mistake or something. There was too many of us, so we moved on and separated. I left there and just felt my way through Jew town, local shops. Walking through there I happened to knock off a nice little old sports coat, 'bout seventy-five dollar sports coat. So, now I got me, got me something to work with. I get fifty dollars for it and I'm happy. (After all) it didn't cost me nothing.

The chances of "scoring" merchandise are reduced when a number of opportunistic hustlers gather in the same areas. In groups, hustlers become highly visible to delivery persons, businessmen, and others. For this reason, the opportunistic hustler often works alone. This does not mean, however, that the opportunistic hustler will not participate in other types of hustling activities. Being an opportunist also means that one must be versatile enough to take a partner if the situation requires it. Rickey, 19 years old, from Chicago, was, in his own words, versatile and described what hustling entails:

> Hustling is the main way I get most of my money to buy drugs. Mostly theft, you know. But you can keep coming on these same spots, so you have to be versatile. I have a couple of guys who are burglars, and they come and get me for my strength. Not that I'm a good burglar, but if the joint is cased out . . . I got another guy who steals cars, and he want me to drive a legitimate car and block anybody else from ah, a side street, you know, block something.

Few situations are exempt from the exploitations of the opportunistic hustler. For example, Rick, a 27-year-old heroin user from Philadelphia, describes the opportunities he found while interviewing for legitimate employment.

> I went to see about this job and I went to this here office. And as I came, I noticed the lady at this place was sitting on the steps and had left her wallet on the desk. So, I said that I wanted to go to the bathroom. When I came back out, they was all upset, asking who came past the desk. They didn't even ask me 'cause I acted like I was standing there and I didn't know what was going on. I kept my mind straight. I went back to the interviewer and asked what happened. I had the money, she had forty dollars in the bag.

Even when the opportunistic hustler has a legitimate job, it does not mean an end to his hustling activities. He is as likely to exploit the opportunities found on his job as he is to exploit those found in any other setting. This point was made by Leroy, a 31-year-old government employee from Washington, D.C.:

> I working for the Department of Energy, in all kind of big old government buildings. My ID get me through the door so I just flash my ID on the guard. Walk past him and usually the door be open in the building. I worked for the government long enough, I know that one door be open to a section. Open the door and you go in there, you know. I know a guy that buys IBM typewriters. The ball that goes around. You don't have to steal the whole typewriter. You just gotta be patient and get them balls. He gives me four dollars a ball. I work for the government and that's my main hustle. Getting them balls, you know. Take fifty of them and the dude gives you four dollars a ball. So that's fifty times four, that two hundred dollars.

Rick, who also considers himself a "strolling" thief, shows again how the naivete and trust of others is essential to the success of the opportunistic hustler.

I'm just like a strolling thief. I'm looking for whatever is not guarded. You know, most people are not geared to that way of thinking. And I just take advantage of their trust, you know.

A truck driver fails to lock his truck; a novice drug user trusts the addict to buy drugs; a wallet or purse is momentarily left unguarded. These are all situations that are ripe for exploitation by the opportunistic hustler. He manages to support a heroin habit by being alert, in the right place at the right time and ready to swing into action.

The Legitimate Hustler

Unlike the opportunistic hustler, the legitimate hustler seldom engages in illegal activities to support his heroin habit. Instead, he raises the money he needs for drugs by providing services or goods to residents in his neighborhood. These services are often an assortment of odd jobs done for people with whom he is familiar and who are familiar with him. The goods that he provides might consist of different kinds of merchandise that he sells at the various locations in his neighborhood. The legitimate hustler is different from others in that he earns, rather than steals. This sets him apart from most hustlers in the heroin lifestyle.

Like the opportunistic hustler, the legitimate hustler looks for any opportunity that promises to help support his habit. He also shares the distinction of being a jack-of-all-trades among hustlers. That is, under certain conditions the legitimate hustler will do whatever is necessary to obtain his drugs. However, as noted, the legitimate hustler is rarely involved in illegal activities. Rather than engage in illegal activities, hustlers like Bobby, a 27-year-old employee (Washington, D.C.) of a messenger service, devise a scheme whereby drugs are exchanged for services rendered:

I drive for a messenger service. Yeah, I have a run for the government that takes me out of the district, about twenty miles out of the district. Basically, what I do is deliver and pick up documents. And, after I make that run, which is eight in the morning, I usually make it back [to the neighborhood] within an hour. So, that gives me, for all practical purposes, till the afternoon when I have to make a second run. So, I have free time. So, uh, I got a system because of the car that I drive on my job. I want to make it clear that I don't do no stealing or stuff like that. I met this guy who had just received his income-tax check. He had a special place that he wanted to go to have it cashed and told me that it was worth $200 to get it cashed there. So, I took him. He gave me some stuff and bought two quarters. So, we got down on one quarter and he took the other quarter and split it in half. If I wanted to oil [shoot it] then I could and if I wanted to walk with it I could. So, I chose

to walk with it. Ya know, it's like that. Cats I know will say, "Well, take us so-and-so," and that's a shot.

Legitimate hustlers like Vick, age 26, from the Philadelphia area, maintain their habits by borrowing—"robbing Peter to pay Paul." As he explains:

Just like I say, you robbin' Peter to pay Paul in a sense. Just like I borrow twenty dollars from you and tell you I'm gonna give it back to you tomorrow. I know I don't have no way of getting your money tomorrow unless I borrow it from somebody else. So, I borrow it from somebody else and give it to you. That keeps me and you straight. And, I borrow it from somebody else to pay the other guy. On payday, I take off the slack.

The legitimate hustler's ability to acquire money or drugs by transporting or borrowing from people means that he is familiar with them and that they are familiar with him. An important feature of his hustling behavior is that the targets he selects for hustling are usually people he knows or who live in his neighborhood.

He must often do an assortment of odd jobs to raise the money he needs to buy heroin. No job, regardless of how menial it might be, is beyond consideration. As George, a 23-year-old handyman, from Washington, D.C., points out:

I might do anything. I might clean somebody's house for him. They will give me five or even ten dollars. Yesterday, I cleaned the upstairs of my girlfriend's house. I hadn't even finished when she gave me the money. Other times, I might be helping some dude move or clean a car. I fix people's television sets and, if I get the chance, I do some painting. Someone has a leaking pipe; I fix it. I know people [in the community], different people that want to improve their house. Wall papering, plastering, panelling. I do all that. You know, I might do anything I can to get my money. But as far as going out there to steal and all that, I don't do anything illegal, nothing illegal.

The legitimate hustler generally gets up around the same hour as most hustlers, somewhere between the hours of seven and eight. He may smoke a reefer, wash, eat breakfast, and if he hustles with someone, contact or wait for his hustling partner. Ramon, a 32-year-old enterprising salesman from New York, describes the early morning routine of the legitimate hustler:

Friday morning I woke up at eight, washed, ate breakfast, bacon and eggs, and waited on a buddy of mine so that we could go hustling.

But the hustling does not start until about ten. As a matter of fact, it is not uncommon for hustlers like Ramon to begin at an even later hour:

[My buddy] he came by about noon. We left my house and went on up to the wholesale place where we go to get merchandise cheap. You know, for wholesale. We come out and sell them cheap and make a profit.

Like other hustlers, the legitimate hustler's initial hours are primarily dictated by the hours in which neighborhood business or residents begin their days and start to congregate in front of homes or in local bars. Billy, 30, of Chicago, talks about some of his activities:

We just walk around, just in the area, in the bars and stuff like that. You know, from bar to bar. You run into people on the street, especially in the afternoon and on payday. People are all over the place, you see people sitting on the steps, you know. You selling merchandise, you ask them and you bargain with them. Yeah, in the afternoon, you be joking with them. You know, the kind of personality you gotta have [in order to] sell stuff on the street. Salesman, that what it is. Selling the merchandise, making money back from what we put out our pockets.

The Skilled Hustler

The skilled hustler occupies a position of high status because of the type of his hustling activities. The activities most frequently reported as skilled hustles include burglaries, picking pockets, and specialized forms of shoplifting. These kinds of hustles are more highly regarded because they involve more risk and are generally more lucrative. Users who support their habits through these activities are believed to be more skillful, knowledgeable, and sophisticated than other user hustlers (Biernacki 1979).

Like the legitimate hustler, the skilled hustler usually begins his day like most working people in the United States. He rises early, somewhere between the hours of seven and eight, and follows a regular routine in preparing for a day of hustling. In spite of the early hour at which he awakens, the skilled hustler seldom begins hustling until around nine-thirty or ten. During the intervening time, he generally contacts his hustling partner and together they develop some plan of action. James, 28, a shoplifter from New York, describes this part of the skilled hustler's morning:

I made a call to my man, a partner of mine, to see what was happening. After that, I was downstairs about eight-thirty and I started to make my hook-up. It takes me between eight, no between eight-thirty and I'd say, uh, quarter to ten and I board up. You know, hook up with who I'm gonna play with. I'd say it's between quarter of ten or fifteen minutes to ten and whoever I'm playing with, we're hooked up. We usually try to determine which way we gonna go—north or south. We burn them west suburbs up over there so we don't even put that in our mind. So, we go south.

The skilled hustler seldom begins hustling without at least one other person. He gives far more attention to selecting the target for hustling than other hustlers do. Fashionable department stores, apartments where the occupants have left for the morning, and people in congested and impersonal settings are potential targets for the skilled hustler. Timing is extremely important to a skilled hustler's plans. He must know when his targets are most vulnerable. Department stores are more vulnerable at specific times during the day, people leave apartments at specific times and "pigeons" are found on the streets during certain periods of the day. Glenn, a 33-year-old pickpocket from Chicago, explains how he operates:

> We start playing from the word go—this is our game. About quarter to ten. Then, you know, a woman or man, they try to get their shopping down before the noon hours. So, we get out like that. I stick, you know, or he stick, either one. We're picking pockets. Like I say, it's quarter to ten and we're having our plan.

Occasionally the skilled hustler will deviate from his normal hustling routine and vary his methods (Waldorf 1973; Biernacki 1979). However, he usually stays with established methods that can be counted on to provide the kind of money he needs. One of the more skilled methods most often used by the hustler is "tail-choppin'." As Zulu points out, successful tail-choppin' is dependent upon the aid of an accomplice.

> Tail-choppin' is when you go into a store and . . . you have somebody with you—mainly I prefer a woman. You go into a store where they have maybe just two counters and don't have no more than three people workin' in there, so you can pull one of the salesperson or maybe two of them away, while you deal with one. I prefer jewelry stores and clothin' stores, because they are not really that big [but] you got to look the part. . . . If the woman can pull the salesman away while I'm lookin' at a tray, then I'm gonna swing. . . . I'm gonna swing and when he look up I'm gone.

Another hustling method employed by the skilled hustler is described by Ray, 19, a self-defined burglar from Chicago:

> My man and me, our thing consists of apartment B & E. You know, apartment breaking and entering. Ah, we pick the locks, open the locks. There was a few apartments that we tried, knocked on the doors, ya know. A few people were home at the time. There was one apartment that we knocked on the door and nobody seemed to answer. I got into the apartment; jimmied the window, went into the apartment. Nobody was there. I opened up the door and let my man in. We jammed the lock because this way if anyone did come with keys, they couldn't get in. We robbed the people of jewelry

and cash, no TV because it's too heavy to carry. We were in and out in about ten minutes. We got out by the fire escape.

The Dope Hustler

The dope hustler supports his habit through a variety of activities associated with illicit drug sales. Most often, he is a low-status pusher or "juggler" (Waldorf 1973; Preble & Casey 1969), who gets drugs on consignment, takes out a small amount for personal use and sells what remains to fellow addicts in his immediate neighborhood (Biernacki 1979).

Slim, 38, of New York City, talks about this type of hustling:

> My main thing, I sell stuff, man. You know, I try to get me a package and I'll convert it into bags and sell it. Like yesterday, I went to see the man, tell him, you know, man, there's a lot of customers out there and, shit, nobody got no good dope. And, he give it to me on consignment, you know, get enough for ten bags on consignment. So, I dumped [shot] two and went on the street and sold the other eight. You know, make a little money to take home. Yeah, that way I can use and make a small profit.

The dope hustler seldom realizes a large profit from his activities. He might try to keep twenty to forty dollars for every one hundred dollars of heroin he sells. As James, 26, a juggler from D.C., points out, the amount of money from such activities fluctuates with the amount of heroin that the dope hustler takes out for his own use:

> Uh, my brother and me, we went downtown and, uh, picked up a big packet. We get the dope from the man. He gives me the dope to sell, so I sell his dope and get my drugs, money, and his money out of it. So, we picked up fifteen, that's $480 street value in drugs. I got me some bags, got off, and came back on the street to sell. We sold a lot of drugs that day. Sold about, about fifty people. Made about $400. I sold about $400 worth of drugs but I only made like $75.

The dope hustler recognizes that drugs and/or money can be obtained by providing certain kinds of services to dealers. As a "tout" or "steerer" (Preble and Casey 1969) he persuades other users to buy a certain dealer's bag of heroin. Frank, a 28-year-old tout from Philly, talked about his trade:

> Well, my main hustle is, um, like we bring so many customers to a certain dealer and we'd get something from him. Like, I'm with a couple of guys that sell dope and every customer I get they take five or seven dollars out of whatever they make and that's mine. Like, sometimes they give me a half a quarter in the day when I first come out, that's twenty-five dollars. I got to

make five customers to pay that twenty-five dollars that they gave me for that morning shot. During the day I might get about five more customers, right. That's another half a quarter, it goes like that. At the end of the day, my drugs and money is there.

The dope hustler also provides services to other drug users who are unfamiliar with the heroin scene in his neighborhood (Biernacki 1979), buying for people who want to avoid being seen in copping areas or who do not have good connections in the neighborhood. Philly Ben, 27, a self-defined "middleman," describes the typical activities of a copman:

> Like sometimes there are people that don't know where to cop. We get their money and cop for them and get a taste. My biggest advantage is that I know, uh, I am real tight with most of the people that get in big quantity. I always know when the [good] stuff is comin' through. I always have people who want me to get it for 'em. I'm like the middleman, I got a credit line with most guys.

Thus the dope hustler supports his habit by trading services for small quantities of heroin and/or money. He relies upon his knowledge of where good quality heroin can be bought and his familiarity with the heroin scene. This knowledge gives him an advantage over others who would like to engage in similar types of activities. Philly Ben describes his assets:

> It's like a trading thing. If you want to buy some such and such, okay, I can get it for you. I may get it, uh, cheaper than what you can get it, I know the man. So I make out like that, you know. You may want some stuff and you may want it in quantity. I'll go get it from people I know. I get good quality stuff cause I know the people. Everybody know that and I come out making something out of it. I may do that two, three, four times. A guy might be used to paying seventy-five dollars for a bundle, I get it for him for fifty-five, cause I know the man.

Some hustlers are paid at both ends of the transaction. The buyer and the dealer pay for his services (Goldstein 1981). Sometimes the payment is in drugs and sometimes it is in cash. The dope hustler is also in a position to con naive or unsuspecting heroin users. This type of con may be as simple as the one described by Sluggo, 22, of Chicago:

> I used to sell and people come up to see and ask me if I still have some stuff. You know, am I still selling stuff. I tell them yeah and sell them bunk. You know, flour, milk sugar, quinine—bunk.

Or, as in the case of the "baiter's game," the con may be slightly more complex and require the involvement of others. Andre, a 27-year-old player from Chicago, describes the way this game is played:

Yeah, I hit the streets and, uh, run into a couple of associates of mine and try to figure out what we are going to get into. So, uh, we play a game we call baiter's game. We have a bait man out on the street, like he is selling drugs. We have another man as a come-on. A third party would be a man with the front money. Okay, in this game, say myself, I would play the come-on man. I see a customer coming down the street who wants to buy some drugs, you understand? I tell him that my partner got some, which ain't nothing but quinine and milk sugar, or something like that. It ain't no real heroin. It's just, you know, bunk, mixed straight up quinine and milk sugar. Okay, so, this guy ask me what's happening. I say, well, uh, I don't know what is happening. I say, but, I say I think my man got some. Just as I say that, my man steps out of the shadows, he play like he is really high. You know, he put on a droopy look on his face, and a slippery walk. The third party, the come-on man, he come up with two or three dollars and say to the dude that he is going to cop. This is to really convince the tricker, as we say, that this is legitimate, you know. So, okay, to make a long story short, we get the money, the man go about his business. We play this game off and on, off and on, and we make up to, sometimes, $300 or $400, you know.

As a general rule, the dope hustler's cons do not require much skill or imagination (Agar 1973). But this does not mean that skill and imagination are absent from the activities of the dope hustler. As Irv, 26, from Philadelphia, points out, "prescription busting" requires a considerable degree of imagination:

My main thing, uh, I bust prescriptions. See, the guys that I know, they don't do nothing but drink syrup. They mainly into cough syrup. That's how I got turned on to my hustle. I bust prescriptions, you understand? I just go in a doctor's office and, uh, just go in there for something, see the prescriptions and take a few. I just write out for syrup and go to different stores and get the prescription [filled]. The prices vary from store to store. Mainly, I go to the stores, the ones that cost less. I get like eight ounces for like twenty-eight dollars from certain stores, or like some charge three dollars for an ounce. Ah, the first stop is always the cheapest stop. You know, you might get it and sell it on the street. You get like forty dollars for eight ounces on the street. Yeah, you know, it's like five dollars an ounce. With the money I make, I go down and buy me some dope.

In addition to being imaginative and inventive, the successful prescription buster must also possess some of the same skills as those of the accomplished forger. He must have reasonable handwriting skills and know how doctors write prescriptions. Irv, an accomplished prescription buster, talked about the way he learned to write prescriptions:

Some people had a few prescriptions. I told them to write out a couple, you know, write one out for me. I just copied their handwriting. I just keep writing until I figure it out. So, after that I just write out for syrup. If you know the name of a syrup, it's fairly easy.

Targets for the dope hustler are usually restricted to fellow addicts or naive heroin users. Because of the nature of his goods and services, he is generally sought out by others. As a result, he tends to exercise a considerable amount of control over his hustling schedule. For example, pushers like James may begin at a relatively early hour:

> I got out of bed about eight o'clock. I was in the street by eight-fifteen. Went by my brother's and we went downtown to 23rd Street. We picked up a big package of stuff and we was selling around nine o'clock.

On the other hand, hustlers like Karl, 20, from New York, begin hustling at a much later hour and do not have to leave the apartment to sell their goods:

> That morning I got up about seven-thirty. I looked out the window, smoked a cigarette, cut the television on. Then, I cut that back off and laid back down for a while and listened to the radio. I went back to sleep and woke up about eleven that morning. See, I don't have to leave the house. Naw, I have a source bringin' me the stuff, you know. I deal right out of my apartment. I don't have to do no running, just lay down, like twenty-four hours a day.

In summary, the dope hustler has a relatively low status position in the hierarchy of drug dealing. He is not the high status dealer who realizes large profits from his activities but is a scuffling hustler who obtains just enough money or heroin to support his habit on a day-to-day basis.

Problems of Hustling

Among the many obstacles faced by the HLS men are the various preventive measures that people take against their activities. For example, John, 33, a burglar, in New York describes how his hustling is made more difficult:

> They put more fuckin' locks on the doors. All those locks. Sometimes you go to burglarize, man, they got alarms, everything. You hit the door, you hit the window and the alarm goes off. I am gone. I run by this lady so fast, I think she will catch pneumonia just from the wind. It gets harder.

To protect their homes and apartments, people in large urban areas often invest in security devices. It is common for store managers to install antishoplifting devices to protect store merchandise. And although these devices may simply slow down the highly skilled professional thief, they represent still another obstacle to the hustler. And of course there are always policemen and undercover agents to contend with. As Rick points out, these measures have more serious consequences for the low-level juggler:

It's a hassle. Some days you stand out here on the street or on the strip and sell your wares and don't get hassled. Other days every few minutes you look up, a whole flock of motherfuckin' pigs riding around. So, you gotta run and stash your shit.

Nathan, 28, from D.C., aptly points out what is commonly felt in the drug world: that it is those at the bottom who get most of the attention from the law enforcers:

Who controls those types of things, the White man. The Jew boys, the Italian boys, them are the ones that got control, who sit in Congress and stuff like that; they make the laws and any time a Black man get involved in anything like, into makin' some money and it happen to be dealing with drugs, those are the ones who do thirty, forty, fifty years; and the White man that was at the top of it, he don't get nothing. The main thing is, what are we doin' to control the importation of heroin into this country. We're only fuckin' . . . with the low man on the totem pole. . . . What are we gonna do to the people who is bringing the drug into this country. That's where you start. Don't start with me or Joe Blow. Me and Joe Blow between the both of us we ain't got twenty dollars. Don't start with us. . . . You get the man that gets the money from me usin' . . . get him.

One of the reasons for the diversity of hustling activities is that repeated use of the same method of hustling poses increased risks for the addict hustler. As James, a 28-year-old skilled hustler from New York City, points out:

Normally I steal. But it gets more difficult, you know. You go, there's only certain places, you know, where you can steal cause you burn your stuff out. Sometimes you gotta walk, walk, walk, you know, until you get in the right store. I went to Gimbels, I went to Macy's and Alexander's. I had to make all those stops, they know me. Some of the people in the store they already know your face. They know what you're coming in there to do and they watch you. You have to move around. Some days you don't get nothin' from boosting cause they watching you, you know. Some days you can't really come off, you burn your stuff out.

Over time, the shoplifter runs out of stores that he can steal from because he becomes known by store owners, salespersons, and detectives.

Repeated use of the same method of hustling also poses problems for con men. But the consequences of recognition can have a far greater impact. A case in point is provided by Andre, who used the baiter's game:

By him knowing me, understand, facewise, he's going to eventually confront me. Well, I seen him about an hour later [after conning him] and my repercussions came. You know, I was standing up there by the corner and all of a sudden one of my friends said, "Look out." I turned and there I met a lead pipe hitting me dead in the face. He knocked me to the ground, busted my eye, cracked my nose, the side of my face and split my head open. After I got out of the hospital, they wanted to keep me, I ran into a friend. I told him, it's a baiter's game. I knew eventually it was going to happen if I continued to do it. You know, someone going to get wise, recognize me, come looking for me.

HLS men recognize the extreme problems that injury or extended hospitalization can create for them. They talk about the problems posed by street predators, making reference to the jungle-like nature of the street and the predators who prowl on them. And as is the case in any jungle, the men are aware, that if they relax, if they are careless, other hungry predators will not hesitate to make them their prey. Jake, a 28-year-old from Philly, underscored this aspect of street life:

The lifestyle is tough. It's becoming more dangerous and I have to think of how I'm going to protect myself. Other people in the game, he's a drug addict too, your life be in danger cause most of the time he don't care about hurting other people. They all got they main thing, that's dope. They cut your heart out for that dope. If they thought you had some dope on you and they needed it bad enough, they cut your heart out to get that dope.

Jugglers perhaps have most to fear from the street predators since they usually have dope or money. But no user can forget the rules of street life. Those who relax and become careless become prey. Ray, 19, from Chicago, discovered this fact while attempting to cop drugs for friends:

I was trying to cop and some weightwatchers came up. They seen I had a lot of money. That used to be my main thing. I'd go cop, bring it back and we'd all get high. Anyway, I goes up the street, trying to cop, run into a dude who said that he had something. I asked him if he'd let me check it out. It was all right. But he didn't have enough of it for the kind of money I had. So, I wouldn't go for it. So, while I'm negotiating with him, we go up this alley, he takes out a knife and sticks it in my middle. He don't say a word, he don't have to. I got the money in my hand and I drop it. The money was on the ground and he don't mind tripping me loose to get the money. So, when he took the knife out of my middle, I grabbed his hand. When I grabbed his hand, that's when he tried to stick me. He had me around the neck so I know I can't let go of him now. I pulled and grabbed the blade, covered it with my hand. I pulled and grabbed the blade, covered it with my hand. But I couldn't hold it, see. We fought and I tripped and fell on the ground. When I tripped, he sliced my hand and I hit my head on the ground. He's standing over me, trying to get the money, so I kicked him. I kicked up and he stabs me. He got me several times. After that, I don't really know. I think he picked up the money and ran. I don't know. The next thing I remember, I'm looking up and there's red lights coming this way. I must have passed out. It was the police and they took me to the hospital. They told me I had to stay because of all the blood I lost. But, you know, they ain't got no shit in hospitals so I snuck out as soon as I could.

The problems that the HLS men face in hustling are not new. Nor can it be said that they are problems that affect activities of only heroin users. Security and crime-control measures have been improving. Technological advancements have made hustling activities such as stealing, burglarizing, and drug dealing more risky, and thus the job the hustler faces is more formidable. As a result, HLS men are not able to meet their daily heroin needs by specializing in only one hustling method. They know that any slip up can cut short their lives in the heroin lifestyle. To maintain heroin habits over time they must have alternative sources of funds or drugs and a variety of hustles. The four-fold typology of hustlers identified reveals a complex interweaving of behavioral styles which comprise the essential activity of hustling money for heroin. In addition, this discussion shows how hustling is closely integrated with the larger lifestyles of both heroin users and the non-heroin-using community. Finally, the types are also important in understanding the social and economic function of hustling and its impact on inner-city communities.

Reflections and Implications

The crimes and hustles described in this chapter are born mainly of poverty and exist mainly in the communities of the poor. One might argue that, in a certain sense, no one knows the value of money better than those who do not have it. In 1984, for example, (according to the Census Bureau) 34.4 million Americans—15 percent of the population—live below the official poverty line (currently $9,862 per year for a family of four). For all of these people, a decent, visible means of support are primary values. But toughness, getting big money, and getting some wine "are values [they] adopt after the 'props' supporting decency have for some reason been judged unviable, unavailable or unattainable. . . . When jobs are not available, living up to the rules of conduct based on values of decency becomes difficult." (Anderson 1976)

Obviously this is true of HLS men. Although over half of them cite legitimate enterprises as frequent sources of income, only a quarter are able to claim them as a primary source. The others must depend on crimes of various sorts and for most that means some form of thievery.

Our typology of hustlers makes one wonder about the impact of addict hustling on society and on the communities in which these men live. Crime and heroin use are certainly linked. For example, it is known that crime increases when the cost of heroin escalates and when a heroin user is in an active phase of use rather than abstinent. However, the HLS data lend support to the contention that one cannot project the level of heroin-supporting crime simply from the number of known users and the theoretical cost of their habits. Further, in light of the average cost of these men's habits, one must wonder about the nature of the crime/heroin connection. Is *all* crime a heroin user commits heroin-related or only that share which directly pays for dope? One cannot seriously argue that, were it not for their heroin use, these men would be legitimately employed and their criminality suddenly disappear— not when unemployment rates remain staggeringly high in the minority communities: over 21 percent of Black adults and about 41 percent of Black teenagers are unemployed in our central cities (communication from the Bureau of Labor Statistics, U.S. Department of Commerce, for October 1983). Ball (1982) suggests that the heroin/crime connection should be measured by the difference between the crimes committed while actively using heroin and those committed while "on the street" but not actively using heroin. There is a certain logic to the argument. He concludes that heroin use itself explains from 60 to 95 percent of the criminal activity of active heroin users. But even if we grant the point for discussion's sake, have we really learned much by it? For one thing, it asks us to suppose that the only difference between the two life phases is heroin use or nonuse, which may not be the case. It should also be noted that in Ball's argument a heroin user would be considered *abstinent* if he used heroin *no more than* three times a week. Suppose a former user is released from prison, a detoxification facility or a treatment program and that he qualified to be considered abstinent. Also suppose that he is jobless as are most "ex-users" like him. It is not hard to imagine that, jobless, he feels the increasing pressures and financial burdens of life and that two things happen concurrently: he feels both forced back into hustling *and* pulled back into the lifestyle of heroin use. Once the four-times-a-week threshold is passed, Ball's argument demands that the heroin use be blamed for the crime. Yet, one can argue that both are effects of other causes, such as, poverty and psychosocial pressure.

A further limitation of this approach is that measures of criminal activity say nothing about its seriousness or cost. They tell us nothing about violence, victimization or dollar value. One crime is not just like any other. Although this does not acquit them of guilt and social responsibility, HLS men do express reluctance to be violent. Also, we must consider the fact that their skill levels are not very high. Depending on skill and luck, it might take a greater number of petty crimes to scratch together twenty dollars than five hundred. HLS data suggest that heroin crimes are more likely to involve small amounts of money. This would be consistent with habits which, on the average, are supported by only twenty-five dollars per day.

Furthermore, our typology shows that one out of every four HLS men have legitimate income and one in five deal with the drug's distribution system itself. In the case of dealers, touts, and connections, the cost of their activity is supported primarily by the other hustlers' and workers' dollars, not by additional illegal dollars. The fact is that only about half of the HLS men pass on the bill for their heroin habits to the rest of society. But society is a vague term. One might ask more precisely who is victimized and at what cost. Here, again, HLS men provide some insights.

Consider the respective crimes and targets of the two types of hustlers: opportunists (19 percent of HLS men and 30 percent of all hustling activity) and skilled hustlers (12 percent of the men and 19 percent of all hustling). As detailed earlier, the skilled hustler can manage sometimes safer and usually more lucrative crimes such as thefts from businesses and more affluent residences. In Pennsylvania alone in 1982, according to the FBI Uniform Crime Reports, skilled-hustler-type crimes accounted for some $88.3 million. (This is by all perpetrators, not just heroin users.) In that same period in Pennsylvania, opportunist-type crimes accounted for about $62.7 million in losses. The opportunist hustler, however, tends to be a solitary predator involved in street crimes and petty larcenies. It is well established that the targets of these poverty-driven crimes are the poor themselves. These predators prey on their own communities.

The predatory presence of opportunistic hustlers in their communities undoubtedly oppresses the poor, degrading their lives further by adding dread to their destitution. Yet, one might argue that quality-of-life issues are marginal in the hard-scrabble world of predator and prey, the world of the survival economy. Theirs is a world of staggering unemployment, illness, malnutrition, and death. Black children, according to the Children's Defense Fund, are twice as likely as White to die before the age of one and four times more likely to be murdered before the age of four. It is indisputable that the survival economy desperately needs an improved quality of life or that opportunists add to its burden of fear. But it also desperately needs increased financial resources. In that regard the typology of hustlers allows one to speculate whether the communities of the survival economy, despite self-predation, might not realize a net gain, at least in simple terms, of resource transfer from hustling.

But one need not defend hustling in order to question whether heroin lies at the root of the crime problem. A study of the HLS men and their hustling challenges two fundamental axioms of public policy on heroin. The first is that heroin use leads to a drug tolerance invariably manifested in escalating drug habits. The second is that escalating habits drive the users' economic behavior. The story of the HLS men's patterns of heroin use presented throughout this volume, but especially in chapters 5 and 7, is in direct contradiction to the first contention. Lives of heroin use can, in fact, be self-regulated and lived within manageable limits. As a consequence, HLS men call into question the second assumption. Their pattern of life and hustling gives solid support to Heather Ruth's study of heroin users' economic dynamics (Ruth 1973).

In her study of New York City addicts, Ruth contends that "heroin users adjust their habits over time to reflect attainable goals in response to economic pressures [rather than] physiological demand for heroin." Her study shows that users' incomes consistently outpaced their drug expenditures. But more importantly, when users had the added financial burden of dependents, such as mates, it was their drug expenditures that dropped rather than their incomes that rose. One could not expect to see that pattern if their heroin use was beyond their control. Ruth's conclusions are inescapable. First, income is a consistent predictor of a user's weekly expenditure for his own heroin. Second, and further illustrating the plasticity of the heroin habit and the humanness of its users, "a significant number of heroin users prefer the psychic (and social) benefits of having adult partners—usually of the opposite sex—to maximizing their level of heroin consumption at constant levels of incomes."

Heroin use is not the root of the social and economic patterns and ills of the user and the community. It is the other way around. Treatment programs and enforcement policies will never be adequate to the task as long as they insist on focusing on mere surface patterns of heroin use. The hustler types discussed in this chapter are important examples of aspects of heroin use that exist under the surface. Social and economic factors on the larger scene create and perpetuate this hustling which, in turn, is integrated into the social and economic fabric of ghetto life and the heroin lifestyle. Enlightened public policy and effective treatment must realize that hustling and heroin use exist as integral parts of lifestyles that are socially shaped and economically driven.

Note

1. Data used in this chapter consist of responses by the sample of 124 men interviewed to the following kinds of open-ended questions: What are the different ways you obtain money to buy your drugs? What is your main hustle? How did you get money for your last buy? Answers to these questions were supplemented by responses to the open-ended questions and the general descriptive accounts of their hustling activities. For example, when interviewers asked the men what they did on a typical day, respondents described their hustling activities in some detail. We therefore analyzed: (1) descriptions of main hustles and of the actual processes of hustling, (2) discussions of problems HLS men encountered while pursuing their hustling activities, and (3) information suggesting how the hustling activities affect the lives of people in the larger community.

References

Agar, M. 1973. *Ripping and Running: A Formal Ethnography of Urban Heroin Addicts*. New York: Seminar Press.

Anderson, E. 1976. *A Place on the Corner*. Chicago: University of Chicago Press.

Ball, J. 1982. Lifetime criminality of heroin addicts in the United States. *Journal of Drug Issues* 12(43):225–239.

Biernacki, Patrick. 1979. Junkie work, hustles, and social status among heroin addicts. *Journal of Drug Issues* 9:(4):535–551.

Chambers, Carl D. 1974. Narcotic addiction and crime: An empirical review. In *Drugs and the Criminal Justice System*, eds. James A. Inciardi and Carl D. Chambers. Beverly Hills, California: Sage Publications.

Finestone, Harold. 1964. Cats, kicks, and color. In *The Other Side: Perspectives on Deviance*, ed. Howard S. Becker. New York: The Free Press.

Goldstein, Paul J. 1981. Getting over: Economic alternatives to predatory crime among street drug users. In *The Drug-Crime Connection*, ed. James A. Inciardi. Beverly Hills, California: Sage Publications.

Gould, Leroy. 1974. Crime and the addict: Beyond common sense. In *Drugs and the Criminal Justice System*, eds. James A. Inciardi and Carl D. Chambers. Beverly Hills, California: Sage Publications.

Helmer, John. 1977. The connection between narcotics and crime. *Journal of Drug Issues* 7(4):405–418.

Maurer, D. 1949. *The Big Con*. New York: Pocket Books.

Nash, George. 1972. You got over any way you can: A look at the criminal addict. Unpublished.

Polsky, Ned. 1969. *Hustlers, Beats and Others*. Garden City, New York: Doubleday.

Preble, Edward, and Casey, John H. Jr. 1969. Taking care of business: The heroin user's life on the street. *International Journal of the Addictions* 4:1–24.

Ruth, H. 1973. Mathematica. Unpublished.

Slim, Iceberg (pseudonym). 1969. *Pimp: The Story of My Life*. Los Angeles: Holloway Publishing.

Smith, R.B., and Stephens, R.C. 1976. Drug use and hustling: A study of their interrelationships. *Criminology* 14(2):155–166.

Spradley, J.P. 1970. *You Owe Yourself a Drunk*. Boston: Little, Brown.

Stephens, R.C., and Levine, S. 1971. The street addict role: Implications for treatment. *Psychiatry* 34(4):351–357.

Sutter, A.G. 1966. The world of the righteous dope fiend. *Issues in Criminology* 2:177–222.

Valentine, Betty Ann. 1978. *Hustling and Other Hard Work: Life Styles in the Ghetto*. New York: The Free Press.

Voss, H.L., and Stephens, R.C. 1973. Criminal History of Narcotic Addicts. *Drug Forum* 2(2):191–202.

Waldorf, Dan. 1973. *Careers in Dope*. Englewood Cliffs, New Jersey: Prentice-Hall, Inc.

5

Life With Heroin: Voices of Experience

George M. Beschner
Elliott I. Bovelle

> With heroin one is no longer grotesquely involved in becoming, one simply is.
>
> Alexander Trocci, 1961

I t is perhaps easy to understand why heroin users suffer from stereotyping. In describing important social and psychological phenomena, researchers have identified several striking types of heroin users, often focusing on the adventure, challenge, and reward of the heroin lifestyle (Preble and Casey 1969). In a quest for information about the heroin experience, researchers have described the "righteous dope fiend," whose status in the community is based on a lifelong commitment to heroin. This characterization is underscored by the users' ingenuity, versatility, and ability to hustle money to support a "long habit," an ever escalating demand for heroin (Sutter 1966). Researchers have introduced us to the "cool cat," who lives for momentary sensory experiences while showing off his wealth and affecting a detached "sophisticated boredom" (Stephens and Levine 1971). The "stand-up cat," we are told, plays a more specialized role in the drug world. Through intense cultivation of self, this character turns life into "a gracious work of art." He exhibits a harmonious combination of charm, ingratiating speech, class, music, and generosity, while introducing drugs (principally heroin) into the community (Finestone 1957; Fiddle 1967; Feldman 1968). Because of his personal attributes, the stand-up cat feels "equal to any man."

These magnetic personalities bear an unsettling resemblance to the character Sporting Life in Du Bose Heyward's *Porgy*. Of course not all early studies portrayed a glamorous image of heroin users; some investigators focused on the despair and harshness of daily life, pointing out that heroin users suffer from bitter loneliness and alienation (Fiddle 1967; Wakefield 1969).

The Heroin Lifestyle Study (HLS) took a fresh look at these stereotypes, not so much to question their validity in the past as to question their usefulness in describing today's addicts. We found some contrasts between past stereotypes of heroin users and the contemporary lifestyles of poor inner-city heroin users. To sustain a daily habit, contemporary urban heroin users must circumvent or adapt to powerful social forces. Increasingly stringent law enforcement and tighter security in stores have made theft more difficult, while security watches and neighborhood vigilance have made break-ins more difficult and much riskier. At the same time, efforts to prevent importation and distribution of heroin have resulted in variation in availability, fluctuating prices, and heroin of uneven quality, often dangerously contaminated with diluting compounds. Anxiety in the heroin subculture is enormous, causing heroin users to often turn to other drugs as heroin substitutes.

In response to high risk and high costs, many heroin users are bargain hunters who pool their resources with other addicts and barter for drugs and other goods. A large number maintain jobs to reduce the likelihood of arrest. Many heroin users also limit themselves to one shot of heroin per day.

This chapter examines the experiences HLS men have had with heroin—their introduction to the drug, their feelings when shooting heroin for the first time, and the effects they attribute to heroin. In addition, since heroin users frequently pool their resources to obtain heroin, we also look at their relationships with one another and how they have come to cope with the harsh economic realities of their lives.[1]

Initiation: Acolytes and Imitators

In The Beginning

In their "before heroin" period, all HLS men shared four commonalities:

1. They were familiar with heroin prior to using it, usually having learned about it from the person(s) who subsequently presided over their initiation.
2. They were curious about heroin.
3. They feared using the drug, especially intravenously.
4. They recognized the aura of status granted to heroin use by many ghetto youth.

As can be seen in the subsequent discussion regarding their introduction to heroin use, these elements are interwoven in the comments made by HLS men.

The Familiar Presence

Consider the first condition. It is not surprising that HLS men saw heroin use as a familiar, even positive activity, prior to their own addiction. Drug use is common in their communities, if not in their own homes. The study findings show that 72 percent of the HLS men were introduced to heroin by close friends, 9 percent by their brothers, and 5 percent by other relatives.

Once associated with the subculture, the HLS men experienced a sense of inevitability that perhaps precluded regret for their actions. Jug, a 22-year-old Chicago man, gives such an account of his induction. He reports having witnessed heroin use by others for years before trying it himself. Like many who had resisted initial overtures, the time eventually came for him:

> Cats on the block had been using it for years and they had been trying to get me to use it but I backed off. A couple of my partners went down and they pulled a stick-up and they had plenty of money, so they came back after buying dope for everybody. We seen the availability of it and they seemed to know what they were talking about. It was a thing where heroin was always talked about. We all went off in a vacant building, must have been about a dozen of us. We just lined up, rolled up our sleeves and started pushing the dope, you know, everybody got a shot.

Likewise, Umber, a 26-year-old Philadelphian, describes his first heroin use:

> We was sitting around with friends of ours. We all grew up together and they were into it before we were. We wanted to know what kind of feeling that was, the way we watched them high. And they looked like they felt so good. So I stayed for awhile and tried it.

Neither Umber nor Jug gave a specific reason for resisting use as long as they did or for starting to use when they did. Umber fell victim to curiosity and a desire for increased status in his peer group. For Jug, a successful stick-up and fraternal celebration were the culprits. Neither seems to have been aware that they had been drawn into the subculture by heroin users.

Curiosity and elevated status were clear motivating forces for 18-year-old Louis from Chicago. His brother's interest in heroin stimulated his desire to try the drug himself:

> I got an older brother that got high. I used to go out with him. After watching him turn on, it made me want to get high. Made me *curious*, I'll put it that way. You know, and so me and my man went off.

Similarly, Butch, age 28, a New York user still in school at the time, was enticed by older boys:

> When we used to play hooky, we used to have hooky parties, and the older crowd of dudes used to try to come to the party to mess with the women. Then they'd sneak off in the bathroom and start shooting heroin. And they'd come out and say, "Hey, take [snort] a couple of blows, I think you'll like it."

And we'd do, just being naive and wanting to hang out, we did it. At first I really didn't like it. I don't know what it was that continued me with it because it made me more sick than pleasing.

As can be seen, striving to maintain or increase one's status is often accompanied by heavy peer pressure to accept the challenge and try heroin. Two 28-year-olds from Washington, D.C., Nathan and Jim, describe how peer pressure influenced them. Nathan speaks first:

It was our little crew. There was a lot of peer pressure involved in that. Saying to myself, if you can do that then I can do it. It was one of them things, I'll do it if you'll do it.

For Jim:

Using heroin in those days was a fad. You wasn't cool unless you used it and, you know, you want to be like everybody else, you want to be like your big brother, gang fightin'. You want to be hip, and you wasn't in the crowd unless you were getting high.

Some felt even stronger peer pressure bordering on a sense of obligation. From Chicago, Bob age 20 says:

It was compulsory because I have seen others doing it. I wasn't strong enough to back up from it while they was sitting there doin' it.

The Curiosity

This sense of obligation, frequently implied rather than directly asserted, is related to the persistent curiosity HLS men report having felt in their youth. Frank, 28 years of age (Philadelphia), tells how familiarity and curiosity led him into the heroin world:

I was fifteen. My friends had been into it and I was curious as to what happened while I was gone. I had the option to go to college for six months and I had a paying job. As far as the drug scene, it wasn't even on my mind until that particular night; the curiosity was always there. I said, "Here's my chance." I ran into a friend of mine, he was with friends of his. We go back over to my house and I gets dressed and by that time it was after nine o'clock. I ran into a gal, and was teasin' her, "Come on, I want to see what it's like." I got high but it was more of an acting thing from what I see how other people was actin'. They talk, they act, ya know, somethin' I said, "wow." It seemed like "it" at the time.

Similarly, Ron, a 30-year-old (from Chicago), was propelled into heroin use by curiosity, reinforced by familiarity, and helped along by a long standing friend with the required expertise:

Me and one of my closest friends sneaked out one day and I didn't even know he had no stuff. But we were hustlin' together so after we got through selling the merchandise, he went and bought an eighth. He told me to take a walk with him. When we got to his place he pulled out a cooker, a outfit, and filled a jug up with some water and cooked up the eighth. By then I was strictly out of curiosity. I tried it in the pit of my arm. The sensations that I felt behind that first shot of stuff, man, went a long way, because I've been dealing with it ever since.

Gut, an 18-year-old, also from Chicago, was similarly initiated into heroin by older, sophisticated friends who seemed to be experiencing something he was not. In his case, though, fear played an important role. But his fear was not great enough to prevent him from taking the big step:

I used to be around these guys a few years older than I was, and I used to see them when they'd get high. It seemed they'd be floatin'. Ya know, their eyes be closed, they be noddin' their head, they'd be bobbin', they'd be scratching', smokin' cigarette after cigarette, and drinkin' nothin' but these sweet pops and things. I just got curious one day; I was in this old house; so I bought a bag, and I had this guy named Sammy hit me. I remember the day well. It was in the evenin' on payday. I felt fear cause I never done it before and didn't know what to expect. You know, I ain't gonna lie, I was scared.

Buck, age 29, a Washingtonian, reports a slightly varied experience. He had progressed further on his own than the other HLS men, already snorting, but not mainlining. His initiation consisted of a final commitment to using heroin rather than an introduction to the drug itself. This experience is significant because young ghetto men view snorting and skin-popping as nonaddictive, while mainlining is considered to be the final commitment:

The first time I fired, I was with the guys. They told me, why waste your dope, why throw it away. Shoot the dope, you get high faster, you use less dope. And, at the present time, being that I was snortin', the caps was buck action. I kept me five caps in order to carry me to the man. He said, "Try it," and me bein' an old green egg, he hit me. I couldn't hit myself, I didn't know nothin' 'bout that shit. He was a vet, the best. He took me to the pan and put one cap in saying, "We both can get high off of that." So he put the shit in the cooker and cooked it up and hit me. I felt the same way I did when I was snortin', which is like a Utopia, you get loose, you get mellow. It's just like havin' a half a pint of alcohol all at one time. You get fucked up so quick.

The ambivalence expressed by Gut and Buck is common during the initiation experience. This ambivalence results from a delicate balance of feelings—familiarity, curiosity, and fear. Black Charlie, a 30-year-old from Chicago, reveals just how delicate this balance is for young ghetto dwellers who seem to gravitate toward the familiar world of heroin:

I had been taught like any other regular guy out here that heroin is bad for your health and what it can do to you in the long run—you know, killing yourself. So I had a fear for it. The fear was kinda strong for a while because I had been introduced to heroin when I was fifteen, but overcome the fear because I lived in a neighborhood where people was always usin' heroin in front of me. So heroin is just like this to me: hey, if you goin' deal with it, you gotta learn to deal with it in this life.

Like Black Charlie, almost 82 percent of the HLS men were afraid before using heroin for the first time. Many knew people who had gone to prison or died from heroin addiction, and many experienced powerful pressures against heroin use by family, community, and church leaders. Many feared the police and the threat of being arrested.

The Mystique

Apparently, however, the inducements are strong enough to help many people overcome their fear. For the uninitiated, inducements such as peer pressure, media sensationalism, and the mystique and status of heroin use increase the curiosity and add to the fear, creating a sense of awe. For young men who become regular heroin users, the first intravenous shot of heroin is a peak experience. The first shot introduces them to "the life" where their commonplace goals are filtered and distilled until all that remains is the promise of the next high. Thereafter, their lives are divided into "before" and "after." Further, the first intravenous shot separates the initiate from the rest of society, even from users of other drugs, and from heroin users who merely sniff, drink, smoke, or skin-pop. If and when these users give up their addiction, they will retain a separate identity by being labeled ex-addict. Truly the first intravenous injection of heroin is a profound initiation ritual.

The First Shot of Heroin

Fear and Firing

The aura of mystery, danger, and status associated with heroin use is, in part, responsible for the drug's attraction, influencing attitudes toward the first intravenous shot of heroin.

Two clear patterns emerged from our interviews. First, the predominant feeling just prior to taking the first shot was fear. As noted, about 82 percent of the HLS men expressed fear to varying degrees. Second, in describing the rush, 84 percent used terms and phrases suggesting euphoria and ecstasy. This was the case even though about 32 percent of the men said they got sick soon after shooting up.

The fear expressed by so many HLS men is significant because it reflects the community attitudes and personal phobias that must be overcome. Anticipation of the unknown, needle phobia, the risk of overdose, and breaking a powerful societal taboo all combine to generate fear. Lloyd, age 32, and Hunter, age 22, of Chicago seemed nervous and worried as they approached their first experience:

> My heart beat kinda fast 'cause I didn't know what would happen. I didn't know what to look for. (Lloyd)

> Uh, I was nervous and you know kinda scared, I was thinkin'—all I could think about was—I wonder if this is too much, am I gonna OD, you know, real paranoid, I was just scared until it was injected into me, and then I kinda eased on, and I thought it was cool. (Hunter)

The use of the needle can be compared to an attack on the self, with implications of violence. This interpretation is underscored by the terms used to refer to it: "shooting up," a "hit," a "shot," "firing up." A number of heroin users, like Dawson, a 28-year-old from Washington, D.C., report mild to severe needle phobia. As can be seen, beginning with Dawson, they express fear in different ways and with varying degrees of intensity:

> I had a fear of needles, and it was hard for me to let somebody shoot one and I couldn't shoot myself.

Butch of New York City overcame his phobia:

> Sticking that fucking thing in my arm, I was scared to death but I did it. I was scared to death. I grabbed my man by his arm and he called me a faggot. I grabbed him by his wrist to hold onto him when he was getting ready to skid. What did you expect me to do? I wanted to be a bigger man. But I was scared to death, scared to death.

Tommy, 19, from Philadelphia, also was afraid of the needle puncture:

> Now that scared the hell out of me because I always was scared of needles and I had to turn my head. Shit, after I got over that damn thing and did it, it scared me 'cause I put the head in and draw back. It was hitting the blood and I didn't know what the hell was going on. I was going to take that damn thing out but he said, just a little more. And then it fucked me up 'cause after I did it, damn, I didn't know what the hell happened. Everything just happened so fast, damn, I don't know, it just felt numb.

Sometimes fear is based on other concerns. Most HLS men report that they have heard, or been taught, that heroin ruins a person's health and can be fatal. Black Charlie expressed this concern:

I was scared because I had been taught like any other guy out here that heroin is bad for your health and what it can do to you in the long run—your killing yourself. I had fear for it.

Roscoe, age 27, and Tiny Shaw, age 21, also of Chicago, had heard similar tales:

I used to hear about them mutha fuckahs OD-in' and that shit you know. I started thinking why do I fuck around the OD. I was scared, man. You don't know when you goin' to OD off that shit man. Some mutha fuckah might give you some rat poison and fuck you up. I say shit, wonderin' if I'm gonna fuck up and OD or somethin'. Everybody should think about that, man, that go fuckin' with this shit. (Roscoe)

I felt fear, because I had heard that peoples OD, or that if you stick a needle in your arm, an air bubble will go to your heart, so I was really afeared. I had a whole lot of fear 'bout it, but I looked at it like it was a chance itself. So I chanced it, and when I did it, it come to be all right. (Tiny Shaw)

Michael, age 26, of Washington and Karl, age 20, of New York were fearful because they knew people who died from heroin overdoses. Michael's fear was intense:

It was a fear of needles that made me feel scared. Doctors sticking needles in my arm when I was a kid, so that thing was still in my mind. Not knowing, people OD-in' and stuff. Back then people was dying using heroin. They would OD and die because people didn't know too much about it. Some friends of mine died. They were older than me, but they were still friends of mine. They was dying from it, back in the early 70s. They were OD-in' and dying.

Karl's fear was more subdued:

I felt afraid 'cause I saw a lot about people dying from it. I had an uncle who was doing it 'til he got run in, so I really got scared then. I kept saying to myself that I would never do it, but I kept doing it.

But for some, like Dave, age 35, from Philadelphia, stories circulating in the community about death from overdoses merely increased their attraction to heroin:

Yeah. I had my own fear because of stuff I'd heard about overdoses and stuff. I had a little anxiety in terms of tryin' to find out what there was to it. I saw this dude noddin' tough, and I figured the high must be real down, you know.

Fear of heroin, generated in large part by stories in the community about the drug, intensifies the effect of the first heroin shot and contributes somewhat to the resulting euphoria. However, the small percentage in our sample who first experienced heroin under combat conditions in Vietnam faced a different type of fear—fear of death from military action. This fear was greater than their anxiety about heroin. This was the case with Dap Daddy, a 32-year-old from Chicago, whose first exposure to narcotics involved morphine as a painkiller:

I started in Vietnam. I was scared, a rednecked honkie had just shot my best partner for no cause at all. I was afraid for my life, just like any other young Black man over there with these honkies, scared. They were scared, we were scared. Yes, I started usin' heroin because I was psychologically feared of the white man. The first drug I used, it was morphine. I had got shot. It was a bullet straight through the thigh. The medics gave me a shot of morphine and they got me high and all of a sudden I forgot I had got shot and I wasn't scared. So, each time we went in the jungle to a fire fight, I wanted the same feeling from my life.

Dave, age 35, from Philadelphia, had a similar experience. His first medicinal use of morphine led to the regular use of heroin to calm combat fear and to relax:

I got hit, a flesh wound. It wasn't bad, but it was hurtin' and they couldn't get me back to the company to the medic. So, a friend of mine said, "Hey, man you see that little needle thing there, all you do is take that, flip open the thing, pour stuff in the hole, stab that in and push it in your vein and lay back down and you be all right." And, I done it and it felt good. Shit. While I was in the hospital, I was poppin', I didn't give a shit. It was a good high, it takes all the scaredness out of you. When you over there duckin' bullets, it takes it away from you, man. You gonna defend yourself because you don't want to die. But the idea of the drug is that it calms your mind out. On base all you been hearin' is dropped a VS and relax. So, you go to town you scared because you don't know which one is which, you might catch one of them whores out there and she stab you up that night. So, instead of bein' paranoid a little voice say, "Hey, Joe, want some of this?" They bring you a package which you pay twenty dollars for, man, and you can use it for almost a week. Just take a little bit off, and it's stronger. Take a little off, man, clean the little spoon, heat it up. Some dudes just take it and rub it into their skin, that's how pure it was, you rub it into the skin.

In combat, the fear associated with heroin is reversed—the drug becomes an antidote to fear.

The Rush

In describing their first heroin shot, the HLS men mention an ambivalence: despite nausea and vomiting, the experience was overwhelmingly positive (84 percent). The euphoria they achieved from the first shot is described as a "rush," a combination of unique physical sensations, followed by a "nod," a trance-like psychological state.

Umber begins:

> I felt a warm sensation over my whole body. My body relaxed, my hands relaxed, it just felt like I had a shield up, ready for anything that come at me. It was a real good feeling. Made you feel like you didn't really need to care about nothing.

Others describe a similar reaction:

> I was sitting down, and when it rushed up on me, I jumped up and said to myself, make sure you're all right, 'cause it was so fast. As soon as it goes into the vein—Bam—I wasn't used to that, it takes a while before it hits when you're snorting, but when you shot it, it's instant action, you know, there wasn't no waiting around, it's right there, so I was kinda scared. I felt beautiful, you know, it took a lot offa my mind. (Hunter, age 22, Chicago)

> It started as a tingle in my toes and it went completely through my body, quickly through my head and I just relaxed as though I had taken a sedative. It just relaxed me and sorta gave me an upper. Like I said—relaxed—all my problems if I had any seemed to vanish, you know. I found complete satisfaction. Well, as I say, it seems to ring reality. At first I felt exhilarated. Then it really started coming down and I just cooled out into my nod, and that was cool. It was cool. I hate to say that but it was. It was cool, man, that was it, there, buddy, the ultimate high. Fired up, brother. Just like something you been talking about for a long time and you really did it. Kind of like thinking about getting your first coat. All the time you save your money and you finally get it, you know. (Louis, age 18, Chicago)

Although many withdrew deeper into themselves, Nathan felt like reaching out.

> It was like you walk downstairs on Christmas Day and see a brand new bike that you were supposed to get. It was all of the enjoyable things that you would like to feel. I really felt, down right, 'cause it was like I had so much energy. I wanted to do so many different things off of the high, because the high was so enjoyable and pleasurable I wanted to associate that with all the things that I enjoy doin'. I was able to talk to people and adapt to things so easily.

The Sickness

Thirty-eight percent of the HLS men were nauseated after their first shot and 31 percent vomited. Others felt sick either before or after their high. Some implied that sickness was part of the rush. Nevertheless, these men still regarded the first shot as a positive experience. The remarks below reflect this as well as the variation in the descriptions of their feelings of sickness.

Ace, age 34, of Philadelphia reports:

> I threw up in his store. When I first felt it, I threw up and it was a nauseatin' feelin'. I said, Well, this stuff is a gas, I'll die a junkie. So we goes to his crib, right? He puts me on the couch, and I sleeps it off. When I wakes up all that nauseatin' thing is gone. It's a pure high then, and that was easy. It was enjoyable.

Walter, another Chicagoan, age 25, had a different reaction. First he experienced the sensation of being transported and then was overcome by sickness:

> I knew the first time I stuck that spike in my arm, I was hooked. I had a little fear from what I heard 'bout it, but I had that in the back of my mind that's always happenin' to somebody else, that ain't gonna happen to me. I ain't gonna get strung out, I don't quit. When I first took off I was up there and I felt real down, and everything seemed dark, I guess I almost went out. I just kept on goin' in to a deep nod, spent the whole night, and then in the mornin'. When I woke up I got sick, couldn't hold nothing in my stomach, you know, but I guess I thought I was cool, this is a high.

Some HLS men regarded the nausea as a minor irritant that did not affect their positive sensations. Chico, a 34-year-old from Chicago, struggled with nausea before reaching euphoria:

> It hit me in the stomach, and I got nauseated. At the same time, it hit me in the head. I was trying to keep from throwin' up, you know, but the nausea overcame me and I started throwin' up, all right. So after I threw up, I got the nods, and my mouth would get dry. So I'd drink some water and I'd have to throw up again, you know. After a while, the nod laid with me for a good six-seven hours, you know. It gassed me, man, and like I say, after I stopped throwin' up, the nod was bad. It was a positive experience, at that time. I was looking for the nod, looking for the high. And I found that.

As noted earlier, nausea does not necessarily represent a negative response to the initial injection. Like the intense fear and anticipation, nausea can enhance the euphoria associated with the first shot of heroin. Some users report that even the sickness itself feels good.

For Bull, age 27, of Chicago, the sickness enhanced his total experience:

> The shit was so good, man, it made me throw up, and I was fucked up, man, I was nodding and shit, but I was feeling good. But I was fucked up . . . it had me feeling . . . at first I felt like I was drunk, but after it wore off I was grooving. I'm talking about when I first shot it, man, I was fucked up, but then, after a while, you know how you get the rush at first, you know, and then after that, sorta cool out.

James, a 49-year-old musician from Chicago, literally identified the sickness with the euphoria:

> When I was snorting, it would take a little time before I get my nod, but when I shot it, it hit me right away and I threw up, but it felt good to throw up and it scared me, you know. Seemed like I just stopped throwing up. It was just a good feeling. The first three or four times I put the needle in my arm, I threw up, but after about the seventh or eighth day, I didn't throw up anymore. It was a good feeling of throwing up which left me feeling good, but I would always throw up.

In summary, the initiation to heroin use and the commitment to a heroin lifestyle carries with it a range of feelings and responses. As we have seen, they revolve around fear, curiosity, peer pressure, and status enhancement. These feelings are undoubtedly generated by societal views of heroin use and by strong family and community pressures against heroin use. These pressures, which emanate from such sources as the church, social movements, and community leaders, are part of the straight community's ongoing efforts to curtail drug use. Further, the presence of the police and the threat of being arrested also prevent many of the members of these drug-tolerant communities from becoming addicts. However, these same pressures paradoxically add to the magnetic attraction of heroin by enhancing the mystique of heroin use and elevating its status. This, in turn, serves to increase the curiosity and fear, bordering on awe, with which the uninitiated regard the phenomenon of heroin use.

For those few young men who do become regular heroin users in these communities, the first intravenous shot of heroin becomes one of the most significant experiences in their lives. That first shot introduces them to the life, where the commonplace goals and values of the straight world are filtered and re-arrayed into a complex lifestyle that focuses on the promise of the next high. Further, the first intravenous shot of heroin also marks the beginning of a process which sets off the heroin user, in a social and psychological sense, from those who use other drugs and even from those who sniff, smoke, or skin-pop heroin. Finally, the heroin user must readjust his relationship with the straight world. Even if he stops using heroin, it is likely he will always be labeled an ex-addict. Nevertheless, most initiates into heroin use do not stop after that first "ultimate high." They go on to shoot more dope and, as we will see, continue to search for that first shot feeling.

Effects of Heroin

The Search to Recapture

A small proportion (12 percent) of the HLS men said that their second experience with heroin was better than the first. This reaction may be due to greater familiarity coupled with reduced fear; combined, these feelings increased the men's confidence, defined the suspense, and sharpened the experience.

Ronald, age 31, of Chicago, explains the dynamics of his second shot:

> It was easier. I didn't have no fear of the needle or nothing, like I was really anxious, really ready to do it this time. The first time I was a little hesitant, but the second time there was not fear involved at all, you know, couldn't get it quick enough.

Solo, 26, of New York, reports essentially the same reaction:

> No, the second shot, ya know—ya know what to look for. It's like a broad, you pick her up and make love to her, she's good in bed, right? So the second time around you know what you're going to get. Ya dig it and that anxiety, that challenge, that doomf, doomf, doomf, doomf, my adrenalin is pumpin', I know, man, when I stick this in my arm, Jack, I'm gonna be there where I want to be.

Such positive reactions, however, were far from typical. Most of the HLS men remember their second shot of heroin as the beginning of a long descent from the peak experience of the first injection. It also marked the beginning of a futile attempt to recapture that first experience—in short, the beginning of a never ending search for the perfect high. In the statements that follow, HLS men acknowledge with nostalgia the powerful memory of their first shot of heroin, their attempt to duplicate the experience and finally, the futility of the effort:

> I got a hot flash, and my stomach turned, broke out in a sweat, ya know. It was good. I wish I could get that feelin' again. That's what I'm still lookin' for, I guess—after all these years, that same feelin' I had the first time. I'll never get it again, but it seems like I'll alway be tryin' to get it. That's why I can't explain it, man, that's how deep it is, man, ya know, the first time. You can't explain it. (Ike, Philadelphia)

It's not like the first one—the shock or the element of surprise or the feeling that I got from the first one, I don't think you can ever get it back. (Ben, age 27, Philadelphia)

Uh, the high I got the second time, it was cool, but it wasn't as cool as the first time, because I had already experienced it and I knew what to expect, what to look for, you know, so it wasn't no big surprise, you know, oh, it was good, you know, but it wasn't like the first time. You be always tryin' to get that first high back. (Hunter, Chicago)

I didn't have that nausea, that feeling that I was going to throw up. Other than that the high was similar only this time I nodded a little bit more. Other than that, it was just about the same. I liked it better the way it felt the first time. Things weren't exactly like I wanted them to be. (Ron, Chicago)

At first I went into a nod I was so high, he had to walk me around to keep me from going out. I was like dreaming, but I was awake, but I was dreaming. Dreaming about girls and stuff. I felt good, relaxed, everything. It's a good feeling. That's why everytime I get high, I think about the first time. Always trying to get back. That's how people get addicted, trying to get that feeling they first felt when they first tried it. (Pete, age 26, Philadelphia)

This poignant testimony establishes the connection between the powerful, unforgettable first shot of heroin and the persistent attempt to reproduce it. Clearly, the search for euphoria is an important motivator for addiction. It is not the only one, however. Many researchers have established that euphoria is not the primary motive for regular heroin use. Rather, heroin users seek calmness, stability, peace of mind, and even serenity, that fall short of transporting the user to a euphoric state (Wakefield 1969; Brecher 1972; Waldorf 1973).

It is perhaps not surprising, then, that many of the HLS men report that heroin makes them feel "normal" and "relaxed."

The Heroin High

As with other modern lifestyles, nearly every aspect of the heroin lifestyle is complex and riddled with ambiguities, making it hard for users to explain and even harder for outsiders to understand. This is particularly true of the heroin high. The high initiates users into the heroin lifestyle and continues to draw them further into the drug's subculture. Yet the high remains an enigma, even to heroin users themselves. Great literary geniuses such as Samuel Taylor Coleridge, Thomas De Quincey, and William Burroughs have had trouble capturing in words the essence of the high. This should be kept in mind as we read how HLS men describe the effects accompanying the heroin high, that elusive central goal around which heroin users' behavior revolves.

Contrary to popular belief, veteran users do not consistently achieve a high. According to the HLS men, heroin does not invariably produce elevated feelings or intense, pleasurable sensations. Often, though not always, most seasoned addicts experience positive feelings, moods, and sensations when using the drug, and most users report heightened sensitivity accompanied by a sense of increased personal capability (not possible without the drug), and with enough regularity to reinforce continued heroin use.

Continued drug use is also reinforced by the feeling of normalcy that heroin induces, allowing the HLS men to relax and sometimes to "escape." Although they often experience little joy from heroin, these men believe that heroin use is a unique experience, altogether different from most other drug use. They struggle to describe its unusual effects. Jim, of Washington, D.C., put it this way:

> Rather than taking off, you feel deeply implanted. Rather than *going on a trip*, it [heroin] brings you back home. You don't go out like a jet or a rocket, you accommodate yourself to this world.

These effects appear to be medically soothing—not much different from feelings attainable through meditation, but perhaps more pronounced.

The perception of timelessness, or the ability to control time by suspending it, is a typical sensation resulting from the heroin experience. Under the influence of heroin, some HLS men feel they can control time, that they can move inside of time, anticipate the beat of time passing, slow time almost to a stop.

Other HLS men report feeling as if they were retreating deep into the self:

> It is a highly personal experience. You feel like you are deep inside yourself. (Nathan, age 28, Washington, D.C.)

> I felt like I was floating, like being back in the womb. (Larry, age 26, Chicago)

The high also insulates heroin users from the outside world; this effect is a primary attraction of the drug. Under the influence, HLS men feel that their harsh and hostile environment cannot penetrate their lives. They can escape from their problems, from other people, and feel better. Temporarily, these men can achieve a feeling that eludes them in the straight world—a feeling of well-being. Seventy-two percent of the HLS men report such feelings and appear to gain a sense of calmness, serenity, and acquiescence as a result of their heroin injection:

> It [heroin] gives me the feeling that I don't have a care in the world. (Zulu, age 33, Chicago)

Ya know somethin', I ain't got no job or nothing but at least I got something to block out this bullshit and kill the problems I am having and make me sleep better. (Tap, age 26, Philadelphia)

Hey man, my shot helps me escape, makes me feel better . . . lets me feel as though I am free of problems. (Tiny, Chicago)

You feel good. You don't feel like nobody is messin' with ya . . . ya just want to sit there and relax, and cool off and think. (Gut, Chicago)

It's my relaxer, *my shot* for the day . . . so I can feel *normal*. (Dap Daddy, Chicago)

Getting high is the *norm* for me . . . I just get *normal*. (Ace, Philadelphia)

The high further contributes to a sense of well-being by adding feelings of increased competence. George, a 23-year-old from Washington, D.C., cited earlier, in addition to noting a calming reaction from heroin, also reports feeling an increased ability to communicate:

I seem to be very hyper-type individual . . . when I'm high I feel like I'm communicating better with people.

Hollywood, a 27-year-old Chicago man, reports his sense of heroin-induced confidence as a kind of generalized optimism:

If you have heroin you're going to do everything on a smooth basis.

The feelings of normalcy and expanded competence contribute to the observations users often have of other users but not of themselves. Catman, age 34, of Philadelphia, described the classic "nodding," "drooling," ineffectual addicts, indicating that he felt apart from them. Their experience with heroin differed from his as much as his daily life differed from that of nonusers:

I see other people, sitting around and nodding, dribbling at the mouth, and all that kind of stuff . . . It [heroin] don't affect me like that, man, I just feel straight.

In conclusion, the HLS men tell us that heroin does not consistently produce euphoria, but it does routinely provide feelings of normalcy, stability, and competence as well as an unusual transcendental feeling. These experiences, although not the euphoria experienced with the first shot, are enough to keep heroin users deeply rooted in the heroin culture.

The Best Experiences

We also asked each respondent about his best and worst experience while high on heroin. The largest percent (31 percent) reported their best moment as those occasions when they were able to get a greater quantity of high quality heroin and as a result get an exceptional high. These moments generally came about as a result of lucky encounters rather than through efforts of their own. Another 6 percent reported getting drugs of high quality as their best experience.

Ron, from Chicago, describes a fortuitous encounter as his best experience:

> We went to a crap game and I had won some money, and lost some money. When I came out, I met a Mexican who gave me some heroin, that was fantastic. It was like being high a different way, because it was stronger. It was the premix or something. I wasn't nodding as much. I mean, you couldn't nod with this particular drug. I really fell in love because this was heroin.

Kevin, a 20-year-old from New York, reports:

> The best experience I ever had usin' heroin is when I done got a nice quality of powder and I knew I don't have to hustle no more. Because I done got my beautiful high and I got money to get high some more if I want to. Bein' so high and knowin' that you got money to get high again without goin' through the changes of hustlin'. After the high wore off I just, ya know, I falls asleep, when I wake up I'm wonderin' can I do to all over again.

Anton, age 20, of Washington, D.C., provides us with yet another example:

> We were listenin' to music and testin' the heroin. And, everybody kept wantin' more and more, said they wasn't high. And, I say, "Forget that. I want to do it myself." And, I had one of the one's who was usin' it inject me. It was so good. I had triggers in my toes and everything, I said, "I don't need no more testin'," and from then on I tested it myself. Shew. Felt like a millionaire, it's somethin' you want to feel every day, 365 days per year.

James and Bull of Chicago along with Ben of Philadelphia reported a sense of personal peace:

> The toughest time I can remember is I went to a jam session on the West Side and I sat in with some fellas who were much older at the time and they were real good musicians. I seemed to be able to play with them the way I wanted to. It was a feeling of well-being like I could really play. Just an experience of euphoria, happiness. When I had it in me it seemed like the feeling of well-being—everything was all right. (James)

The best experience I ever had when I was high off of heroin was when I went out to this lounge and I was tired and I was really having a good time. I was feeling good. All the ladies was giving me action and shit. And I guess that's about the best time I had when I was high. It's quite a while back, but I still remember it. Dancing and having fun and getting high and just partying. (Bull)

The best experience I had when I was high on heroin was just layin' back, listenin' to some jazz, my I was in complete solitude and I was in my own apartment and had everythin' that I wanted. I didn't have to want for any material things. If I wanted to talk to somebody, I had the phone. All my bills was paid, and the abundance of peace was just really blissful. I refer back to that as my "dope dream." I was just complete. You know, because I'm the type of person in order for me to be happy I have to be at peace with myself. I value peace of mind above everything. (Ben of Philadelphia)

The next largest category (27 percent) of best experiencces involved relationships with women, of more than usual intensity:

I was in a go-go listening to, you know, a pretty nice sound. It was 11:00 P.M., decent music and a lot of females. You want to be somebody that you're not, so you just trying anything you can. The music controls the average beast. That puts your mind at ease right there. You feel good. You ain't feeling like one of them bad days where you got to go out and rob somebody, take somebody's money and things like that. They let you take control of them. When we leave the disco, we end up in the hotel. We went to the hotel right across the street, laid up in the hotel all night. We didn't have nothin' to hide, and we had some dope. Didn't have no bam though. It's that bam that keep you awake all night. (James, age 27, Washington, D.C.)

Others were simply sharing, first the heroin and then a feeling of closeness with another human being. Lee of Philadelhia and Hunter of Chicago reported this kind of experience:

The best experience was when me and my old lady was both high together and we didn't have no problems. Everything was just smooth, and we both on the same level, you know. We got the same high and just sit back, and be high, both had some money in our pockets. (Lee, age 29)

One night me and my woman got high at home and it just made us both feel like we wanted the world, you know. We wanted to give each other the world, and it just made us feel like that there wasn't nothin' that we couldn't do, we wanted for each other, you know, and you know, just wanted, just thought of life as a dream, you know. (Hunter)

The reported best experience while high of other respondents were even less dramatic—12 percent indicated having a particularly good time while partying, 9 percent said it was when they had money in their possession, another 9 percent could not identify a best experience that stood out, and 6 percent gave other responses.

What is most interesting about these "best experiences" is that if judged by middle-class standards, they are not so unusual. It appears that the environments in which heroin users regularly function offer such comparatively limited possibilities that even the best drug-induced experiences are not so far removed from the pleasant experiences of most people in more well-to-do lifestyles.

The Worst Experiences

The experiences are not all viewed as positive, however. Almost 40 percent of the HLS men said that their worst experience was overdosing. Another 20 percent reported severe sickness approaching the trauma level of an overdose as their worst experience. Almost 11 percent reported that their worst experience resulted from having witnessed a friend or relative overdose while high themselves. Collectively, more than 70 percent cite some aspect of the overdose syndrome as their worst experience while high on heroin. The following three accounts are typical responses:

> Once I had the feeling of OD-ing. I had this feeling and it frightened me because all of my limbs became limp and it was like I couldn't use them. I always had a fear of that. I remember a couple of friends walking me. Seemed like they was walking me for half the night until I came around. (Joe, age 29, Chicago)

> It was in '74. We decided to get a couple of quarters of dope and get high. So we went downtown and copped the dope and we went to a oil joint. Everybody was shooting dope. People talking about what was going on, you know, in the area and stuff. We sat down and fired the quarters and I went out. I lit a cigarette and felt myself go into a nod, and that's all I remember until I woke up. And when I woke up everybody was standing around me and slapping me on the face and stuff. They carried me out to the car and I was sweating and I felt scared. Everybody was telling me I should go to the hospital. They kept trying to make me walk and stuff. I didn't go to the hospital, I just stayed with somebody. (Max, age 25, Washington, D.C.)

> I started falling down on the floor; didn't know what was wrong. Didn't know he just called me something and said, get 'em up, make him walk. Twenty minutes later, we done had the ambulance and the police, and it was a trip. (Derrick, age 22, Washington, D.C.)

Sometimes supportive friends or experienced users must employ brutal remedies to revive an overdose victim:

The worst experience I ever had was when we was in OD. We were at a person's house. When I woke up and came to my senses I didn't have no clothes on, had ice between my legs and my fingers was painted where they had stuck needles and stuff, trying to bring me around. I finally came around and was thankful that the young lady administered the first aid to me. (Icepick, age 35, Washington, D.C.)

I overdosed at a shooting gallery. I had bought three dime bags of brown dope from the Bronx and I called myself bein' slick. I went up there and thought I could handle it by myself and it wasn't like that, ya know. I shot the dope and, that's all I remember—just pushing it in. The next thing I know, I woke up and they had ice through my legs, they was givin' me the salt shot and they was smackin' me and walkin' me around, and givin' me milk, because I was only sixteen years old at the time, and I guess they didn't want me to die on them. (Shorty, age 18, New York)

If a heroin user is not with friends when the overdose occurs, or worse, is in a hostile situation, results may be brutal, as in the case of James, a 29-year-old from New York, left for dead:

I went out. I OD'd. When I fell out, I hit my face and messed my eye up. I almost died. That's the worst experience I ever had. When I went out they left me for dead. I woke up and there was this little kid holding me, holding my hand. I was hot, man. I ended up in the hospital and I came around pretty good. I was lucky that time.

And Andre, age 27, of Chicago, left buried in the snow:

I had a blackin' out feelin' . . . felt it comin' on . . . faster . . . faster, want to say somethin' but can't 'cause it come on so fast. Right, next thing you know, I was hittin' the floor. How did that experience end. I wound up lying in the snow after bein' drug around in it. I was buried in the snow.

The HLS men who reported severe sickness as their worst experience (20 percent) often identified the cause of the sickness precisely. This was more severe sickness than was reported following the first shot and generally approached the trauma level of an overdose experience.

Bob, a 35-year-old from Chicago, identifies his own inept administration of the heroin shot as the cause of his illness:

The syringe I was usin' slipped, you know, and upon injection it slipped all the way from the top to the bottom. It went in BAM, like that, too fast. It hit my heart like ten tons of bricks. I thought I was gonna die. I got up, I turned on the fan, raised up the window, I started runnin' in place because it was OD-in' me because it was thrown in me so fast. I resisted, I was fightin' by keeping movin', I thought I was really been movin', I thought I musta been movin' really fast, but I musta not been movin' that fast, by my circulation an' moving and jumpin' and, you know, fightin' like that and bringin' in the air, increasin' my heartbeat—I knew I had to do that or I'da been gone, that was the worst experience and the next day my heart was still hurtin' from the pressure of slammin' it in me like that.

Andre (Chicago) "shot hot" and got sick:

> It comes from shooting the heroin too hot. You know, say you don't cool it off after you cook it and put it in cool water, you just don't leave it there long enough, for your body temperature, to mix with the heroin, and it will be chilled. You start shaking and you know, whatever you know. Your teeth chatter and you feel like your head will just explode, you know. And the only relief you get, the only relief for it really is, to shoot some more heroin. I usually just let it wear off itself. It generally ends with me just getting enough money and going out and coppin' again, and shot the dope, and it took the feeling away.

But Henry, a 28-year-old from Philadelphia, got sick as a result of injecting impure heroin:

> The worst experience I ever had when I was high was when, uh, I bought some drugs from some people on the West Side, that was supposed to be heroin, but I think it must of had some procaine or something mixed on it, you know, 'cause when I shot it, it just zoomed real fast, real fast you know, and it made my thumb and my tongue real numb, you know, and my heart was beating real fast and I was just, you know, I tried to drink a glass of milk, and I was, you know, spilling it all over myself, I ran outside in the cold, and oh, man, that was a trip, you know, but a friend of mine was with me.

These traumatic overdose experiences commonly resulting from mistakes during administration and from the injection of impurities can leave deep emotional scars on the OD victim and on friends who witness an OD.

The following case, for instance, approaches the macabre. It embodies the fear of physical harm, the brutal measures sometimes required, and the detachment and indifference which veteran addicts can display:

> We was all over at my house. We had shot some dope. He shot up and he went too quick. Next thing I knew he hit his head on the sink. POW. I was scared to death because I'm off on my dope that day too. I figured maybe he took my dope. I turned my back and all the sudden . . . he smashed his head. A nigger told me to put ice on his nuts. We didn't have no ice tray. The refrigerator was froze so we took this little thing like an ice pick and a hammer and broke the frozen part off from around the refrigerator. So we using the ice off the freezer and putting it down there. Then they said to put cigarettes in his eyes to keep his eyes open. They said it was going to burn.

Tried to walk the man. The nigger don't call the ambulance. He had been fucking around longer than we had so he had known all this shit. He said you don't want the police coming to your house or nothing like that. So we got the nigger, the ice down there, and he was jumpin'. The nigger put the cigarette in the back of his eye and his eye bulging. I mean, it was a trip. It was a cold trip. Then the niggers picked him up and got to walking him. This nigger was throwing up. He couldn't hold up, they were dragging him. His feet was dragging. It seemed like he be coming to or something like that. His pants was down. They dragging him in the alley, up and down the street and smacking him on the face. Those niggers looked stupid out there, man, pulling this man. (Torre, age 28, Washington, D.C.)

In the next account, Solo, 26, (New York) reports being left with a feeling of helplessness. His statement also demonstrates a troublesome contradiction. On the one hand this was his worst experience and on the other hand his own experience with the drug was good because of the high quality:

My worst experience was when I was with my friend who OD'd. I was high— had gotten off first and told him, "Be cool, man, don't shoot, this is gonna be too much for ya." My system's strong and he had been clean, this mother-fucker. He was clean for six months and he wanted to get high, "Come on, man, one time, one time." And we proceeded to get high and there was nothin' I could do, he was turnin' purple. I tried everything I knew, even called the ambulance. The ambulance came and I stayed with him. That was in '71 man. The stuff was good, the heroin was on the money.

Tiny, from Chicago, had no such ambivalence, as he tells of the death of a close friend. His description is important because it reflects a sense of loss and futility that has none of the more typical detachment and indifference that characterize many reports by veteran addicts:

He was purple in the face, and I could feel he had died. That was the worst experience I had had, because he was like a brother to me. He was as close as anybody could get without being kin. Just to see him dead. I couldn't help, couldn't do nothing, just cold, just died, shit, you know, the color just left his face, and left him cold black. It really upset me, it had me mentally sick for a long time. That was the worst experience. He's been dead 'bout nineteen months.

Tiny's reminiscence is in sharp contrast to Ike's (age 35, from Philadelphia) cool, precise, somewhat detached report:

We were fucked up with drugs and didn't even know the man was dead. He OD'd. He hit himself and he stood against the wall, and then slowly slid down the wall. He was the first one to take off and he said, Damn, this stuff is good man. So when he slid down the wall we didn't pay him no mind. We took the works from him and did what we had to do and got high. We did things to him and he still sittin', we thought he was noddin', we didn't know nothing about people dying. We heard about OD-ing but it ain't never happen to none of us. His wife came in the door and asked what he was doin'. She couldn't bring him around and asked us to put him on the bed. It wasn't no hot shot or nothin' like that. He made them sounds, but what the fuck, we didn't know. Like I said, we was green, ya know, just got into it, what did we know about it. 'Cause, if we did, we woulda tried to do somethin' for him, ya know. Or even call the police and just left him, but we didn't know. That was the worst experience.

Finally, in addition to these overdose-related worst experiences, 11 percent of the HLS men said their worst times occurred when they were being arrested while high or getting into fights (4 percent). Another 5 percent noted that causing disappointment to family members through the humiliation of being observed by them "on the nod" was the worst experience. Almost 9 percent of the respondents did not describe a worst experience.

Thus, for most of the HLS men, a worst experience with heroin can be dangerous, confirming their anticipatory fears. And these experiences can be brutal and terrifying, sometimes resulting in witnessing the death of friends or acquaintances. However, the painful experiences and even possible long-term harmful social and psychological effects do not appear to dissuade users from continuing to take heroin.

Heroin and Sexual Activities

The effect of heroin on sexual functioning has been well documented. We know, for instance, that most regular heroin users engage in less sexual activity than their nonaddicted counterparts (Wieland and Yunger 1970; Mirin et al. 1980); that heroin users of long standing generally have reduced libido and diminished sexual capacity; that opiate addiction usually reduces sexual desire and sexual pleasure (Rubington 1967; Brecher 1972; Weil 1973); and that heroin use reduces anxiety about sexual inadequacy (Chein et al. 1964). From a clinical perspective, biochemical data show reduced libido and diminished sexual capacity in men as normal outcomes of regular heroin use. Also, extended use of heroin suppresses the pituitary gland, blocking the release of the luternizing hormone (LH) which, in turn, causes testosterone levels in the blood to drop (Mendelson and Mello 1982).

When HLS men were asked if heroin affected their sexual performance, 87 percent reported that it did. Of these, 51 percent indicated increased ability to sustain an erection when high on heroin. However, nearly a third (32 percent) of the 51 percent were unable to climax. These men generally appeared to derive little pleasure from sex and had ambiguous motivations for engaging in sex with women, as shown in the following accounts:

Heroin gives them the sexual endurance they need to dominate the woman. You don't care whether you come or not. It's just coming home man 'cause he don't have no confidence in his performance level. How else can you build up your masculinity and ego. (Tap Shoes, age 25, Washington, D.C.)

The girls that really like me, I know they'll give me something, and I have sex with them. That's the way I have sex now, I'm not doing it for pleasure, really. That's the last thing I want. No pleasure. (James, New York)

It [heroin] makes me have a peace of mind. In other words, it don't just knock my hat off, it makes me last longer. And it makes her feel good too because I can't last that long if you ain't. With drugs inside I feel like I could do anything. Without that I don't want no sex because that's a substitute for sex for me. When I'm in the bed with my woman and I'm on heroin, it's like I can stay on it a long time but after so long it won't release, you know, my sperm in her. Then I can't get back on it. If I have enough drugs in me, then I can't get back on it. (Larry, Chicago)

In addition to ambiguous feelings about pleasure, frustration is also a central theme in the dialogue about heroin's impact on sexual performance and sexual relations:

It prolongs it, it makes you, keeps you going for a longer period of time. Sometimes I feel it's bad. Sometimes I want to get it over with, you know. And sometimes, like, I don't even get no feeling out of it. I don't even get no sensation. Sometimes, with me, what it's got to be, it's got to be a ritual. You know, I really wasn't enjoying it, I just in the habit of, like doing it like that, so that when that time period would come along, I do it. (Paul, age 27, Philadelphia)

You can't feel as good about sex when you shootin' dope as when you ain't had none. Heroin holds, man. It keeps me from nutting. If love is gonna be hell, there's too much damn work to be messin' around. (Catman, Philadelphia)

When I got drugs in my system, I can't reach a climax, you know, I can just go on and on and on, but I don't get to the point where I reach a climax, I go on and on and on and nothin' happen. (Hunter, Chicago)

I do heroin right, I find it hard for me to get an erection. So, before I go see her I try to limit the day, you know that I might not do it [shoot heroin] until four or five hours before I see her. You know, try to get my body where it kind of builds it back up. 'Cause, then I get there. Like when I be laying in bed, I can't tell her, "Not now baby," you know. (Stitch, age 26, Philadelphia)

Other HLS men report a different experience. Two claim that heroin is often an aphrodisiac, especially when combined with cocaine. One of these men further explains that general health and motivation, not heroin per se, are the critical factors in sex:

Sometimes it [heroin] drives it and sometimes it kills it. It depends on when I got hooked up and what I use. When I'm doin' stuff and coke there's no problem at all. (Ron, Chicago)

It's all in your mind, man. I don't care what nobody say. You got somebody you care about and you want to get down with them you gonna get down. But a dope fiend or a drunk, somebody's that high all the time and don't take care of themselves, that's a different story. I don't know about that 'cause I don't get that bad. I don't dig it. But as far as drugs, I ain't never had no problems with that. (Ike, Philadelphia)

Still others, in the minority, recount exceptionally good relationships with women while high; over a quarter (of those who said heroin affected their sexual performance) claim that their best heroin experience involved sex, especially when both partners were high:

Maybe just once, man, with this girl named Michelle. Both of us got high, man, and I really liked the experience that came with it because we was fuckin' for about nine hours, nonstop, and I was gettin' higher and higher. It seemed like I was in a cloud, ya now. That's about the best experience I really even had, ya know, off of it. The other part, ya know, you'd be high and she'd be high. (Gut, Chicago)

One night and I had a little woman, you know. And she really gassed me and I gassed her. We had a little sex party, just between me and her. And it was like no other sex party I ever had with her. Made dinner and you know, had a little wine, and we just held each other, and we just had a nice, pleasant evening. We fell asleep in each other's arms, after we had sex, and then we woke up the next morning. (Andre, Chicago)

Social Relationships and Economic Realities

To this point our discussion has focused on the shooting of heroin and the behavior of HLS men while high, based on their perceptions and feelings. Before concluding, it is worthwhile to report briefly on two other areas which are an integral part of using heroin in the inner city—social relationships and the cost and availability of heroin. It is through social networks that heroin users obtain daily information on the availability, cost, and quality of drugs. And it is through "associates" that financial resources are often pooled to buy heroin and it is with "walking partners" that users often hustle money, cop, and shoot their drugs. These relationships affect the amount and quality of heroin each man can get each day.

The Dudes on the Corner

The existence of extensive social networks seems not only plausible but necessary, given other reported experiences with heroin. For example, the men rely on user friends to pool resources to cop heroin, to provide a safety net to protect against their vulnerability to ODs and other heroin-related sicknesses, and as a source of supportive social interaction. Given their mutual needs regarding heroin, extensive social networking is understandable.

The following are typical comments of those who reported more than four close addict relationships as the men describe the value they place on these relationships when getting their "shot off" . . .

> You know, you know, durin' the time . . . I try to have somebody with me when I'm takin' off, you know, just in case somethin' happen, you know, fuck around . . . getting my shot off. Have somebody with me just in case I go out or somethin'. I want somebody there that know what they doin'. Don't want no amateur, man, mutha fuckah don't know about the game, I go out and this mutha fuckah around goin' to leave me, man. (Rosco, Chicago)

. . . and for providing a defense against conflict and exploitation . . .

> I would say I'm tight with about three or four, tight. Just by seeing them every day, you know. And, you know, being with them, and seeing that they was, you know, had values close to mine. We ain't gonna rip off each other, so to speak. (Tommy, age 19, Chicago)

. . . and for mutual support . . .

> We talk about, you know, trying to get ourselves together, you know what I mean, trying to tie it up, deal with the drug problem, you know, as times moves on, you know what I mean, ah, try to go into a thing of, hustlin' together, you know, to make money, to make ends meet, you know. Ah, trying to ah, pull each other together more, trying to stay out of the police way, you know, ah, ah, ah, how to work together, you know, so to speak, in terms of getting our habit going, you know what I mean. Ignoring the, the, we need each other more than anything, you know. So you know, like birds of a feather we flock together, you know, so (got tight with them) copping every day. (Walter, Chicago)

. . . and for enriching the heroin experience . . .

> It's much better gettin' high when ya with somebody, somebody that you dig, a good hustlin' partner, you know, the high seem to be much better. When you get high, you need somebody you wanta talk to. You don't talk to any motherfucker, you want to talk to somebody you know. Somebody that lives 'round you, somebody you been 'round for a few years, and that's my partner, you know. And he's cool, and when I get high I enjoy being with him. (Jimmy, age 30, Chicago)

However, Be Be from Chicago, while discussing the process of "getting tight," also reveals some of the problems with staying tight:

> It only takes about two or three days [to get real tight with them]. When you see the same person every day, you know, and you up there trying to get the same thing, and both of you are addicts, all of you are addicts—you tighten up real quick like that. Because a lot of times, you know, you go to cop and you get burned. You also got your fellow addicts out there trying to be a little slicker than you, trying to beat you, you know? And, after one or two times, they do that, there is just some that you completely forget about. You don't run around with them no more. Because you will end up, you know, fighting or killing each other or something like that. (Be Be, age 33, Chicago)

Perhaps this is one reason HLS men who are loners, that is, more detached and distant from their peers, approach others with suspicion and reluctance. Yet these men frequently report having had at least one or two close social relationships beyond the traditional walking partner. Consider the revelations of HLS men who remain loners to avoid exploiting their loved ones . . .

> I'm only tight with a few. Most heroin users, man, when you get off, really off into it, it's hard to really trust. That's when you get to the point of no return. That's when you become what they call a dope fiend, a hype, or a person who's just out there livin' for the high. That means that you'll take anybody off to get the money. That includes mother, brother, sister, close friends. So, therefore, when you get off into that type of atmosphere you don't want to be too close. (Red, age 36, New York)

. . . because they are selfish and suspicious . . .

> No, man, just tight with some niggers. If they got a pile of the shit and I'm around when they're doin' it, they'll give me a pump out of it, ya know. But, I ain't tight with no group of them, ya know. Because too many of them too tight with their own selves. (Gut, Chicago)

. . . because they fear exploitation . . .

> They are out for what they can get. They'll use you, they'll use the next time man. They'll try to use me if they can, so therefore, I play it by myself. Me and my partner Bull we go back so many years that he straight with me, but these guys out here on the streets, you walking down the street, they may wave, say hello to me. We are not tight. We not shit. (Jimmy, Chicago)

Despite such feelings, most of the HLS men cope with the pressures of the heroin subculture by cooperating with others to pool resources to purchase, borrow, and barter for heroin. Thus, the network of social relationships goes beyond the traditional, lone walking partner and is evidently a byproduct of the need for cooperation, support, protection against exploitation, and first aid for overdoses and related sickness. The importance of social networks for purchasing heroin will become more evident as we examine the economic realities of the heroin marketplace.

Facing the Economic Realities

In 1967 I could sniff a bag and it would hold me. We could just sniff at our leisure and it was a two dollar a bag. There was fifteen bags in a bundle and we would take two or three of those and put them in pieces of tinfoil and pass it around and sniff it. (Jay, age 35, New York)

At first I would get high on weekends. At that time drugs were so plentiful and so cheap we could get together two-fifty and get a five-dollar bag that would keep us high all night. (Butch, New York)

You couldn't shoot no half quarter bags by yourself in the sixties. I'd turn on the whole neighborhood with a half quarter for heaven's sakes. Then a two dollar bag would get me straight. Now you got to shoot fifty dollars to feel the same as the two dollar bag in the good years. Now they talk about Afghanistan and Iran dope and China white. I ain't never seen it. Where is it? Bring it to me and let me shoot some of this shit. (Solo, New York)

Solo's estimate of the escalation in cost since the late 1960s may be somewhat exaggerated, but his perception of street price for bags during that period is close to the heavily diluted three- to seven-dollar bags documented by Waldorf (1973). Preble and Casey (1969) estimate that it cost approximately twenty dollars a day to maintain a heroin habit in the late 1960s. Holahan (1972) reports that in the early stages of dependence, many addicts' had habits that required only ten to fifteen dollars a day. In a more recent ethnographic study conducted in California, Rosenbaum (1982) found that a bag of heroin, which is less than one-quarter of a gram, cost approximately twenty-five dollars.

The HLS data suggest that at least half (51.5 percent) of the HLS men are spending no more than twenty-five dollars a day for their heroin. Thirty-four percent are spending between twenty-six dollars and thirty dollars, and 14.5 percent said they spent over thirty dollars a day. There are, of course, numerous difficulties in accurately estimating such figures.[2] However, these figures do suggest that at least the majority of the HLS men are able to get by on twenty to thirty dollars per day. It is difficult to know for certain if the economic realities of the 1970s and 1980s have forced users to reduce their dose (73.5 percent of HLS men typically shoot up only once a day) or if they would shoot only once a day even if heroin were cheaper or if they had more money. It seems likely, however, that twenty-five or thirty dollars a day is a considerable amount for these men, most of whom are unemployed or sporadically employed and who do not engage in big-time illegal activities. Finally, our data suggest that while the price of heroin has increased over the last two decades (and perhaps the quality has gone down) its increased cost has not been as dramatic as have inflationary processes in many legal consumer goods.

Nevertheless, it is understandable that poor, Black, inner-city heroin users would be extremely sensitive to the changing price of heroin. At least one member of the HLS group reported economic considerations as his primary motivation for beginning intravenous use of heroin. Buck, of Washington, explains:

> It may seem strange, but I am a tight motherfucker, ya know, and the boy told me I'd be savin' money and usin' less dope. So, bein' that that seemed like a thrifty idea, you know, me savin', I figured I'd do it that way. Instead of snortin' three caps in a day, I could just use one and get high. For a dollar I be high all day down there.

Perhaps as a result of inflated drug costs and the establishment of more effective security measures (such as community crime watches and antishoplifting devices) and the generally tight economy, HLS men report other cost control methods such as shopping around to take advantage of variations in price, spot buying, or buying only from reputable dealers to ensure the acquisition of good heroin. Here the HLS men tell of making ends meet, getting rewarded for being a regular customer, establishing credit and simply buying smart:

> I had about half a quarter. The cost varies from forty-five to fifty-five dollars but I can usually get it for thirty-five. (Icepick, Washington, D.C.)

> The cost of heroin depends on the time and money I've got. If I got twenty dollars I get a sixpack, but if I don't have twenty I gotta deal with what I can get. (Stitch, Philadelphia)

> From being in drugs a long time me and a lot of dealers is close. Like when it might cost the average person twenty-five or thirty dollars, I might get for ten, you understand. (Ace, Philadelphia)

> I got credit line with most guys I cop from. I don't usually cop from these little guys out in the street. I know guys that got the big shit so I don't really have a problem. But if I would only have like twenty-three dollars, they would give me one or two b's anyway. (Ben, Philadelphia)

> See, I know where to get it from. They might give it to me cheaper. I give him fifty-five dollars because I know the guy and he'll probably give me a few bags. (Vick, age 26, Philadelphia)

There are a number of other techniques HLS men use to cope with current economic realities, especially when their "money is funny." One technique is to pool resources. This is a common practice among heroin users even if one has only a small amount to contribute to the pot. Ike (Philadelphia) says only a minimum contribution is necessary for participation in this process:

> If you come out of the house with just five or ten dollars man, you can get things workin'. When you come out there broke, you ain't gonna get nothing all day long. You come out with ten dollars, and you can work something. It comes to you. People might come and say, "Look, we got this here."

Or some maybe lucky enough to come up with free heroin. Vick (Philadelphia) gets his heroin free in exchange for "hitting" people—injecting them with heroin. A few heroin users have needle phobia which prevents them from injecting themselves, while others have burned out the veins which they can conveniently reach themselves:

> I get high all the time for nothing. 'Cause I hit people. Some people, they all swelled up and they hit each other. I hit them on their arms, legs, butt, and everywhere else.

And others, like Gut (Chicago), reduce their own costs by taking advantage of someone else:

> I ran into this girl I hadn't seen in a few years. I beat her out of twenty-five dollars and bought me a bag of dope and took about ten dollars of the shit out of the bag and gave her some domino (sugar) on top of it.

Yet another technique, which, although a recently acquired practice, is perhaps the most common, is to use cheaper, more readily available drugs to maintain a tolerable level of consciousness and to extend the influence of the heroin:

> It's not like it used to be, 'cause there is so many drugs around, you can always get something, you take this and that, and sell it to get something else. So many people get high off of different things, you wouldn't really know the difference what you get high off. Before it used to be you could tell a person who is on heroin by appearancewise. (Tap, Philadelphia)

Substitute drugs used during periods between heroin shots are viewed as helping to extend the effects of heroin. The most common substitute mentioned by the HLS men is marijuana, which is generally passed around free or used in exchange for something else. Marijuana is used (sometimes in combination with alcohol) as a relaxer in the morning. Ron (Chicago) gets his day started with this combination:

> Woke up and smoked a joint. Went into the bathroom where I have my works laid out. Had my little ol' shot of heroin. I try not to go home without it. I injected it into the vein and laid back. Got me a glass of wine and hit the streets. I was feeling pretty good.

And Jim from Chicago:

> I went back and bought myself a bag of reefer—this was about eight o'clock now. Smoked some and came back in the street and messed around with the fellows. Drank some wine and went in and partied for an hour. That was about eleven o'clock.

Reefers are frequently chain-smoked. James (Washington, D.C.) used them in this manner frequently and casually:

> During the course of the day I went here and there but didn't pick up no real money. I guess 'bout three or four o'clock, I stopped and took a break. Smoked a joint and went back around four-thirty. I went back home when I got done. Watched a little TV, ate a little food, and smoked a few more joints.

So does Pete, from Philadelphia:

> I stayed on Tenth Avenue, smoked some reefer. Went back home for a nap, got up and went back to the store with a friend. Listened to a music box, smoked some more reefer and then went out riding with this friend.

These few examples provide an indication of the range of techniques inner-city poor Blacks have developed to cope with their need for heroin and the economic realities of their lives. It seems reasonable to argue that the HLS men carefully control their purchases of heroin by skillful use of their relationships and by the coping techniques just described.

The HLS data show that the heroin experience is not as dramatic or as glamorous as many past studies (cited earlier) have led us to believe. The "cool cat," and "righteous dope fiend" characterizations, which have influenced the public image of Black heroin users, do not seem to fit the Black inner city addict of the 1980s. Certainly, these types of men exist, but our findings reveal a substantially different profile of contemporary heroin users. The HLS heroin user is a struggling, disciplined, "controlled heroin user" who generally takes one shot of heroin (of varying quality) each day. Between shots he uses cheaper, easier-to-obtain drugs. The high that he gets from heroin is not usually a transcendental euphoric feeling, but rather, a feeling of being normal and relaxed. Heroin functions as an equalizer, enabling him to perform in keeping with his view of how non-addicts act and to avoid treatment. The HLS men are not raving, crazed, dope fiends, whose habit increases continually. These men control their heroin use through self-medication.

As noted earlier, it is difficult to determine whether these men maintain their controlled use because of the harsh economic factors they live with or because they simply have the self discipline to control their heroin use. They obviously do not want to epitomize down-and-out dope fiends, nor do they want to be arrested or forced into treatment. Also, it is clear from our data and other studies that the heroin life offers certain benefits and fills important needs—without it these men would have to undergo tremendous social and psychological readjustments. It is possible that the vast majority of today's inner city Black heroin users fit this HLS model. Perhaps it is only the large number of men who have avoided going into treatment that fall into this category. Whatever the case, it is important to determine the extent to which the struggling, disciplined, one shot-a-day Black male heroin user prevails. We will return to this issue in the concluding chapter.

Notes

1. Data for this chapter were derived from the answers of HLS respondents to specific open-ended questions about their experiences with heroin. The authors first listened to twenty-five tape recordings (each approximately two hours in length) and then read all of the completed transcripts (N = 124) in order to understand how the men responded to the questions and to determine the kinds of data particular questions yielded. After the transcripts were coded, responses to questions were extracted and organized in subject areas that emerged from the data. Where appropriate, some data were quantified. However, the thrust of the analysis involved a systematic search for common themes and patterns in the open-ended responses. This required that the quotes from all 124 interviews be assembled around the relevant questions and then organized according to specific patterns of reported behavior. Thus, the quotes used in the chapter are representative of the themes and patterns we identified as most consistent and salient in the experiences of the HLS men.

2. The authors arrived at these figures by analyzing the responses heroin users gave to four different open-ended questions regarding the cost of heroin: how much they reportedly paid for heroin on a typical day; how they obtained money to buy heroin; how they got money for the last buy; and how much it cost them to use per week.

References

Agar, M. 1973. *Ripping and Running: A Formal Ethnology of Urban Addicts.* New York. Seminar Press.

Brecher, E.M. and Editors of Consumer Reports. 1972. *Licit and Illicit Drugs.* Boston: Little, Brown.

Chein, I.; Gerard, D.L.; Lee, R.S.; and Rosenfeld, E. 1964. *The Road to H: Narcotics, Delinquency, and Social Policy.* New York: Basic Books.

Feldman, H. 1968. Ideological supports to becoming and remaining a heroin addict. *Journal of Health and Social Behavior* 9:131–139.

Fiddle, Seymour. 1967. *Portraits from a Shooting Gallery.* New York: Harper and Row.

Finestone, H. 1957. Cats, kicks, and color. *Social Problems* 5(1):3–13.

Holahan, J. 1972. The economics of heroin. In *Dealing with Drug Abuse: A Report to the Ford Foundation,* 290–291. New York: Praeger.

Mendelson, J.; and Mello, N. 1982. Hormones and psycho-sexual development in young men following chronic heroin use. *Neurobehavioral Toxicology and Teratology* 4(4):441–445.

Mirin, Steven; Meyer, Roger; Mendelson, Jack; and Ellingboe, James. 1980. Opiate use and sexual function. *Journal of Psychiatry* 137:909–915.

Preble, E., and Casey, J. 1969. Taking care of business: The heroin user's life on the streets. *International Journal of the Addictions* 4:1–24.

Rosenbaum, M. 1982. Getting on methadone: the experience of the woman addict. *Contemporary Drug Problems* 11(1):113–143.

Rubington, E. 1967. Drug addiction as a deviant career. *International Journal of the Addictions* 2:3–20.

Stephens, R., and Levine, S. 1971. The street addict role: Implications for treatment. *Psychiatry* 34:351–357.

Sutter, A. 1966. The world of the righteous dope fiend. *Issues in Criminology,* Fall. 2:177–182.

Wakefield, D., ed. 1969. *The Addict.* Greenwich, Connecticut: Fawcett Publications.

Waldorf, D. 1973. *Careers in Dope.* Englewood Cliffs, New Jersey: Prentice-Hall.

Weil, A. 1973. *The Natural Mind.* Boston: Houghton Mifflin.

Wieland, W.F., and Yunger, M. 1970. Sexual effects and side effects of heroin and methadone. In *Proceedings of the Third National Conference on Methadone Treatment,* 50–53. Washington, D.C.: NIMH.

Zinberg, Norman. 1982. Nonaddictive opiate use. In *Criminal Justice and Drugs: The Unresolved Connection,* eds. Weisman, James and DuPont, Robert, Port Washington, New York: National University Publications.

Part II

6

Brickin' It and Going to the Pan: Vernacular in the Black Inner-City Heroin Lifestyle

Austin S. Iglehart

We laid around, shot the beast . . . up and down in the street, bullshit in the street, messin' around . . . I seen a guy I know coming from work and borrowed a pound off him. So that there was cop street. We got the half, and then we had problems who's gonna oil it . . . none of our cribs was cool . . . galleries ain't where it's at . . . two dollars a person to get in. They works, the shit all dirty . . . most of the guys like old houses—I case them out if I can. (Mr. Ben, age 27, Philadelphia)

Those outside the Black heroin lifestyle may be totally confused by the above statement. Yet, within the Black heroin subculture, it is easily understood. Mr. Ben was socializing and talking. He borrowed five dollars, which meant he now had enough money, approximately twenty dollars, to buy a half a quarter-teaspoon of heroin. Where to inject it then became a problem. He and the other heroin users couldn't use their living quarters for activities unacceptable to outsiders. The shooting galleries, which, for a fee, supply shelter and paraphernalia for injection, weren't desirable, perhaps because the paraphernalia is often unsanitary. Most people Mr. Ben knows prefer abandoned houses; he tries to investigate them in advance to make sure each is a relatively safe place in which to inject heroin.

This chapter discusses what Black, male, inner-city heroin users talk about with one another and how they communicate, and assesses how the HLS men's language helps them cope within their social world. We will see how language is used in informational exchanges, in some situations, and as a manipulative tool to insulate and protect the user within his world and from the larger society outside. Special attention is given to the user's use of slang, and the vivid nature of its imagery. Through a better understanding of his idiom, we begin to see the intricate dimensions of the user's social world. Accordingly, emphasis is placed on analyzing the social and psychological functions of language and language use patterns, rather than simply the individual meanings of words. The role of Black English in shaping language patterns specific to the heroin lifestyle is discussed. In addition, the range of topics the HLS men say they discuss regularly provides a solid background for the analytic discussion of the functions of language in the process of information exchange. The chapter concludes with a discussion of the potential implications of this analysis for understanding heroin users.[1]

Role of Black English in Black Heroin Users' Speech

The concentration of heroin users in Black inner-city areas has clearly shaped the speech of all heroin users in the United States. Abrahams, in his book *Talking Black* (1976), wrote that "what is needed (to understand Black English) is a framework in which larger patterns of interactions . . . may be considered." Much of the Black heroin user's way with words comes from Black culture. Terminology and metaphorical imagery used by addicts are often drawn from Black slang, and reflect Afro-American cultural values as expressed in dynamic, performance-oriented speech.

Black English was derived from a variety of influences including standard English, Africanisms, and linguistic remnants of slavery and rural Southern lifestyles. Black English is essentially homogenous nationwide (Abrahams 1976). Williams and Brantley (1975) coined the term *ebonics* (a combination of the words and phonics) for ". . . *creative* Black expressions, [emphasis added], both verbal and nonverbal, highly stylized in nature, rhythmic in sound, diversified in meaning, and indigenous to Black people. These speech patterns have been developed by Blacks as a means of communication with one another."

Thus, Black English speech and performance traits, phrases, and metaphors may be part of the Black user's idiom. In the title, for example, "brickin' it" or "throwin' bricks at the penitentiary" (committing illicit acts to get money or drugs) is an easily understood term known by some outside the user's world. James, age 29, from New York, explains:

> I'm not afraid of the penitentiary—I threw enough bricks at it. I be wonderin' what's the hell's going to happen when I walk out that door in the morning . . . I know I'm throwin' the brick. I don't know if I'm going to get busted, killed, or what.

"Going to the pan," however, is a term basically limited to the Eastern U.S. addict lifestyle. Similarly, in Mr. Ben's opening comments at the beginning of this chapter, "galleries," "works," and "a half" are specific to the heroin lifestyle, while "cop street," "a pound," "case," "crib" are not. Fiddle (1967) states that ". . . addicts share a . . . culture with its own language." While addict peers share slang containing specialized ingroup terms, much of ⌐

their language is derived from the communities in which they live, and may be understood by nonaddicts within that community. Black English incorporates Black inner-city street speech. Moreover, the often dramatic publicity by the media about drug use has made the general public increasingly familiar with both drug use and the drug terminology used in urban areas.

In *Runnin' Down Some Lines* (1980), Edith Folb, commenting on language used among her sample of Black Los Angeles teenagers, noted that the explosive growth in the use of illicit drugs had made them (drugs) a major topic of conversation. Whether or not individuals used drugs, "many utilized an exceedingly rich and intricate drug lexicon to relate their experiences and feelings." This trend has been observed in other segments of U.S. society. Dillard (1975) found a "preponderance" of "narcotic terms" in the language of the streets. Widespread drug use of any type seems to be reflected within a few years in popular slang. For example, current slang for a bad experience is a "bummer," derived from a "bum trip" on LSD from the 1960s. Street vernacular often involves some drug terminology, terminology that has meaning within and outside of the Black addict subculture. For example, to "cop," a "front," to "nod," and getting a "taste" all have such dual meanings. Some phrases, such as quitting something "cold turkey," have become well known in the general idiom. Thus, considerations other than actual drug use may sometimes motivate use of drug slang. Addicts may draw from, as well as contribute to, this shared pool.

There are many ways that slang terms may move from one group to another. In the illicit inner-city black-market economy, a drift of jargon, action-oriented slang, and graphic metaphorical imagery occur in a two-way flow of communication between straights and criminals, and between hustlers on the street (Dillard 1975). Also, during imprisonment, addicts and nonaddicts share close quarters and communication with each other, mixing language of the street with the powerful and defensive slang of prison (Futrell and Wordell 1981).

Thus, some of the important factors shaping the slang used in the Black inner city are: drugs; incarceration; influential opinion makers in the Black community, such as disc jockeys (Folb 1980); pop culture; and the church. In addition, their language has elements of poetry and striking, vivid speech patterns which derive from the predominant experiences of U.S. Blacks in their shared conditions of poverty and ghetto life. Black English generally has evolved out of and reflects Blacks' experiences in the United States and provides a larger context for the development, sustenance, and function of the heroin addict's slang.

HLS Men's Topic of Conversation

This section discusses the range of topics HLS men say they most commonly talked about with other users they were "in tight with."

The men were first asked if they were "in tight with any group of heroin users." They were then asked an open-ended question about topics they discussed most frequently with those friends. A follow-up open-ended probe encouraged mention of other topics. Finally, the user was asked about a wide variety of topics in a forced-choice manner. The open-ended questions seemed to offer the most promising line of research, because they eliminated demand characteristics inherent in the closed-ended approach. Both the primary and the follow-up open-ended topics spontaneously mentioned revealed that nearly three fourths (73 percent) of the men who answered this question said that they discussed drugs (mostly heroin).[2] This pattern of discussing drugs, is, of course, predictable, and verifies Fiddle's (1967) point that all discussions between addicts inevitably tend to revolve around heroin. Clyde, a 29-year-old from Chicago, made a similar point (using the term "drugs"):

> . . . every direction you go in, the conversation gonna wind up about drugs. If you change it, drugs is gonna 'filtrate into your conversation some kinda way. And basically, that's all you're gonna be talkin' about. [And if you keep trying to talk about other subjects] . . . then you're a drag to them. "Oh man, I don't have time for that motherfuckin' bullshit . . ."

In addition, a high percentage (58 percent) of HLS men across all cities report discussing hustling. Sluggo, age 22, from Chicago, said "You talk about how many cats you beat." Pablo, age 25, from New York, gave a typical response:

> Just hang around. We talk about who got the best dope, who got the best coke, who got the acid, who got the grass. . . . How, this dope that we got from this guy, or do we did rob today. You know, somebody got killed, you know. Just general conversation, mainly. Like how you all makin', how we gonna do it, or where we gonna get it from. Or who got stuff.

While more men reported discussing drugs and hustling than discussing women (41 percent), sex (23 percent), or kicking the habit (21 percent), these and other topics appear to be part of typical conversations. This is reflected in the responses below which also illustrate both the commonalities and graphic distinctions between users and straights.

> We talk about lots of things . . . politics, sex, money, heroin, houses, bank accounts, just goes on, cars, racing, going to the racetrack, gambling, going to New Jersey, Georgia, Chicago . . . (Bobby, age 27, Washington)

> . . . current events . . . problems they might have. We talk about our problems; we get each other's views on things like that there. We talk about women. We talk about everything, its' not no set conversation just on one

thing. . . . We talk about sex, and maybe one of us might have had a girl that night, maybe they talk about her. Or they talk about how the dope is comin' in different places to get good dope from . . . politics, we discuss that now. We're more into, how the fuck would you say it, we're more into the political line in itself. We think more about what's gonna happen to this country . . . what if a nuclear war starts, where would we be. Would we have to go and fight for this country? (Jay, age 35, New York)

The responses to the forced-mode questions also revealed a significant number of reported conversations on sports, leisure activities, personal problems, and places they are going or would like to go. Thus, the things "in tight" users talk about among themselves, except for drugs and hustling, are relatively conventional.

Information Exchange: The Content and Form of Language

To maintain his illicit lifestyle, the user must continue to obtain information, avoid sickness, and hustle successfully. Information on where drugs are, their quality and price, where the police are, where he can get money, is only part of what he needs. In street life, a man with good information is respected, or "with it;" the one lacking good information is "out of it." Whether or not the addict sees himself primarily as a "stomp down, righteous, hope-to-die dope fiend," or as a drug user in control of his habit, the strong subcultural experience of heroin addiction, with incarceration and withdrawal sickness always possible, adds extra importance to his information exchanges. The following discussions present a number of important ways language functions in the Black inner-city heroin lifestyle.

What's Happening; Runnin' it Down

"What's happening?," a common greeting on the streets, means much more to the addict. Status and reputation are enhanced through being "in the know" and "running it down." Specialized vernacular unique to heroin's use may also serve to enhance the heroin user's status. Banks (1975) defined "running it down" as to "tell someone . . . tell me." This is a phrase that means to ask for and convey information. Its verb also incorporates a sense of action, a key element of Black slang (Kochman 1972). "Runnin' it down" has the sound of something with force and momentum, information of significance to the speaker and, in his mind, to the listener. In turn, it's an invitation, sometimes a demand, for the listener to reciprocate. This type of talk is a major component of Black street-corner conversation, as noted by Abrahams (1976).

Respondents used well-known terms to describe informational exchanges. Ronald, age 31, from Chicago, said his associates were "trying to hip me." Folb (1980) equates this term with "schooling someone . . . making them aware of what's happening, what's important to know in order to survive." Karl, a 20-year-old from New York, said that friends tried to "pull my coat," a term with the same meaning. Abrahams (1976) describes this informational style of Black language as necessarily an intimate affair, between two or more individuals, with a prescribed decorum which includes certain patterns of posture, eye contact, and body language.

In the following example, Torre, a 28-year-old employed in Washington, D.C., talks about the necessity of providing accurate information within the ingroup:

> With my walk boys, we can rap about things we can't with others, like on your job. You can exaggerate on your job, you know, you ain't had no pussy in a week but you say, "Yeah, I been fucking every night." They don't know if you lie or you don't. But your walk boys, they be with you. They know what's going on.

However, friendship and intimacy aren't necessarily required for an information exchange in the heroin user's conversations. Rather, communication is often based on the shared experience of drug taking, and the fact that this shared experience is an illicit activity. In the words of Icepick, 35, of Washington, D.C., users live by their "diabolical wits, ripping people off."

For this they need good information to function effectively. Survival for the user often hinges on the actions of law-enforcement personnel in his area. Thus, one user may school another in the actions of the police, as reflected in the following comments:

> Yeah, we talk about the police all the time. Their routes, just about got a time table on them. If nobody else, we got it on them. (Mr. Boxies, age 31, from Chicago)

Michael, age 28, from Washington said "[We] . . . talk about . . . police, but don't care too much about them." However, Roscoe, age 27, from Chicago disagreed: "[Do we] . . . talk about the police? Every mutha fuckin' day, them dog mutha fuckahs, yeah."

The reason these conversations occur regularly is noted by Zulu, age 33, from Chicago:

> Some days you can stand out here on the street or on the strip and sell your wares and don't get a hassle, other days every few minutes you look up, a

whole flock of motherfuckin' pigs is ridin', so, therefore, you gotta run or stash your shit.

In addition to providing information on the police, users' communication networks provide a mechanism for obtaining and sending vital information. Mr. Ben from Philadelphia said that disagreements between users can cause trouble, and angry heroin users can: "get mad, and put the word out on you." Users out on a "dope stroll" eagerly seek information through these networks. Little D, a 26-year-old from New York said: "I usually go to someone I can depend on telling me the bad is good."

Packages of heroin are referred to in terms of dealer's labels to help identify quality and facilitate repeat sales. These trade names include "Black Sunday" and "ET," reflecting the influence of popular culture. Some are plays on words: "tragic magic." Some are named after weapons or fast, powerful planes: "Hydrogen Bomb," "F–16," "747"; and some are linked with pleasure or fantasies: "Santa Claus," "Paradise." The network is also used to spread the word of overdoses. Icepick, from D.C., said "You hear about Jim's dynamite [heroin] and you see two or three dudes OD'd and Jim split."

Ironically, word of an overdose means that other users immediately want to buy the same heroin, assuming it is extra powerful, even though it may "put them on the curb." Mr. Ben from Philadelphia said: ". . . [they] say so-and-so just OD'd, 'where'd he get it from, what he cop?" They want the OD bag." Butch, age 28, from New York, said: ". . . a bag that somebody OD'd off of a few minutes ago, you run and buy *two*."

"To run it down," then, is to impart information to someone. Prerequisites are shared experiences and serious issues, and the whole communication process is generally focused around the illicit events in the user's lives. Whom they talk to, what they say, and what they hear are of great importance in maintaining their lifestyle. However, this information need not always be straightforward, as shown later in the segment on "signifyin'."

Stylin' and Talkin' Shit

In addition to the content, the form and style employed by speakers is important in perpetuating the status order and other aspects in Black street life. Indeed, Kochman (1972) has noted "stylin' " (how it's said) influences one's status. Status in street talk may be determined by speaking styles and choice of words, as well as by the content of the communication. Abrahams and Gay (1975) noted that in the Black inner-city culture, status is usually not a question of raw coercion, but rather a product of an individual's ability to manipulate words and phrases in a stylish and skillful way, and that "the man of words is the one who becomes a hero of ghetto youth." He cited Muhammed Ali's popularity in the ghetto as being enhanced by his colorful use of language. Predominantly male, speakers in Black street life, with little formal language training, often rely on other ways to express themselves, emphasizing action and the clever use of metaphor, and unselfconsciously modifying words used in standard English. Abrahams (1976), in *Talking Black*, noted the importance of delivery—tone of voice, posture, and how syllables are accented. (Street talkers may call Whites "Eur-o-peans", for example.) He continues: "Style is conveyed, not only through dress and manner, but through a dramatic ability to persuade, even manipulate others, achieved primarily through the effective use of words."

Sutter (1966) comments on the importance of the manner in which the addict conducts his business on the street. HLS responses demonstrate many of the performance aspects of speaking. In part, participation in the HLS provided a forum of stylin'. Jake, a 29-year-old, from Philadelphia was asked if he had enjoyed the interview. He said he had, because "It was able to show a side of me, man—versatility, you know. My greatness."

Added to the valued performance traits of stylin' are demands specific to the heroin lifestyle. While some users may not have great verbal facility, the stereotype is that the heroin user (usually on the lookout for trouble and a way to get his next fix) is an adept and skilled talker. James, age 27, from Washington specifically said he wanted to get into heroin use to be "one of them boss talkers." Jimmy, a 30-year-old from Chicago said that when high on heroin: "I made sense when I was talkin'." Louis, age 18, from Chicago said: "Dope fiends . . . they know everything. You ask a dope fiend about something, he can tell you, he's going to give you some kind of answer."

Heroin, like alcohol, may lessen inhibitions and motivate some to "talk that talk." Almost half of the heroin users interviewed in New York claimed that one reason for initiating and continuing heroin use was because it facilitated a "gift of gab."

The following colorful and stylish quotations taken from the HLS men's comments indicate their facility with language. In these examples, traditional phrases are slightly modified, imagery promoting action is accentuated, and metaphors, similes, and ingroup references are skillfully used to sketch the user's views.

Ron, a 30-year-old from Chicago, compared straights to addicts, and saw no chance of compromise in lifestyles. He noted: "Two different outlooks on life . . . east cat meets west." Chico, age 34, from Chicago, said bluntly of straights: "people live in glass houses . . . they be throwing rocks."

Solo, age 26, from New York, described the post-heroin high of another user this way: "He was nodding and kissing his ankles." He then went on to comment about his ambivalent feelings toward addiction:

> That white powder, tragic magic. Ya know, it's like bein' on a chain, when he calls ya, ya come beggin'. It's like a woman so fine, when she calls ya, ya come. That's what we call "White Lady, I'm in love with her."

Torre, describing his sex life and marital fidelity, said:

> I don't mess around unless my name is on the gig.

Lucky, age 29, from New York said that because of heroin:

> instead of me standing up straight, sometimes I'm so far over I walk the walls.

Bosco, age 33, from New York commented on the basic resources available to heroin users:

> The ground they walk on is what they have to deal with every day.

Language and Manipulation: Signifyin', Mackin', and the White Man's English

Folb (1980) found that "fully one quarter of the vernacular expressions transcribed from conversations and interviews with young Blacks describe or characterize some form of manipulative or coercive activity." Similarly, Finestone (1957) emphasized the importance of quick thinking and smooth talking among his sample of young Black drug users. He noted that most of his sample favored persuasion, indirection, and manipulation. In this section, such manipulation is illustrated in the contexts of signifyin', mackin' (a special form of flirting), and the use of standard English, all modified by the heroin experience. Even the best interview format is ill-equipped to capture the language of such manipulation; the HLS data will have to serve as a sketch in lieu of a blueprint.

Signifyin'

Signifyin' has become a traditional part of the Afro-American subculture. This use of innuendo can be a manipulative tool very important in street life confrontation. Mitchell-Kernan (1972) defines signifyin' both as verbal dueling and as an encoding of messages for a variety of purposes in different contexts. Folb (1980) points out how signifyin' is used to deceive others in con games and verbal trickery.

Although covert aggression is often the key element, signifyin' may be used primarily to transmit information. "Dropping lugs" is a particular form of signifyin':

> Most dudes on heroin they drop lugs. They don't come out and force tell me somethin', you got to listen to what they sayin'. If you don't catch it, they

ain't gonna repeat it. Yeh, "Hey, I was your friend, and I did try to tell you, man." "I did try to hit with you that somebody's tryin' to take your old lady." You hear lugs. Some cat be sayin' somethin' smart out of the side of his mouth and chuckle, ya know. It's for you to find out what he really means. "Hey, man, hold it. What you mean?" (Dave, age 35, Philadelphia)

This form of signifyin' is informational, but also may include other elements of performance and manipulation. In the example above, it may be that to tell Dave directly about the competition for his old lady's affections would be unwise. Also, the person who doesn't need to know or shouldn't know about the situation may be excluded. Dave must have credentials on the corner to challenge the speaker to elaborate. Finally, the speaker may deny that the statement was a form of innuendo if the listener objects. (Such denials may or may not be accepted.)

Clyde explains how a non-drug-using friend expresses his concern about Clyde's usage:

He never relate to my drug problem, but he have dropped lug like "God damn, you had money yesterday, where the hell did all that money go?" So, he would drop those little lugs which indicates that he feels somethin' is happenin'.

Similarly, James said:

They just kinda indirectly drop lugs, "Well, I don't care what you do. You do what you want to do, but *I* think *you* should . . . and if I was you. . ."

Dropping lugs, like much of Black English, is well suited to heroin users' speech. Clearly, the indirect exchange of information may be advantageous for men whose drug habit must remain hidden from mainstream society.

Mackin'

The use of language as a manipulative tool was best illustrated in the HLS transcripts by direct references to heroin use and talking with women. Buck, age 29, from Washington gives an overview: "Niggers like to dress jam, chase women, get high and talk shit."

When chasing women and talking shit are combined, the manipulative form of speech which results is called mackin'. Mackin' is a flirtatious combination of different speech styles and idioms, a mix of different moods and moves utilizing situational cues. This term is not new, and the process has been described in detail by Folb (1980). She noted that mackin' is perfected as an end in itself, as well as for seduction. Torre, talking about mackin', said he asked women about their past sexual experiences:

If they say things, I figure they might do it right, so I try to figure out a way to try to get them to do me—I crack a little joke, and give them a couple of them little real foxy eyes.

Many of the heroin users interviewed mentioned that heroin facilitated mackin'. Buck said it helped him "talk a little slick shit in her ear." He goes on to explain: "You don't give a fuck and you say things that you might not be known to say or seem like you—just seems to come to you."

Karl, age 20, from New York noted:

The person using dope, he usually mouth more than a person that not using it. He could go to a dance and pull more girls or rap more people than a person that's not into heroin. A person that's not high, he just mouth closed. He ain't got too much to say.

This parallels the loss of inhibitions between people at a cocktail party. However, mackin' in Black street life is a far more stylized and intense activity than its White counterpart (Folb 1980). Not only did respondents mention that heroin facilitated their ability to talk persuasively to women, some even mentioned this perceived enhanced ability as encouraging them to continue using heroin. Thus, it appears that an existing process in Black street language is again well-suited to the heroin user, perhaps this time as a result of the actual effects of opiate drugs.

Standard English

Spoken standard English has two recognized dimensions. One is "broadcast English," the type of speech used by national media commentators on radio and TV. The other is the type of standard English accepted in a given area, such as the form of spoken English used by John F. Kennedy (perceived as standard only for the State of Massachusetts). Our discussion encompasses either definition.

Folb (1980) noted that most of her sample of Black Los Angeles teenagers had the ability to use varying forms of the standard English dialect. Standard English may be an asset (in hustling) or a liability in street life. The amount and form of standard English dialect varies according to the addict's social context, life experiences, and his degree of familiarity with his environment.

Roger, age 26, from New York said his schooling, emphasizing standard English, had made it hard for him to be accepted on the streets:

The school I went to, I was the only Black boy in my class. All the rest of them was White. I picked up they way of talk . . . [when I got to the city, Blacks] used to call me a little White Black boy. Street talkin'—I didn't know nothin' about that.

Ron used a common pattern, shifting from a more standard English dialect to Black vernacular:

> I went into several stores and obtained merchandise that I would later sell during the day for my habitual use.

Within a few moments, though, he said:

> I laid for a minute, I made a few dollars . . . copped again. I went back to the crib and got on.

Little D specifically noted that standard English was a useful asset in his hustling:

> They [other hustlers] think they need me 'cause I don't try to talk flip out my mouth—I just talk average.

Anton, age 20, from Washington, was able to talk his way into an exclusive party in the city's Georgetown section to pick pockets:

> I went up to Georgetown . . . it was getting to be about nine o'clock, and these Europeans was having like this outside cocktail, so I sat down and I ordered a glass of orange juice and talked a little.

Thus, it appears that the dichotomy in usage patterns between standard English and street vernacular noted by researchers among Blacks generally also occurs among the HLS men. While not surprising, this is a factor which helps shape their speech. Further, it serves to remind us that, to some extent, the language they use is voluntarily assumed. The next sections explore some of the factors which sustain this usage.

Language as Self-Identity and Labeling: Junkies and Dope Fiends—That's What Bonds Us Together

Language serves a variety of ingroup functions. This section shows how language aids in labeling shared experiences and outsiders, and in providing access to drugs and drug lifestyles.

Minority Status: Bein' Niggers Together

A common bond for the HLS men is minority group status in a society perceived by many to be racist. This ingroup experience of being Black and poor was reflected repeatedly in the HLS men's comments and is the basis for what Louis referred to as "bein' niggers together." Roscoe said: "I do just like the average nigger do ain't got no job–go look for a job, [then] get him a taste, [and] start talkin' with the fellows." Likewise, Lee, a 29-year-old from Philadelphia emphasized shared bonds in explaining what he did in his leisure hours at home. "I listen to records . . . things like that, watch T.V. I enjoy doing what anybody else would do. No different, I'm Black and I'm poor."

Other common themes besides race and poverty (most described themselves as "poor" or "very poor") involved dealings with Whites and police. Dap Daddy, age 32, from Chicago, commented on his initiation into heroin. Note the role of his identity as poor and Black ("street nigger") as a means of separating himself from Whites ("honkie") and police:

> I was a poor street nigger, and the brothers that I thought were my friends, my peers, were actually hypes. From jumpstreet, nothin' went right . . . even before he finished [injecting me with heroin], here come the honkie, here come the police. Like I had to run then, I'm still runnin', and I'm runnin' my life away.

Similarly, Karl said:

> [They] view us as monsters—a breed of monsters and they, like, trying to capture us. Trying to capture our souls.

The language of the heroin user is linked with other elements of Black culture. How does an addict verbalize the feeling of waking up addicted, with all of its attendant feelings? Sometimes it may be easier to adapt poetic imagery to convey feelings. Clyde, an older musician from Chicago, uses the lyricism of jazz:

> You feel like Billie Holliday say, "I thought you was gone, but here you are with the dawn," ya know? So, that's the way you feel, just like she say, "Good morning, heartache," and you don't want to face another day.

While the language quoted in this section does help define a minority status for the HLS men, it also contributes to a bonding effect which is discussed in the next section.

Junkies and Dope Fiends Together

Heroin users are always acknowledging commonalities among themselves. They use a variety of terms to describe themselves and other addicts: users, addicts, junkies, hypes, druggies, and dope fiends. These terms are often used without any implied stigma, as the term "nigger" may be used among friends.

"Thoroughbred dudes, real dudes that have really been there"—these are the preferred companions of the HLS men living the life. The shared reality of being heroin users together was mentioned by Boscoe:

> We have something in common. We're junkies and dope fiends and that's what bonds us all together.

This shared identity, one might conclude, could provide a basis for talking over things, to cope with mutual problems. Sometimes this appears to be the case, as Jimmy Jones, age 30, from Chicago says: "When you get high, you need somebody you want to talk to. You don't want to talk to [just] any motherfucker." Paradoxically, however, there is a lack of trust among users, an important distinction between associates and friends. While the picture is complex, it appears that one's identity as a user is not usually enough to provide continuous or intense ingroup support. As the hours without heroin mount up, the need for a fix, or at least a "gap" or something to get the edges off, becomes more important than anything else. Torre said:

> Ain't no dope fiends tight, man. They all got their main thing, that's their dope. And that's it—if they thought you had some dope on you, and they needed it bad enough, they cut your heart [out] to get that dope.

Likewise, as Roscoe (asked if he was in tight with any heroin users) said:

> Yeah, I'm mellow with all them mutha fuckahs, you know. I don't trust none of them.

Roscoe, when discussing coping, goes on to make a key distinction between identifying with others and trusting one another. Coping, he explained, tends to occur within the context of interacting with friends but a fellow addict is more likely to be viewed as an associate. Joe, a 29-year-old from Chicago, provides more insight about associates:

> Associates is people you don't really say is a friend, just guys that like to do the same things. You count your friends as friends.

Further, Icepick noted that:

> Associates . . . don't go to each other's houses . . . it's a street thing.

Buck said:

> I don't like to have close friends. I don't get to know people that good. Now, I've got some good associates . . .

The user discusses problems only with selected people in his social environment. Roscoe said:

> If you gotta mutherfuckah you in tighter with, if it's somethin' you want to talk about, you say, man, let's rap just for a minute, I got such and such thing on my mind, you know. Hey, long kick it, you know, nigger try to help you if he can.

However, not all the users felt that this was an option. Shorty, age 18, from New York said:

> Talkin' about your troubles, they don't want to hear it—they sayin' right away they got their own troubles, so that's out.

The HLS men did mention friends, some of whom weren't heroin users. Some users seemed uncomfortable with the concept of friendship, stating they weren't tight with anyone. Chico said: "I ain't got no close friends and I don't rap with the neighbors." The closest parallels with conventional friendship were the relationships HLS men said they maintained with regular crime partners, whom they referred to as "walkies" or "crimies." Solo said about his crime partner:

> Shit, that's my man . . . I'd live for him, and I'd die for him.

Torre expressed a similar reaction:

> When we go to get high, we go to the cooker together, we get high together, we cop together, we go get chicks together.

Bosco said:

> I got no close friends. [But] my crime partner and me are like brothers—like everything we do, we do together. We don't look at it as having affection.

Thus, while the HLS men do not trust other users and express varying degrees of discomfort with friendships, they appear to have very close "like brothers" relationships with their crime partners, although there is not necessarily affection in the relationships.

Identities as heroin users and crime partners are not the only devices that serve as important bonding mechanisms. The labeling and stigmatizing of outsiders is often vividly reflected in the HLS men's language. Straight people were described in New York as "wacky-tackies," and in Washington, D.C. as "L7's" (this expression when hand drawn forms a square). More traditional terms such as "squares," "lames," and "suckers" were also used frequently by men in all four cities. These tend to set heroin users off from the larger straight society.

A simple and expressive term illustrative of the whole genre discussed here turned up informally in conversation with a New York addict. He was asked, "Do you have any special nicknames for people who are being treated in methadone clinics?" He immediately replied: "we call them Methadonians." This is an excellent example of ingroup labeling among addicts. Short and precise, it clearly labels the methadone clients and highlights street language's fondness for word play. The HLS users viewed methadone users as being radically different in their lifestyles, and "Methadonians" conveys the impression that they (methadone users) have (through the use of methadone and other lifestyle changes) become aliens in their environment. Other terms heroin users used to describe methadone clients included "zombies," "blimps," "meth-heads," and "murdocks." One New York user called methadone clinics "death banks."

There are also regional variations in heroin users' language which tend to contribute to ingroup cohesion and identity by city. The police serve as an example. Terms to describe law enforcement agents varied from neutral to highly negative in all four cities, from simply "the police," and traditional terms, such as "rollers," "pigs," and "fuzz," to "the honkie," and "them dog muthafuckahs." Police were also called "5–0" and "10–4" and "the Romans" in New York.

Other such differences include the following. In New York, Philadelphia, and Washington, D.C., "oil" was defined as shooting narcotics; in Chicago, the expression retains an older meaning as a synonym for alcohol. New York users called junkies "stuffers"; in other cities, the term wasn't used (although "stuff" is a universal term for heroin).

The purest examples of regional variation in the addict's idiom may be the wide variety of brand names used by dealers to mark their products. Such names in Detroit in the fall of 1982 included: Motown, the Bomb, KO, Firecracker, Oh Baby, Bag of Fire, Young Boys, Inc., and Huggie Bear. Names used to mark heroin in New York in the fall of 1982 included: Omen II, Quicksilver, COD, Black Magic, Mad Dog, Crazy Eddie, Freedom, Death Boy, Silent Partner, and Mexicana.

Scoring: Going to See the Cop Man

One of the tenets of the user's world is that one heroin user can recognize another, through an unspecified process. The shared aspects of the heroin lifestyle which form the basis for these beliefs can be found in the experiences of obtaining and using heroin. The manner in which these experiences are shared and compared among heroin users will often involve colorful and sometimes original language.

Copping is an area where the language of the user is of particular importance. Although one can hustle alone and shoot up alone, copping heroin involves a verbal interaction with other heroin users. Money or goods, "tracks" (scars from intravenous use), or shared experiences: some or all of these may be necessary for obtaining heroin. However, language is an essential tool used by the addict to purchase heroin from strangers, re-establish such rights with current associates, and negotiate the price, quantity, and perhaps the quality of the heroin.

In contrast to the conventional business world, appearances aren't important. Solo said:

> You don't care how you look. The cop man ain't gonna give you an extra
> bag if you look clean or if you come with this fuckin' suit on.

However, the cop man is concerned that the buyer, especially if not a regular customer, be conversant or fluent in the language of the subculture. Users will be expected to know the system of distribution in the region appropriate to the money they have to spend. Bags, bundles, spoons, sixpacks —the list of terms is confusing to the outsider but second nature to the user. Many types of weights and measures appear to be stable over time although the quality of heroin varies. Terms tend to reflect prices ("a dime"), and certain premeasured amounts ("bags" or "teaspoons"), or quantities of premeasured amounts ("bundles" or "sixpacks"). Except for those addicts involved with dealers that use scales (and consequently transact business by weight), both price and quantity are somewhat arbitrary.

Copping also involves the risk of being cheated by being sold adulterated or poor quality drugs. Terms for these types of drugs include "garbage dope," "blanks," "bunk," and "flour dope."

Names used for heroin itself are relatively unchanging—heroin, sometimes sarcastically pronounced "her-o-wine," or, more commonly, "hair-on," smack, shit, skag, stuff, doo-gie, junk, scoobie-do—are colorful but not new labels. Ironically, Solo actually didn't realize that "smack" was heroin the first time he used it. He said: "I wasn't hip to the terminology—I didn't know what it was—it made me feel good, and I thought it *was* smack, it wasn't no heroin to me."

Injecting heroin was termed "shooting up," "oiling up," "getting off," "taking off," "getting high," "getting down," "getting on," "geezing," "firing," "fixing," and "pokin' the stuff." Terms used by the HLS men to describe the injection apparatus were "works," "outfit," "tools," "joints," and "gimmicks"; injections were made with syringes, needles, or pins ("spikes").

Paraphernalia in which to heat the liquid was "the cooker," "the pot," or "the pan." The apparatus in which the heroin is heated has special significance to the user, as it closely precedes the injection process. James said: "Dope fiends

without money, they be floppin' around, waitin' for you to go to the cooker."
Users on the East coast use the expression "going to the pan" (in which the
heroin is heated) as a term for the ritual of getting high. A lucid description of
this ritual is provided by Solo:

> This is my ritual. I set up everything, get the quarter [teaspoon], the joints [in-
> jection apparatus]—I always clean them out—music, got to have music—when
> you get high, you start dancin'.
>
> I make sure nobody's near me [while heating the liquid], too many
> hands in the brew will spoil the pot, the cooker will be fallin' on the floor.
> Happened to me too many times. So—I'm the chef. I hook it up, I measure it,
> and I'm the medicator—"let's go folks." Automatically, I got one [shot], my
> set of joints—"all right fellows, chow." And we just get high, that's the
> ritual.

Language, then, plays an important role for the user in obtaining and injecting heroin and is one of the keys to his lifestyle. The terminology, which
has been relatively stable over time, also provides an additional potential
bonding mechanism between users, and therefore contributes to their social
supports and self-identity. In evaluating the terminology described in this section, it should be remembered that terms and usage patterns which depend
primarily on situationally specific cues, and on associative, ingroup knowledge, are similar to mainstream social interactions.

To the extent the user's language is considered exotic or bizarre, outsiders close themselves off from insight into a very human process. The user's
role in our society and the drug subculture are, at least initially, voluntarily
assumed in a manner similar to other societal activities. There are rewards for
all of us in the mastery of specific terminology in any field; this applies to the
HLS men too.

Some similarities and some differences between users' speech and society's
are discussed in the next section.

Some Closing Thoughts

> The heroin addict's language and his communication patterns generally ap-
> pear to have for him a magical potency. . . . The language of the addict is a
> complex one, depending on the addict and tends to bridge several strata of
> society . . . (Fiddle 1967)

The influence of Black street culture on the user's communication patterns has been noted. Accordingly, it may be seen that substituting "Black
inner-city resident" for "heroin user" would not change the validity of the
above quote. Although the quote's thrust is correct, it is the heroin *lifestyle*

(and the lack of meaningful alternatives, such as jobs) rather than the drug itself which endows the user's language with any "magical potency."

Language is important in forming, initiating, and perpetuating a Black heroin user's lifestyle. It reinforces shared experiences as they are conceptualized through language; it provides information and status; and it promotes a sense of membership in the community.

In attempting to understand the user's subculture, we must now turn from analyzing the functions of his language to a broader analysis. What do the differences and similarities between addicts' speech and contemporary standard speech tell us about the relationship of the heroin subculture to mainstream society?

Researchers have noted the enduring nature of Black street vernacular (Folb 1980, Abrahams 1976). Slang, particularly terms describing process in this vernacular, come and go, often in cyclical patterns; older terms, however, usually retain at least some validity. Examples of enduring process terms in the streets would include "runnin' it down," "signifyin'," and "talkin' shit," all well known for decades.

The HLS data suggest that the same phenomenon occurs within the heroin subculture. Numerous terms for drug use and drug users documented by Major in 1970 were found in the HLS data. Many of these terms originated over fifty years ago, and their original meanings are unchanged. The continuity of some of the heroin user's vernacular over time is important in understanding a fundamental point: social factors which have molded and spurred the use of argot have worked in combination with existing Black cultural traits to promote a unique argot for the Black user through rather traditional processes. Heroin's role in this process appears subordinate to almost every other factor.

Heroin Users' Language as a Bonding and Protective Mechanism

One of society's myths is that the unique aspects of the heroin user's speech are designed solely to confuse police or nonusers. Clearly, this is at best an ancillary function of the vernacular.

Ambiguity in the language of the streets is common, both intentionally (to exclude outsiders) and unintentionally (non sequiturs, and so on). Further, in Black English, numerous factors work towards creating and maintaining this ambiguity. For example, the use of metaphor has been demonstrated by Holt (1975) to be an integral part of Black speech, demanding the close attention of the listener who wishes to understand it. Blacks' extra emphasis on performance in speaking and in public play (Abrahams 1976) are also factors contributing to the ambiguity found in some Black English and in Black neighborhood rap sessions. In part, this is for stylistic purposes, and in part, it ties in with the shared experiences and ingroup nature of Black street life.

The defensive quality of Black English and Black slang, as documented by Major (1970) and Mezzerow (1972), is important in understanding the language of the Black user. Originating with slavery, and nurtured by white racism, it is heightened by emphasis on imagery demanding participatory involvement by the listener for comprehension. Mezzerow (1972) comments:

> Guys talk that way when they don't want to be spied on, resent eavesdroppers, when they're jealously guarding their private lives, which are lived under great pressure, and don't want the details known to outsiders—detectives, square ofay [White] musicians, informers.

The ultimate defense language would be a type of English dialect, incomprehensible to the uninitiated. A stigmatized criminal subculture would seem a perfect candidate for the development of such a language, and the concept of a heroin subculture, with its own unique language, has been popular in the literature. Agar (1973) has commented on "straights" unable to understand the conversation of "junkies." Burroughs (1977) wrote that: "A [final] glossary . . . cannot be made of words whose intentions are fugitive."

The pressures of stigmatization and the ongoing pressures of law enforcement impel users to create and use specialized slang. In the author's opinion, however, their language has little or nothing to do with deceiving straights.

Distinctive traits in the heroin user's language originate and remain in use primarily to bond the group together, express shared concepts, and to protect its members. To be overheard using any form of criminal jargon by the uninitiated may carry stigma and risk to the speaker (Futrell and Wordell 1981). This is obviously different from Black English. Blacks may flaunt differences with standard English in front of standard English speakers they don't know, or "style out" among other Blacks they have never previously met. The heroin user seeks to *conceal* such differences in interactions with all outsiders, while freely using specialized jargon among peers. Therefore, the jargon will be of little use in deceiving straights.

The following examples of this type of jargon, submitted by one of the HLS interviewers in New York, reflect the heroin user subculture's speech among its members. These are examples of speech that hardcore committed heroin users thought straights would not understand:

> Let's hit midtown and sting, then we'll cool out with some boy, girl, and freaks.

> Translation:

> Let's go into the central part of the city to steal or hustle from someone, then we'll buy and use some heroin and cocaine, and find a couple of girls that really like all kinds of sex.

Hey Fred, you got any bank, I know where some death product is.

Translation:

Hey, Fred, do you have any money, I know where some quality heroin is.

Nate, we'll hit 16th street, take care of our business, then brick it.

Translation:

Nate, we'll stop on 16th street, purchase and use some heroin, and then go raise some money illegally.

Again, much of the user's speech, even when an attempt is made to provide examples that straights would not understand, is drawn from Black English. Further, the terms specific to drug use seem to be primarily traditional terms.

Through language and the way it is spoken, a speaker ascribes status to himself. Sometimes such ascribed status may deliberately be of a lower-class nature (Abrahams 1976). Language for regular heroin users not only governs interactions with others in the heroin subculture, but represents a conscious assertion of one lifestyle and rejection of another. Although these men aspire to the American dream, they described themselves as poor to very poor, and as being thought ill of by general society. The reality of their position in society, as well as their drug use, affects their speech. They have little incentive to use standard English.

Becoming a heroin user, and gaining some facility with the language, may not be particularly difficult. Burroughs, Jr. (1984) comments on the manner in which the lifestyle is assumed by an initiate. In the street vernacular, he notes:

[The addict lifestyle is] the fastest learned occupation in the world. . . . You can take the dumbest son of a bitch you can find long as he can count past a hundred and walk and talk.

Since the creation of the criminal addict in the United States, society has generally been aware that users have developed specialized jargon to function in their subculture. Typically, criminal jargon quickly evokes hostility as the dominant culture becomes aware of its existence (Futrell and Wordell 1981). Perversely, however, the slang of minority groups may have an impact disproportionate to their relative numbers upon the majority of society (Major 1970). It is possible that the terminology of illicit heroin use has had and is having such impact. Knowledge of heroin street terminology may precede availability of the drug, and be key in initiating use. If this is true, the study of a population's knowledge of drug terminology and ingroup slang may help predict future trends in drug-usage patterns.

The thrust of this chapter has been to shed light on how language functions in the heroin lifestyle. It is also hoped that the reader will have gained an appreciation for the stressful social sources of the user's creation and use of language, thus viewing it less as a means of deceiving and showing hostility toward straight society, than as a bonding, self-defensive and protective device. This view could contribute to breaking down existing social, moral, and psychological barriers to attainment of a deeper and more accurate understanding of contemporary heroin users and permit straights to begin to have a more humanistic understanding of heroin users.

Notes

1. In order to identify prominent patterns of linguistic functions, all 124 interview transcripts from the HLS men were studied. This analysis resulted in two types of findings. First was a simple inventory of the topics the HLS men said they most commonly discussed with other heroin users (reported later in the chapter). Second was a listing of nine categories which defined and demonstrated the manner in which language functions within the social worlds of the HLS men. After further content analysis, the nine categories were reduced to the three most prominent functions, derived from the frequency with which they appeared in the men's conversations about their activities: information exchange, manipulation, and self-identity. Thus, this chapter is not an analysis of all language-use patterns revealed in the data, but only of those appearing most frequently, and those judged to be most important in revealing how Black inner-city heroin users communicate with each other and how this communication helps develop, frame, and perpetuate the heroin lifestyle. As part of the analysis the author asked a number of current Black heroin users in both New York and Detroit to verify his own interpretation of meaning of words and phrases which appear in this chapter. In addition, a draft of this entire chapter was reviewed by former heroin addicts and by experts on Black English (including John Baugh, Ph.D., Department of Sociolinguistics, University of Texas at Austin).

2. Information on this question was obtained from only those men who said they were "in tight" with someone (N = 93). Of that figure, 46 are from Chicago, representing a response rate of 88 percent. In New York, 23 of 29 interviews were usable, a rate of 79 percent. However, response rates from Philadelphia and Washington, D.C. were lower; 15 out of 23 in Washington, D.C. (65 percent), and 9 of 22 in Philadelphia (41 percent).

References

Abrahams, Roger D. 1976. *Talking Black*. Rowley, Massachusetts: Newbury House Publishers.

Abrahams, Roger D., and Gay, Geneva. 1975. Talking black in the classroom. In *Black American English*. New York: Dell Publishing.

Agar, Michael H. 1973. *Ripping and Running: A Formal Ethnography of Urban Heroin Addicts*. New York: Seminar Press.

Banks, Carl Jr. 1975. *Dictionary of Black Ghetto Language.* Los Angeles: Saidi Publications.

Burroughs, William S. 1977. *Junky.* New York: Penguin Books.

Burroughs, William Jr. 1984. *Kentucky Ham.* Woodstock, New York: Overlook Press.

Dillard, J.L. 1975. *Lexicon of Black English.* New York: The Seabury Press.

Fiddle, Seymour. 1967. *Portraits from a Shooting Gallery.* New York: Harper and Row.

Finestone, Harold, 1957. Cats, kicks, and color. *Social Problems* 5:3–13.

Folb, Edith A. 1980. *Runnin' Down Some Lines.* Cambridge, Massachusetts: Harvard University Press.

Futrell, A.W., and Wordell, C.B. 1981. Language of the Underworld. Lexington, KY: University Press of Kentucky.

Holt, Grace. 1975. Metaphor, black discourse style, and cultural reality. In *Ebonics: The True Language of Black Folks,* ed. R. Williams. St. Louis, Mo.: Institute of Black Studies.

Kochman, Thomas. 1972. The kinetic element in black idiom. In *Rappin' and Stylin' Out,* ed. Thomas Kochman. Urbana: University of Illinois Press.

Major, Clarence. 1970. *Dictionary of Afro-American Slang.* New York: International Publishers.

Mezzerow, M., and Wolfe, B. 1972. *Really the Blues.* Garden City, New York: Doubleday.

Mitchell-Kernan, Claudia. 1972. Signifying and marking: Two Afro-American speech acts. In *Directions in Socio Linguistics: The Ethnography of Communication,* ed. John Gumperz and Dell Hymes, 161–179. New York: Holt, Rhinehart and Winston.

Sutter, Alan G. 1966. The world of the righteous dopefiend. In *Issues in Criminology* 2(2):177–222.

Williams, Robert L., and Brantley, Mary. 1975. Disentangling the confusion surrounding slang, nonstandard English, Black English, and ebonics. In *Ebonics, The True Language of Black Folks,* ed. Robert L. Williams. St. Louis, Mo.: Institute of Black Studies.

7

Not the Cause, Nor the Cure: Self-Image and Control Among Inner-City Black Male Heroin Users

Richard W. Morris

> When I wake up in the morning, I just enjoy being with the whole of my family. You know, they fix me breakfast, lunch and dinner. They take care of me. If like I don't have no money, they give me the things I want. If one day I gotta come out on the street, that's when things gonna change. That's when I get into other things. Like I can stay in the house for weeks without getting high, then I hit the streets and I get like crazy. Everybody is saying "hey, hey, hey, hey" because they know I know how to make money. So they be forcing it on me and like its hard to turn down. (Michael, age 28, Washington, D.C.)

S tatements like this are often used to promote an image of the heroin addict as weak-willed and helpless against the forces of a destructive environment (Chein 1966; Stephens and McBride 1976). In this case, the man appears to lose control and start using heroin when he is confronted with peer pressure. Most of the HLS men spoke of moments when they were unable to resist the temptation to use heroin. For them, heroin offers many desirable effects: a sense of well-being, a return to feeling normal, a rush of strength and power.

However, the HLS interviews suggest it would be misleading to assume that these men have relinquished control of their lives to heroin. It would be equally wrong to assume, as others have (Glover 1956), that they are filled with self-hatred because they use heroin. The fact is that while many of the HLS men have regrets about their dependency, and most admit a desire to stop or curtail their heroin use, they also maintain a sense of self-respect. Many have great expectations for themselves. Although they feel frustrated at their lack of success in meeting these expectations, they still feel they have control over their lives. Some achieve a sense of mastery over their lives, as expressed by Tap, 27, from Philadelphia:

> I have more drive now than I used to have [before I used heroin], because I didn't have to hustle. Now, I have to. Now I do realize one thing: anybody can make any amount of money they want to. All they gotta do is want to.

This chapter describes how these men, who hustle for and use heroin regularly and who interact daily with other heroin users and nonusers as well, maintain a sense of self-respect and control over their lives. After a brief discussion of questions used in this analysis, the chapter introduces the concept that the HLS men constantly struggle to live a narrow path between the street and the straight worlds. The contradictions which emerge out of this marginal life-style as evidenced in the men's comments about themselves are identified and discussed. The analysis is continued in the next section which examines the issue of "marginal status," and the ways in which the HLS men relate to both the street and the straight worlds. The chapter ends with comments on the type of heroin user studied and possible implications for the treatment of this type of user.

Self-image and control are qualitative phenomena and difficult to measure. Most people, whether heroin users or nonusers, are unlikely to respond with elaborate detail when asked how they feel about themselves and their lives. Therefore the HLS interview schedule contained a number of open-ended questions designed to elicit how the HLS men felt about themselves, their lives, and the straight world around them. For example, HLS interviewees were asked such questions as: "What degree of control do you think you have over the events in your life?" "What changes, if any, in your feelings about yourself have occurred since you began using heroin?" "How would you say straight society in general views heroin addicts?" "Think about straight people you actually know—even your own family. How do they regard you and your use of heroin?"

The answers to these and other questions were used in combination with the overall content of each interview to provide insight into the way the HLS men feel about themselves and their lives.[1]

The Street and Straight Worlds: Contradictions and Self-Image

> I get tripped up between love and dislike [for myself]. That really gets tripped up. I'm not doing this to kill myself. I'm doing this to hide from things that's hurting me. I'm not on no death trip. (John, 28, Washington, D.C.)

Issues of self-image and personal control among Black male heroin users raise a number of contradictions. These men profess a sense of power over their lives, yet they also confess a sincere confusion about how or when to exerise that power. Most of them refuse to blame society for their dependency, but readily describe the extraordinarily difficult circumstances of their lives. As a result, many claim to rely on heroin as a means of relaxing or seeking refuge from a hostile world. Many seem to have developed particular methods to avoid becoming what they view as crazed dope fiends. The HLS men generally acknowledge the concern and support of loved ones, yet they carry a burden of guilt for having exploited those who have been closest and most generous to them. These men speak about their suffering and hardship, but in their reasoning, it seems that no single person, event, or agent is the sole cause of their suffering.

Icepick, 35, from Washington, D.C., sums it up:

I have 100 percent control [over my life], if I want to use it.

Given the public image of heroin use it may appear a contradiction that these men see themselves as struggling for self-improvement while at the same time continuing to use heroin. On the surface, it is a contradiction that they see themselves as victims of social injustices, and also as perpetrators of crimes against others. It is perhaps also confusing to the outsider viewing the heroin lifestyle that users may regard themselves as heroin addicts but refuse to label themselves as "junkies" or as "dope fiends."

To understand the contradictions in these men's lives, it is necessary to examine the meanings HLS men attach to events in their everyday lives. This reveals an overriding commonality in HLS comments: that these men are moving within and between two worlds, the street world, and straight society. Both worlds provide them with social models, values and perceptions which determine their behavior, and standards by which they judge themselves and others. Both worlds provide them with stresses and threats, but also with challenges and unique sets of skills with which to meet those challenges.

The contradictory nature of their perceptions is more evident in the context of self-image as the product of a person's adaptation to the environment. Heroin is readily available in the neighborhoods where these men live. In these poor urban spaces, social supports exist for heroin's initial and continued use (Feldman 1968). Heroin use is equated with economic survival in their minds and is viewed as giving them "more drive" in accomplishing the chores of daily living, those chores which are essential to maintaining a satisfactory self-image. In their social networks with other users, opportunities exist for intimacy and adventure, and for acquiring a sense of competence and self-confidence. Even among nonusers in these neighborhoods, there appears to be a tolerance for heroin use.

But tolerance of heroin by nonusers is not perceived by users as complete social acceptance, and being a user is not the only game in town. At least as strong as the values which support a heroin lifestyle are other values which support achievement, familial life, ambition, and determination. Supporting and amplifying these themes are the constant media advertisements which convince listeners that a middle-class lifestyle, with its focus on material wealth, is attainable by all who strive for it. Therefore, the social context within which the heroin lifestyle is played out is characterized by two social models which foster distinct but somewhat overlapping sets of values, expectations, and behaviors: those of the street and those of the straight world.

The street world is composed of neighborhood friends, running and using buddies, and other associates who can be seen regularly hanging out in popular gathering places. The straight world is recognized by users as people who do not use drugs and who do not hang around on the street, including family members. Also, straights are looked at as people who do not understand heroin use and who hold only disdain and/or pity for heroin users. All heroin users have some contact with the straight world, even if only for instrumental purposes, such as to buy groceries or resolve legal issues. They generally have some degree of social affiliation with straight people, relying on them for emotional or financial support. How HLS men negotiate their interaction with the straight world will influence their patterns of heroin use. More importantly, however, the nature of this interaction and the HLS men's perception of society is the key to how they feel about themselves and how they control their lives.

Living between the street and straight world leads to apparent contradictions in their statements about themselves. Their comments can be summarized as follows:

> the claim of aversion for drugs and the lifestyle of the street which is counterbalanced by the thrill of being on the street where one is drawn into a group of peers and valued simply for participating in the activities of the group (most importantly, drug use).

> the sense of being trapped in a predicament and wanting to permanently abandon the situation, but knowing that, in the group of fellow users, one can demonstrate particular skills which win approval and function effectively—even if illicitly—to accomplish certain goals (for example, hustling money).

> a personal feeling of weakness and doubt that one has the necessary fortitude to avoid drug use, which is challenged by the empowering effects of heroin intoxication and of regularly being accepted by a social group.

These simultaneous, contradictory feelings of *aversion* and *attraction* for heroin, of *enslavement* and *mastery* over the street life, and of *weakness* and *power* which accompany heroin use make sense only if we look at the everyday experiences of HLS men. We must look at their lifestyle from their perspective and compare the rewards for using heroin with the rewards for being straight.

Getting High, Getting Normal, and Getting Free: Gratification from Heroin

The statements of HLS men demonstrate that they seek something more than intoxication when they take heroin. George, a 23-year-old, from Washington, D.C. claims to take heroin because it makes him feel as if he is "communicating better with people." Ace, age 34, in Philadelphia, takes heroin because "it is the norm for me. I don't get drunk. I don't get ossified. I just get normal." Gut, 18, from Chicago, says he takes heroin to feel secure: "You don't feel like nobody is messin' with ya." For others, like Larry, age 32, from Washington, D.C., heroin is a medicine: "Like some people would take aspirin for a headache," he says, "I take heroin when I feel bugged." These statements suggest HLS men take heroin for reasons similar to those for drinking alcohol—to keep functioning, to continue participating in their everyday routines. In that sense they would say they take heroin for constructive or normative reasons.

Regular heroin users have rarely been depicted as reflecting on their situation and, after weighing alternatives, *choosing to use* heroin (research by Agar 1973, and Sackman 1976 being important exceptions). It is easy to oversimplify the experiences of heroin users and to assume that their patterns of drug use originate in and are sustained by a sense of helplessness fostered by deprivation in a poor urban development (Merton 1957; Hughes 1971). Heroin users have been portrayed as being easily influenced, as submitting readily to peer pressure, and as inevitably opting for that behavior which provides them with a sense of group membership (Paschke 1970). They are furthermore assumed to be driven to heroin use by the need to escape the pain and alienation of repeated family crises (Stanton 1977), of lost jobs, and of mental or physical illness. In this respect, the image of heroin addicts commonly presented in the media (Mills 1965; Coombs 1974; Morgan 1980) and, even in some scholarly journals, depicts them as helpless individuals who are not totally capable of controlling their lives. While this perspective is sometimes more implicit than explicit, it is stated most boldly by Pittel (1971):

> Drug dependence is most likely to occur among individuals who lack the psychological resources needed to deal adequately with inner conflicts and/or environmental frustrations.

Such a view does not accurately describe the HLS men as they presented themselves in the interviews. Most of these men speak of having a significant degree of control over their lives. Whether describing their first heroin experience or explaining their continued use, HLS men seem to be saying that their use of heroin is a matter of choice. For instance, Irv, age 26, from Philadelphia said:

I asked for some [the first time I used heroin]. It wasn't any peer pressure to use heroin.

Another user, Dave, 35, from Philadelphia, said:

Well, when we first started, believe it or not, all of us tried it. We all tried it for long periods. People who didn't want to be a part of that lifestyle started drifting away from it. People who wanted to, stayed right with it.

Many share the belief that is expressed by Guy, a 30-year-old from Philadelphia:

The stuff is so bad out here now you know that you don't hardly worry about it any more. You either do it when you feel like it or you don't.

Few HLS men said that the proddings of friends, family members, or helping professionals would have any impact on their decisions to use or abstain from heroin in the future. Curiosity seems to have been the strongest factor in directing these men towards their first experimentation with heroin. As Paul, age 21, from Washington, D.C., said:

I was very tempted to try [heroin], you know for the experience . . . just this [one] time.

Curiosity, combined with the conviction that heroin use is not powerfully addicting in quite the way it is popularly portrayed to be, that is, that the user will not be violently transformed into a crazed dope fiend, allows these individuals to continue using heroin while maintaining a sense of control over their lives. Umber, age 26, from Philadelphia also stressed the curiosity aspect:

So curiosity . . . we wanted to know what kind of feeling it was, when we watch them high. And they looked like they felt so good.

Accordingly, curiosity and the desirable or relieving effects of heroin, not peer pressure by itself, draws these men to repeated use. Whether or not this is true, it means that in their own eyes they have some control over their heroin use. It is an oversimplification, therefore, to assume that the continued use of heroin is only a symptom of helplessness and dependency.

Whether they attain a powerful rush or simply relax, many of these men attain real gratification from heroin. At times, this gratification is a total escape from a world that these men view as hostile and unpredictable. It is an attempt to cope with trauma:

'Cause I still have some feelings that I had when I was twelve years old [the time when I first tried heroin]. I remember the first time I used drugs, and like I said, I did it on my own, my mother had called me an ungrateful . . . an ungrateful son of a bitch, that's the first time I snorted, too, cause I had that feeling that that's how she felt about me and I went in my pocket and I used it. (Red, 36, New York City)

A recurrent and convincing theme that accompanies the claim that heroin is used as a means of escape revolves around the many problems that these men face in their daily lives, as portrayed in the following interview.

Interviewer: Did I ask you what type of work you did before you got involved?

Respondent: No. I was assistant to the chef. Assistant chef.

I: Oh, you were cooking. Where?

R: United States House of Representatives.

I: Where?

R: United States Capitol, House of Representatives.

I: Holy smokes, and you blew it?

R: No. I didn't blow it, when Reagan came in he blew it. That's when my problem started with my life. Cutbacks.

I: Oh, so cutbacks got you riffed?

R: Yeah. Even with the drugs . . . because when I was working I wasn't using heroin that much, see what I'm saying? And I guess that's why my wife was putting up with [me] better. And when I lost my job, that's when things began to fall apart. (Icepick)

Heroin, as it was experienced by these men, is more than an escape from disappointment and crisis. It is depicted just as accurately as a journey into intimacy with other people. The HLS men regularly commented on the supportiveness and gentleness with which their peers treated them while getting high together, particularly the first time they used:

[The first time I used heroin] my body got real warm, a hot flash, but I wasn't afraid of it. It wasn't no fear because I knew the people I was around with were ready to do anything and I felt I had enough confidence. I felt as though they wouldn't let anything happen to me. So that's why I didn't have no fear of doing it. (Bull, 27, Chicago)

In addition, heroin use for many of the HLS men occurs in a social or party atmosphere where the drug serves to intensify the social experience, allowing users to interact more freely. For instance, many anecdotes offered by HLS men stress how heroin use is tied with romantic intimacy. Over 26 percent said that their best experience with heroin occurred when they were with a woman. Heroin is regarded as a source of the confidence and eloquence necessary to win a woman's affections:

> I got high one day and I pulled a fox, I pulled a lady, because I know if I was other than myself, I wouldn't have been able to pull her. And I was clean and I was high and I said some words to her that I know I wouldn't [have] said to her if I was sober. And like, I pulled her and it made me nuts, ya know what I mean? That was the best experience of my life. See, getting high is like saying, when I get high I can pull more girls than when I'm sober. (Tap)

In summary, heroin is often attributed to a heroin user's ability to have certain experiences which might be considered very basic to self-esteem, such as companionship, self-strength, and relief from personal distress. As long as they feel that their attainment of these experiences is contingent on heroin, they will be supported in its use. From heroin use they gain certain rewards: (1) the thrill of being in the street where, by pursuing heroin, they also chase adventure and excitement; (2) a sense of approval from their peers and, if their hustling is successful, a feeling of mastery over particular skills; and (3) a feeling of relief, escape, or empowerment which accompanies the effects of heroin, while simultaneously experiencing the distress and complications of heroin use.

The Prick of the Needle: Distress and Complications

The picture of contradictions becomes clear as the HLS men describe heroin as introducing distress and complications into their lives:

> . . . Oh, man, but I don't know how I went on to ever use any more drugs after that; I was so sick that night. (Joe from Chicago, 33, with a 19 year history of heroin use.)

Concerns about health, personal relations, arrest and incarceration, and monetary matters are typical in the lives of these men:

> Respondent: . . . I worry about infection, but I just try to keep things clean as possible. That's all. Try not to use a needle but once.
>
> Interviewer: Do you talk about things you would like to do, such as . . . ?
>
> R: Yeah. Such as, you know maybe owning something, you know. Trying to get your life in order where you can own something and not have to work so hard all your life.

I: What about hooking up, planning and rehearsing some crimes?

R: No, I'm not off on no crimes.

I: What about the police?

R: You gotta watch for them because you be dirty all the time. Got tracks on your arms.

I: What are the circumstances that make you concerned about overdosing?

R: Well, I got a family, man, and I don't want to die and leave them with no father, nobody to take care of them. I try to think about my family. If it happens, you know . . . (Umber)

The many complications which occur in the life of heroin users foster a need for regular interaction with others. These complications are both practical and personal. The heroin user must cope with the practical aspects of supplying himself with heroin: copping, hustling, selling, and maintaining or searching for a job. Those individuals who support their heroin use through illicit means must also learn to avoid arrest. On the surface it may seem that the only health concerns unique to heroin users are those of overdosing and getting an infection. While central in the minds of regular users, there are other health-related concerns which originate in the heroin users' lifestyle, many centering around nutrition. Heroin users would not be able to manage the many complications which their habits impose without support and information from other users. Only users have certain information about obtaining heroin, avoiding arrest, and coping with familial or health problems. This means heroin is also a social activity—successful heroin use depends on social contacts and social networks. Heroin users come together to acquire the social contacts and information which will allow them to manage their use, as well as their lives, most effectively. In order to use heroin and survive they must maintain some involvement with the street social network.

Affiliation with a network of committed users directs heroin users towards certain contacts with straight society, while routing them away from others. There is a tendency among HLS men, for example, to rely on noninstitutional sources of medical information obtained through trusted contacts. The following typical comments come from one HLS respondent when he was asked what he does when he feels ill:

Respondent: I usually . . . my woman is into medicine. I usually lay down and ask her. Before I suffered with aspirins and used street doctors.

Interviewer: What's street doctors?

R: People that use drugs. Like they know everything. Somebody in the place, especially if you go to a shooting gallery, everybody is a doctor, lawyer, or indian chief. (James, 19, Chicago)

Like many social networks, the street network is rich with information about how to manage health problems. Much of this information focuses on drug use. Some of the prescriptions are rather involved; one example is a concoction of vinegar and spinach greens combined with baking soda which is reputed to ward off the symptoms of withdrawal.

Even though they may have some contact with straight friends or family to acquire much of the care they need, the HLS men are still marginal to major institutional segments of straight society. They make every attempt to avoid sources of medical treatment and information where those who provide such aid will try to change their pattern of drug use.

Consequently, the lore of the street encourages them to postpone contact with institutions whenever possible. Contact with doctors is believed by some to entail a risk of having one's involvement with heroin detected, perhaps leading to arrest. However, this fear is not as pervasive as an apparently greater threat, the possibility of mistreatment at public hospitals. Many believe that if they are recognized as heroin users at these facilities, they will not receive proper treatment.

> One day I took my friend to a hospital and we couldn't get nobody to him. We had to take him to a doctor and just because he was a drug addict they sat him down in the corner and he died. I'm serious. They didn't care enough to bring him out, and he died, and the man who was in the corner he died. Squashed me, and it hurt me to my heart. I didn't like the guy, hardly knew him, but he died. His death made me love him. (Jake, 29, Philadelphia)

The HLS men generally describe themselves as being in good physical health. However, the danger of mistreatment at public hospitals causes heroin users to avoid contact with hospitals except when emergencies demand it, and rely on relatives, friends, and home remedies, or on trusted private physicians when they do not get successful results from self-treatment.

Heroin use is actually a form of self-medication for some of these men. For others, to manage one's health meant simply to control the symptoms of withdrawal from heroin:

> I don't have symptoms [of withdrawal] no more because I control it now. Like I said, I don't mess around. When I might mess around two days in the week, and the rest of the week I might just drink, you know, smoke a little joint right there. You know, it all depends, you know, like sometimes, if my money's funny and lot of times, even now, I have a strong control that if I have money I don't spend it on heroin just because I have it. I might just drink all that day. Or drink some wine or liquor or beer, you know. I do all these things. (Kyle, 30, Philadelphia)

Still, these men are not without minor health problems. Most frequently, they reported weight loss since they began using heroin. They also fairly consistently reported having bowel problems and a low sex drive. It was not un-common for them to say that their complexion had darkened or that they had lost a few teeth since their initiation to heroin use. Others experienced fatigue and limited endurance, which they often referred to as laziness. Their posture had changed to slouching in some cases and most men experienced occasional, but manageable, irritability. Also, consistent throughout the interviews is a reluctance by HLS men to attribute their symptoms solely to heroin use.

Balancing the thrill and empowerment that accompany heroin use and involvement in street life are many aversions and complications. These go well beyond the health problems discussed. The thrill of heroin is countered by fear, nausea, danger of overdose, pain of imminent withdrawal symtoms, and the constant hassle of having to worry about and plan for obtaining money and heroin for the next shot. And buried in these complications, at least occasionally, are feelings of being trapped in the heroin lifestyle and a sense of personal weakness.

The Relationship of the HLS Men to Straight Society

The Black male heroin user has been depicted by straights as a desperate loner (Snyder 1970). Rejected by his family and friends, he is alleged to associate exclusively with other addicts. However, as we have seen throughout this book, the HLS men present a different image. For instance, in terms of family and friends, the HLS men appear to have established relationships which potentially can provide them emotional support and advice. In fact, intimacy and a feeling of connectedness with other men and women is a guiding force in their lives. Dave willingly discussed his strong feelings and need for others:

> Well, most of the time it's this older dude [that I talk with]. He was a drug addict too. My old lady, I talk to her. I tell her all that stuff. We sit around and figure things out now, when before it was this old cat. We used to sit around and rap. He'd make me feel better about myself.

And Joe, age 24, from Washington, D.C., says that he has "a lot of friends" and that he sincerely believes his wife "is concerned" about him:

> Okay, I had a lot of friends that I was talking to where I could have said a lot of anger and animosity towards my wife, you know, 'cause like we didn't stay together. But truly down deep inside me I believe my wife is concerned about me, and that she did what she did because she did not want to see I believe what she says, she did not want to see me going the way I was going. She would rather not be there to see.

Many HLS men had considerable contact with nonusers of heroin. Further, the HLS men regularly talk about themselves in relation to straight society. Their comments comparing themselves to straights demonstrate some degree of ambivalence. Some describe the life of straights in an idealized fashion, as if the life of straights were secure and virtuous. Others claim that straights fail to involve themselves in the visceral and pleasurable aspects of life, that their life is unidimensional and somewhat empty:

> The major difference [between heroin users and nonusers] is that they are straight. They're not as happy as you know somebody—there's something missing. They feel more better about blocking out things that they don't have and may never get . . . When things start to fall apart for them, then they need to [but don't] fall back on the drugs. (Jake)

Most HLS men have precise ideas as to how straight society views heroin addicts and they struggle to make a distinction between themselves and "heroin abusers." The following is typical:

Interviewer: How would you say straight society in general views heroin addiction?

Respondent: Something low, dirty. Evil dog. Something to be watched. Scum of the earth.

I: How do you feel about those views?

R: I think they lie. Because, see, all heroin addicts are not heroin abusers, okay? And you get the abuser, he's a dog, right? He's the one who sits in the drug house and shoots all day long. That's an abuser. I'm a visitor, you never catch me in the drug house. Not me, no. (Slim, age 38, New York City)

HLS men seek to become "visitors" in social networks of other users, to establish a degree of contact and membership while remaining somewhat detached from that network. Their attempts to remain partially marginal to both street and straight society are a central part of their strategies for controlling their use and their own lives.

According to the belief system of HLS men, there exists a wide gray area between addiction and total abstinence. They may flirt with the thrill of heroin and engage in the adventure of street life, while maintaining the option to depart from this lifestyle when they choose. Even those who use large doses of heroin for an extended period of time think they can do so without ruining their lives as long as they do not adopt the behavior of the drug-crazed dope fiend. As long as they refuse to see themselves as lowly addicts and maintain a respectable posture in relation to straight society, they are keeping their lives under control.

For these men, controlling their lives is synonymous with regulating their use of heroin. They have a large repertoire of strategies for wielding control over their use which they employ with varying degrees of success. They regularly try to discipline themselves, setting goals and rewarding themselves with heroin when the chosen goals are accomplished. Many of these men will postpone the use of heroin, even if it is readily available, until they have earned the money to pay for it. Some heroin users depend on others to help them limit their use. The peer groups of these men commonly include a nonuser who takes responsibility for holding the dope until the group agrees to use it. Many of these users also subject themselves to periodic episodes of abstinence. Some have the ability to simply avoid drug use altogether for extended periods. Others seem to value periods when abstinence is necessitated by external circumstances. For example, when traveling to an unfamiliar city or even when incarcerated.

In addition to individual strategies for controlling their use, these men have many resources within the street culture to stave off the symptoms of withdrawal. Some of them are regularly drawn towards using low quality heroin which postpones withdrawal, is relatively inexpensive, and does not detract from accomplishing daily tasks. Most of them practice polydrug use as a way to avoid withdrawal. Through combinations of methadone, methamphetamine, barbiturates, and valium, even those with a pattern of substantial daily use appear to be able to endure periods when dope or the money to buy it is scarce. These strategies represent only a few of those which are provided to users through their contacts in the street. If not actually serving to prevent addiction, these strategies serve to raise the level of functioning of the men and allow them to control much of their lives and avoid seeing themselves as "abusers," but rather as disciplined "visitors" to the heroin lifestyle.

Implicit in many of the statements is the belief that an ideal pattern of heroin use means using the drug and successfully supporting a habit, without sacrificing personal relationships or self-advancement through education or employment. In fact, most of the users have experienced at least brief periods of security and productivity in their lives at work and home. It is this ideal pattern of use that HLS men seek to establish for themselves. To control their lives, these users must be aware of the many complications that heroin imposes on their daily existence. Controlling their lives means that they must develop strategies for managing these complications. Heroin use is regarded as an intense experience which, as noted earlier, is just as likely to be self-empowering as self-defeating. From this perspective, heroin users are able to inject heroin regularly, while maintaining the ability to make important choices in their lives. They perceive themselves as weighing the decision to use heroin against several alternatives. They see themselves as taking responsibility for their actions, believing that if they consistently control their use and lifestyle, they will not suffer the destructive consequences of addiction.

Despite his deep involvement with heroin, Michael typifies this view:

I feel positive about the future. I just feel I'm caught up in something of my own making. And it's up to me to get out of it. And I feel as though I can.

Umber has a similar view. When asked if his self-confidence and self-esteem and his "feelings about himself" had changed since he began using heroin, he replied that ". . . nothing had changed." Further, when he was asked if, as a heroin user, he thought of himself as "being sick" he said, "No, because I control it. It doesn't control me."

These efforts to control one's use of heroin are always engaged in with the larger society's values and expectations in mind. Some HLS men appear to measure the proper use of heroin by mainstream expectations such as attending school and being married:

Because the moment I started using heroin . . . If I had used it positively, you know, I would have more things. If I had continued school. I'm quite sure, you know, that my wife wouldn't have left me. I'd be getting a lot of chances. In other words, I've allowed heroin to ruin me. (Icepick)

There is evidence that, for the HLS men, controlling their lives is intricately involved with their hopes for the future. Their expectations for the future involve modest achievements and possessions, with their most recurrent wish being to have security and freedom from a sense of threat:

. . . I'm talking about I'm trying to get out there and get something for me. Like a nice little piece of property where I could have me a nice little home that I could come to, you understand? My lady here and a couple of kids. I don't have to have a brand new car, you understand . . . I don't want a whole lot, I just want . . . something, you know . . . But to put your hand on the door of your house and come in and there's nobody living here but you and your family; and you open the door and know this is yours, it's a hell of a feeling. You don't get a chance to get that, man. So, you get disgusted and discouraged and it's like there's nowhere to turn . . . I'm not talking about drug programs, I'm talking about CETA programs where you can try to get out there and get yourself something the legal way. You start messing around and get out there and getting it the illegal way. Why? For the simple reason that the money they give you can't support what you're trying to get. For myself, I don't want to be as rich as a hawk. Let me live the middle way . . . I can meet that bill and still have food for my woman and kids to eat and sleep. (Dave)

The majority of responses to our questions about hopes for the future expressed goals and desires similar to Dave's and generally acceptable to straight society. Kevin, 20, from New York, was not unusual with his comment;

"Yeah, I'd like to be employed and married and not messing with heroin."
Later in the interview he expressed, as did many others, a deep desire to have
children. Those who had children or expressed a desire to become parents
demonstrated a deep concern for their welfare. When asked about the future,
many of these heroin users stated that they would discourage their children
from using heroin. Zulu, 33, from Chicago, said he would handle heroin
with his children like this:

> I would tell them from my own experience. I would show them the tracks on
> my arm. I would try to show them, not only tell them, but I would take them
> around certain people that maybe at one time was on the top of their game
> and say "Look at them now." I would take them around to areas of the city
> and show them this is what it will lead to if you let it get out of hand. This is
> what you want? Hey, it's not worth it.

Thus, the HLS men appear to have a simultaneous longing for and aversion to the life of straight society. Involving themselves more deeply in street
society and heroin use holds advantages as well as disadvantages. The same is
true for total abstinence from heroin and the pursuit of a straight life. Hence,
from their point of view, it is best to stay in between, not seeing themselves as
depraved addicts or as straights.

However, the HLS men have various and important behavioral, as well
as ideological, contacts with straight society. In this sense, most can be described as marginal not only to straight society, but also to the heroin lifestyle
itself. They describe themselves as being in control of their use. They "keep
clean," dressing neatly whenever possible and hoping to present themselves as
different from the down-and-out dope fiends on the street and to avoid the
suspicions of local police. By more objective standards, these men do not fit
the stereotype of a dedicated hardcore dope addict, one whose entire life
centers around the acquisition and administration of heroin. These men do
not always pride themselves on their illegitimate hustles, and the majority do
not rely exclusively on illicit activities to supply themselves with heroin.
While many do hustle, many also have a legitimate source of income which is
essential to their continued use of heroin. While not without cravings for
heroin, most of these men do not appear to be inescapably trapped in the cycle of frenzied drug seeking, as other heroin users have been described. Perhaps these men are distinguishable from the universe of all heroin addicts by
their insistence (not necessarily reflected in their behavior) on doing something with their lives to maintain control. Ironically, they share an image of
the heroin addict with members of straight society, and they strive not to become like those individuals who were described by one heroin user as:

> . . . downright nasty people. Most of them are [that way] because of the way
> they look and their appearance and their hygiene and, you know. And you
> know, it's really disgusting . . . (Zulu)

In summary, the HLS men's involvement with heroin is not a simple choice of whether or not to use a drug. It is a choice between lifestyles, that of the street or that of the straight world. Both worlds seem to offer attractive rewards, as well as threats and complications. The statements of the HLS men indicate that the rewards and complications are about equal in both worlds. Hence, these men seem partially committed to and partially repelled by their involvement in each of the two worlds. They have developed a set of beliefs among themselves which say that, if they carefully control their use, their daily habits and their involvement with people in the street, they can walk a narrow line between the two worlds, enjoying some of the best of both.

These men provide each other with the ideas about the meaning of controlling one's life. These ideas invariably involve two goals:

> being able to flirt with the dangers and experience the thrill and adventure of heroin use and/or life in the street;

> being able to keep things tight and manageable, so that one has a sense of progress towards normative goals, such as home, family, education, and employment.

Heroin users struggle constantly (to varying degrees) to achieve these two goals. The interviews suggest that, at least for brief yet discernible periods in their lives, these men have been able to achieve both goals. However, they are aware that heroin use makes the struggle to hold one's life together difficult and that not all users will win that struggle. Heroin is also seen as a means of enjoying onself. "If one can hold his life together," they might say, "he has earned a little pleasure." As a result, these men seek a social position which is marginal to the lifestyle of the righteous dope fiend or the down-and-out abuser, as well as to the nonuser straight world. This means they cannot lose control of their use. They would say to members of straight society that as long as they do not behave like the lowly dope fiend, heroin is neither the cause nor the cure of their suffering.

Implications for Treatment

This qualitative analysis of a sample of untreated Black inner city heroin users raises important questions about the prevalence of the types of heroin users the HLS men typify and about how users might best be treated or helped in avoiding the destructive effects of heroin. As they portray themselves, they are able to take control of their lives to the extent that they do not fall helplessly into an endless cycle of getting high and doing nothing but satisfying their drug cravings. These are the hazards which are said to accompany the careers of many heroin users. The HLS men are keeping clean, holding their worlds together. Perhaps they are able to do so because of the social position they have created for themselves at the margins of the street and the straight world.

To the extent that these men do keep their lives under control and avoid treatment, their characters and/or environments may differ from those of other inner-city Black male heroin users. They may simply have more acquired skills in resisting abuse of heroin and in regulating its use. A significant number have social involvements outside the network of street heroin addicts. A majority have some form of social contact among straights, whether it be a family member, a close friend, or the acquaintances and drug-free activities at their jobs. The heroin on the street is regularly diluted, so that daily needs must be kept within modest limits. Other drugs are available which help to stave off withdrawal. Street doctors and the lore of the street provide advice to the user so that he may avoid such hazards as overdose and malnutrition. Perhaps this research project has uncovered a subset of Black heroin users who, with their discipline and strong self-image, their balance of attitudinal involvement and social support from both the straight and the street worlds, and with the array and quality of drugs available, are able to keep their use under control and avoid treatment.

Whatever the case, it is clear that most HLS men possess the belief that they can indulge in heroin use without losing control over their lives. This belief has important implications for treatment of such men, the vast majority of whom chose to avoid institutional treatment. They, and perhaps a great many others like them, feel strongly that they can function well in straight society and are only frustrated that they do not have the opportunity to prove themselves in conventional jobs with opportunities for self-advancement. Heroin is a reward for achievement to many of these men, whether those accomplishments are realized in the street or in the straight world.

Hence, any approach at treating these men must be based on a recognition of the pride they hold in themselves and their real, albeit inconsistent and unconventional, ability to take control of their lives. If the goal of treatment is to get the user off heroin and out of the street altogether, this treatment strategy must include ways of transferring that sense of control from the street and the heroin lifestyle to the straight world by providing realistic and legitimate incentives for achievement and greater opportunities for social support outside of the heroin lifestyle.

Any policy, research, or treatment concerning the type of Black male heroin users identified in this study, then, must recognize the full range of incentives for participation in the heroin lifestyle. It offers more than drug intoxication. It also offers the thrill of street life and a real, if inconsistent, sense of self control. Participation in the heroin lifestyle does not necessarily mean dropping out of the straight world for a life of frenzied drug seeking on the street. According to the testimonies of HLS men, they can "use and then cruise."

If they are disciplined and intelligent, they can enter the heroin lifestyle to enjoy themselves and then depart to take care of the equally important business of dealing with family and/or employment problems, or as Zulu put it, "pursuing the American Dream."

The HLS men tell us however, that not all are successful at walking the line between the street and straight worlds. Yet, it is the fact that they try to walk this line that is significant. They, like those who study them, aspire to a better life. They, like those who treat them, are diligent in their effort to avoid self-destruction. They, like those who design policy which affects them, are seeking to survive and achieve in an environment of drastically inadequate resources. So these Black male heroin users, as do straights, seek control, like Michael from Washington, D.C., who said:

> When I lose control, my little world is gone, you know what I mean? So I'm gonna keep it tight on this end.

Note

1. Initially, all 124 interviews were read and briefly summarized. Forty of these interviews were then selected for analysis. This group represented the diversity of the HLS sample in age, geographical location, history and frequency of heroin use, and degree of contact with other heroin users. Content anlaysis of this group permitted identification of common themes and patterns which emerged from the views expressed by different types of Black heroin users.

References

Agar, Michael. 1973. *Ripping and Running: A Formal Ethnography of Urban Heroin Addicts*. New York: Seminar Press.

Chein, I. 1966. Psychological, social, and epidemiological factors in drug addiction. In *Rehabilitating the Narcotic Addict*, 53–72. Fort Worth: Institute on New Developments in the Rehabilitation of the Narcotic Addict.

Coombs, Orcle. 1974. Fear and trembling in black streets, *New York Times Magazine*, March 20.

Feldman, H. 1968. Ideological supports to becoming and remaining a heroin addict. *Journal of Health and Social Behavior* 9(2):131–139.

Glover, E. 1956. *On the Early Development of Mind: Selected Papers on Psychoanalysis, Vol. I*, 130–160. New York: International Universities Press.

Hughes, Patrick, and Jaffe, J. 1971. The heroin copping area. *Archives of General Psychiatry* 24:394–400.

Merton, R.K. *Social Theory and Social Structure*. New York: The Free Press, 1957.

Mills, J. 1965. Drug addiction. *Life*. February 26, 66–92.

Morgan, Thomas. 1980. Struggling to quit heroin. *Washington Post*. February 27.

Paschke, W.R. 1970. The addiction cycle: A learning theory—peer group model, *Corrective Psychiatry and Journal of Social Therapy* 16:74–81.

Pittel, Stephen M. 1971. Psychological aspects of heroin and other drug dependence. *Journal of Psychedelic Drugs* 4:40–45.

Sackman, Bertram S. 1976. Angela's band: An ethnography of disciplined heroin users. Unpublished manuscript.

Snyder, A.J. 1970. Junkie personality. *Science Digest* 68:62.

Stanton, Duncan. 1977. The addict as savior: Heroin, death, and the family. *Family Process* 16:191–197.

Stephens, Richard L., and McBride, Duane L. 1976. Becoming a street addict. *Human Organization* 35(1):85–93.

8
Just Another Habit? The Heroin Users' Perspective on Treatment

George M. Beschner
James M. Walters

Butch woke up at seven-thirty and lay in bed smoking a joint. He got dressed, fried two eggs, and headed out on his daily neighborhood stroll to find out the day's happenings.

At ten o'clock Butch hooked up with Lucky, his walking partner, and they took the bus to the business district. There they looked for a store where they were not known so they could run their game called "tail chopping." They chose a men's clothing outlet with two salesmen, one busily serving a customer, and began their carefully rehearsed routine.

Lucky occupied the second salesman while Butch walked casually to the front of the store and began looking through items on the rack. Butch carefully folded two leather jackets over his arm, while Lucky convinced the salesman that he was about to purchase an expensive sport coat.

While the salesman's attention was focused on Lucky, Butch moved slowly toward the door, slipping out when no one was looking. Lucky then decided he didn't want the jacket and made his exit, rejoining Butch further down the street.

The stolen coats retailed for sixty-five dollars each; Butch and Lucky had little trouble selling them for thirty dollars apiece, less than they wanted but enough for their daily score.

Back uptown by two thirty, they copped a half a quarter for forty dollars from Blackie, whose stuff was rumored to be better than anything else on the street. They made it to Lucky's crib by three and set about the serious business of getting high. Injecting the needle into the back of his leg, Butch watched for blood flowing into the syringe. The rush came quickly, lasting for several minutes; soon he began feeling mellow. For the next hour Butch and Lucky relaxed and enjoyed the disassociated oblivion of their high—"like not having a care in the world," as Butch described it. They talked about the past and how easy it was to hustle in days gone by.

At six o'clock, Lucky put some lunch meat in a frying pan and made a couple of sandwiches. After the high wore off somewhat, they went outside, bought a bottle of wine and killed some time. Butch got back to his place at ten, turned on the TV, smoked a joint and fell asleep watching an old movie.

Butch's daily routine is typical of thousands of inner-city users committed to the heroin lifestyle. There is now, however, an alternative lifestyle that can be achieved by entering drug-abuse treatment. Through treatment, heroin users and former users can obtain synthetic opiates and free themselves from the daily pressures of hustling to maintain their habits.

Frenchie (who was not one of the HLS subjects) gave up his career as a heroin user, opting for methadone treatment and a lifestyle in sharp contrast to the one Butch lives:

It was early morning in central Harlem when the ice truck dropped Frenchie at the corner of 145th Street and Eighth Avenue. Thirty-six years old, clad in dirty sneakers and a well-worn army fatigue jacket, Frenchie looked tired from a night of delivering ice. Standing on the corner sipping from a pint of Night Train, he anxiously awaited his woman, Sally, who sold goods at the fruit stand nearby and routinely drove him to the clinic. Frenchie was beginning to feel apprehensive. His forehead was wet with perspiration and his hand shook as he lifted the bottle of wine to his mouth. Finally a black '66 Impala pulled up to the corner and Frenchie jumped in.

"Where you been, momma? I've got to get to my program and pick up my thing." At the hospital Frenchie quickly took the elevator to the eighth floor, where it opened on a large waiting room. Frenchie hurried past rows of metal chairs to the reception desk where, without a word, he signed in and went to join his fellow "methadonians."

"What's the waiting time?", he asked anxiously, a common thread in the methadonian's small talk. Luckily the wait was short today and within a few minutes Frenchie walked down the hall to see Bob Taylor for his required Friday counseling session.

Taylor, an ex-addict, looked up as Frenchie entered the room and asked "How you doing, man?"

"I'm holding all right, but things could be better." Taylor looked at Frenchie with some concern and raised his voice. "What are you trying to do to me, man? You sending Night Train at me. How many pints you have today? You know what it calls for, man. I've got to make you understand."

"Man, I just needed something to get me going. I've been working all night, you know. Give me a break."

"You better get yourself together, man, or I'll see that you get a decrease [in dosage]," states Taylor as he hands Frenchie a small glass jar. "You due to drop some urine."

While bringing his urine to the nurses station, Frenchie hears his name called. He walks back toward the waiting room and stops in front of a window marked Medication, which shields a nurse. The nurse checks his cards and shows him an orange diskette. He nods and she breaks the diskette in half, stirring it in a cup of Tang. She pushes the plastic cup containing Frenchie's daily 20 mg. dose of methadone through a small opening in the window.

Frenchie leans back and gulps down his medication. His shoulders sag and he sighs with relief, knowing that the methadone will hold off the sickness for another day. He tosses the empty cup into a nearby container and walks toward the elevator.

This has been Frenchie's daily routine for two years. He is one of more than 75,000 methadone clients in the United States who need a daily dose of the synthetic drug to get through the day (Food and Drug Administration 1983).

This chapter describes how HLS men, most of whom have never been in treatment, view the drug treatment system, what drug treatment means to them, and what inducements would be needed for them to enter and stay in treatment. It concludes with questions about current treatment practices and suggests factors that should be considered in planning treatment strategies in the future.[1]

Although methadone is not the only treatment modality, it is the focus of this discussion because it is the predominant modality in the urban areas where HLS men live. In answering the question, "What do you think about the current treatment programs for heroin addicts?" most HLS men (72 percent) referred specifically to methadone maintenance. Indeed, a majority (68 percent) of the Black clients in federally supported treatment received methadone detoxification or maintenance, compared to only 20 percent who received outpatient drug-free services and 12 percent who received residential care (NIDA 1981a).

A brief history of methadone maintenance in the United States is presented as a backdrop against which comments by the HLS men can be understood.

A Brief History of Methadone Maintenance

Since the early 1900s, controversy about the treatment of heroin addiction has centered around three issues:

1. Whether to treat addiction as a disease or a crime.
2. Whether to provide heroin maintenance.
3. Whether to use other pharmacological agents (for example, methadone, opiate antagonists, antidepressants) or only drug-free treatment protocols.

More recently, a fourth issue has arisen:

4. Whether methadone clients should be detoxified from methadone after a limited period of maintenance or to be allowed to remain on the drug indefinitely.

Despite the early controversy, large-scale methadone maintenance programs were initiated in the late 1960s on the basis of research conducted by Vincent Dole and Marie Nyswander. They believed that addicts suffered from a metabolic imbalance as a result of repeated opiate use, and therefore required ongoing medical care and treatment with an oral dose of an opiate-like drug in a controlled outpatient clinic setting. It was concluded that a stabilized dose of methadone would satisfy and thus abolish the addict's craving for heroin-induced euphoria (Dole and Nyswander 1967).

Although many methadone-maintenance staff and patients did not accept Dole's metabolic alteration theory (Glasscote et al. 1972), support for maintenance treatment grew rapidly in the late 1960s and early 1970s, as community leaders and politicians sought cost-effective methods of treating addicts and combating drug-related street crime. In 1970, relying on advice from physicians, legal experts, and social scientists, the Nixon Administration emphasized methadone maintenance, calling it "the most efficacious treatment weapon against heroin and street crime," and created a vast federal treatment network as part of its strategy to reduce street crime (DeLong 1972).

As a result, the number of individuals treated with methadone increased dramatically. A handful in 1965 grew to approximately 85,000 in 1973. This rapid expansion was impressive considering that little reliable and unequivocal data were available about the effectiveness of methadone treatment (Wilmarth and Goldstein 1974).

However controversial, methadone maintenance soon became an accepted treatment approach. Many clinicians, even some skeptics, viewed methadone as a means of getting addicts into a controlled treatment environment, blocking their craving for heroin, and, over time, rehabilitating them. Furthermore, methadone maintenance was rather attractive to many heroin addicts, because it provided an easily available opiate drug and sometimes served as an alternative to prison.[2]

The numerous follow-up studies conducted since 1974 indicate that methadone treatment can produce significant benefits.[3] One of the most compelling arguments for methadone maintenance is its effect in reducing drug-related street crime.[4] Ball and his colleagues (1982) reported that most heroin addicts are deeply enmeshed in a criminal lifestyle and the cost to society of an addict not in treatment is much higher than the cost to society of treating an addict. They estimated that the average addict commits over 178 criminal offenses each year.

If real property is fenced at one-third its value as has been estimated (Holahan (1972), an addict must steal property worth $60, on the average, to obtain $20 with which to finance his daily habit. Based on these figures, an addict with a $20 habit would have to steal $21,900 a year to pay for his habit.

The annual direct cost of maintaining a client on methadone is approximately $1,500 to $2,500 (NIDA 1981b). If what is said above is correct, based on economic considerations alone, methadone treatment results in considerable savings to society. In addition, studies have shown that methadone maintenance helps reduce illicit drug use (Maddux et al. 1972; Dole and Herman 1977; Tims 1981) and improve employment status (Gearing et al. 1975; Simpson 1980; Tims 1982).

Yet the controversy rages on. Some critics voice concern that the government sanctions and supports a treatment system that perpetuates addiction (Nelkin 1973); others note the disproportionate number of Black and Hispanic methadone maintenance clients (Heyman 1972; Chappel 1974; Bellis 1975; and Epstein 1974) and express concern that methadone is used primarily to control unemployed, disadvantaged, ethnic minority people (Nelkin 1973; Epstein 1974; Dumont 1974).

More recently, serious questions have been raised about the practices of methadone treatment programs in attracting new clients. Ausubel (1982) suggests that, because of carelessness or overzealousness, the addictive status of many applicants is not adequately established. As a result, many nonaddicts are enrolled and are subsequently addicted.

So much for the experts and the critics. Let us see what the HLS men themselves believe.

How HLS Men Perceive Drug-Treatment Programs

Methadone maintenance has not been fully accepted as a long-term treatment alternative by clients in methadone treatment or by methadone program staff (Brown et al. 1972). During the formative years of methadone maintenance, the word "crutch" was commonly used to describe the modality, because it offered little more than the temporary support of the drug. Programs dispensed drugs but few if any medical or psychological services (Siegler and Osmond 1974).

In an extensive study of methadone clients in three states (Hunt et al. 1982), 62 percent had given serious consideration to leaving treatment because they wanted to be drug free, feared long-term side effects, and disliked program rules. There were also some strong inducements to stay in treatment: methadone reduced their craving for heroin, prevented withdrawal sickness, and, for some, provided an alternative high. Further, dropping out involved the danger of losing eligibility for food stamps, and other social services.

Not surprisingly then, HLS respondents sometimes express ambivalence about treatment:

> What I see scares me, man, because the only drug treatment I understand is methadone maintenance, and from what I see of that, I would rather shoot heroin. I have seen a lot of them using it [methadone] and many of them seem to be successful. They come off, man, and they always manage to keep some money in their pocket. They can buy a beer, some wine, and essentials that I can't afford. They can do the little extra stuff right around me that I can't do. I got to be hustling all the time and what I get goes for heroin. But the way they be looking, it scares me to death, man. If I decide to change my lifestyle, I go cold turkey. (Sugar Bee, age 19, Chicago)

As Sugar Bee sees it, methadone maintenance is a mixed blessing, offering a heroin-like drug, reducing the hassle of the hustle, easing the pain of withdrawal, and making it easier for those who want to give up their habits. On balance, though, he rejects it for himself, fearing "the way they [methadone clients] be looking."

Indeed, 80 percent of the HLS men held treatment in disrepute and, of these, 75 percent expressed particular concerns about methadone maintenance.[5] Some HLS men spoke about treatment in a more general way. Although methadone maintenance was not mentioned, it was likely to be the modality to which they were referring. HLS men voiced four principal objections to methadone maintenance:

1. Methadone maintenance is just another drug habit, perhaps even more addicting than heroin.
2. Methadone has serious physiological side effects.
3. Methadone programs are ineffective; clients continue to use drugs, including heroin.
4. Methadone maintenance programs are inadequate in meeting the real needs of people.

Let's listen closely to their criticisms and examine them against the research findings.

The Perception: Methadone is Just Another Habit

About two-thirds of the HLS men (64 percent) who held methadone treatment in disrepute shared the view that methadone maintenance simply shifted a heroin user's dependency from one drug to another:

> Everybody I know who has been on the methadone program have worst habits now, than when they was on heroin. It's because methadone really messes them up and it takes its toll. You put a man on methadone and he be addicted to that. (Leroy, age 32, Washington, D.C.)

Others believe that methadone is at least as strong as heroin, and even harder to kick:

> Well, it's not helping them because of the meth they give them is just like heroin. They even give an overdose of meth—know what I mean. You still drowsy, high, and unaware of things, not knowing what's going on around you. And they don't really care about you, they just want to get you out of the way. They give you meth and that's about it. (James, age 49, Chicago)

> Trying to get off heroin is bad enough. I don't want to get hooked and get me a methadone habit that's even harder to kick. (Michael, age 28, Washington, D.C.)

The Research: Methadone is a Powerful Addictive Drug

In sufficient doses, methadone is a powerful narcotic with effects qualitatively and quantitatively like those of morphine and heroin. Clinic-supplied methadone is generally more potent than street heroin, which is likely to be highly adulterated, although oral administration delays the onset of effects (Bellis 1975). The result is that many methadone clients become more physically addicted to methadone than is the typical street heroin user to heroin, and their withdrawal symptoms are more severe.

Injected, 20 mg. or more of methadone produces euphoria slower in onset but longer in duration than that of heroin (Isbell and Vogel 1948); administered orally, methadone produces similar effects, even further delayed. Clearly, methadone clients experience a wide range of side effects from the drug.

The Perception: Methadone is Unhealthy

Beyond fears of addiction and difficult withdrawal, almost half of the HLS men (48 percent) who expressed concern about methadone maintenance feared methadone's harmful side effects:

> Everybody knows that methadone messes with your bones It take the calcium from you bones. I don't want none of that stuff man. That would be another hassle to contend with. You go from one hassle to another hassle. (Milt, age 20, New York)

> Methadone is just as bad as heroin. I feel that people are just addicted to something else that's even worse. Methadone gets in your bones. I know a lot of people who have died from it. The drug itself is still experimental. They don't know how it's goin' to affect a person who uses it for a long time. (Jimmy, age 30, Chicago)

Findings from an earlier study reveal that methadone clients in treatment have similar concerns about the drug. One third of methadone clients interviewed in a District of Columbia methadone clinic believed that methadone rots bones, and another third were not sure but were suspicious about the drug's effects (Brown et al. 1975).

The Research: Pain Associated with Rapid Detoxification

In the late 1960s and early 1970s, methadone detoxification was more common than methadone maintenance. One study of the health status of methadone clients found a connection between methadone detoxification and pains in the bones and concluded that too-rapid methadone detoxification does result in severe pains in the bones (Kreek 1978). Further, it was noted that clients who experienced these pains feared that methadone was dissolving their bones.

The Perception: Methadone Clients Still Use Heroin

Twenty percent of the HLS men who voiced concern about methadone maintenance believed that it does not preclude the use of other drugs. Some even feel that methadone is inconsequential:

> I don't like methadone programs cause I don't feel they're doin nothin' for nobody. You still using drugs. Those methadone dudes still be using coke, wine, reefer, and whatever else they can get their hands on. They say it supposed to stop you, you understand, but it doesn't. A lot of people who can make no money to buy heroin, get on those drug programs to get more drugs, free—that's all it is. (Chuck, age 20, Chicago)

Others feel that methadone helps users through tough times:

> They ain't even trying to kick, they just usin' it as another means of not getting sick when they don't have no dope. They use it as a substitute. That's the truth—it's a known fact. (Hollywood, age 27, Chicago)

or that it is a handy supplement:

> Most of them cats that's in methadone will still be usin' other drugs. You know, they be usin' anything they can get. They come back out in the streets and they think they foolin' the counselors, but they not foolin' anyone by comin' out and sneakin', gettin' high, they only foolin' themselves. (Shorty, age 18, New York)

*The Research: Methadone as a Supplemental
Drug of Abuse*

Again research confirms the HLS men's perceptions. Hunt and her colleagues (1982) found that many methadone clients use the drug as another euphoriant ("a cheap way to get high") and as a medication, simply adding it to the illicit drugs used prior to and during treatment. A further finding was that some street addicts prefer the euphoric effects they get from methadone to the effects they get from street heroin.

Kaul and Davidow (1981) report extensive polydrug use among methadone clients, particularly abuse of tricyclic antidepressants (for example, Elavil), benzodiazepenes (for example, Valium) and phencyclidine (PCP).

Ausubel (1982) concludes that an overwhelming majority of methadone-maintenance clients regularly and frequently attempt to re-experience the "florid" type of heroin-induced euphoria, by abusing not only heroin and other drugs but also methadone. Not only does methadone guarantee relief from discomforts of living, but it also furnishes the means for obtaining the "more positive hedonistic aspects of drug euphoria."

Methadone clients are also at high risk for alcoholism, with studies reporting that up to half of surveyed patients are moderate to heavy drinkers (NIDA 1981b; Cohen et al. 1977); that alcohol is a major drug of abuse among methadone patients (Bihari 1974); and that 46 percent of studied methadone clients scored in the alcoholism range on the Michigan Alcoholism Screen Test (Siassi and Alston 1976).

Not surprisingly, the methadone-alcohol user has been compared to the Bowery alcoholic who "survives on welfare and panhandling and leads a stuporous life in hallways and on stoops" (Preble and Miller 1977).

The Perception: Methadone Maintenance Does Not Meet Clients' Needs

Most of the HLS men claim to already have their habits under control; 73 percent limit themselves to one shot of heroin per day. They reject the "dope fiend" stereotype in which the habit is ever escalating and the junkie shoots up repeatedly each day. Consequently, the prospect of having to use another opiate, also on a daily basis, is not appealing.

Second, the HLS men perceive treatment programs as being too bureaucratic and not giving enough time to the heroin users' real problems. When this concern is coupled with the fact that 20.6 percent of Black and other male minorities in central cities are unemployed (Bureau of Labor Statistics 1983), it is easy to see why a treatment program's promises of increased employment fall on incredulous ears. Following are comments from HLS men on why treatment is not for them:

> Those methadone programs depend on bureaucracy rather than treatment and people wind up not bein' treated. They're just bein' dispensed medication to maintain them. I don't see how you're dealing with the addict's real problems when you're not dealing with his addiction and what caused the addiction. They treat you like a little, nasty dope fiend. (Tap, age 27, Philadelphia)

> I don't see much in methadone programs they got going. For the most part I think they sorta shooting past it. First of all, you got to go in there wanting to get some help. You got a lot of people around you that messin' around drinkin' meth, but they don't want no help to abstain from drugs. They puts you in a bad environment already. For the most part, I don't think they goin' down, cause drinkin' meth and goin' to the clinic, it takes you through some changes. Them boys that's been wrecked with the stuff have bad attitudes. They gonna make you wait two or three hours on your medication—it's a harassment thing. I can't be goin' for no meth on a daily basis. It would tie me up. I have to go out and get me some money and stuff to survive. I can't be hooked up in no clinic all day. (Chico, age 34, Chicago)

Finally, HLS men gain a sense of self by participating in the heroin life-style, and enjoy a certain kind of respect in the ghetto community; they lose this when they abandon heroin for the treatment setting:

> Man, I've got my hustling to do. By me havin' a habit, I've got to take care of that, you know. Them alcoholics and meth clients have nothin' to do with their time. They have nothin' to do, more or less. That's the difference be-tween me an' them. I always got somethin' to do. (Ronald, age 31, Chicago)

> I'd love to be a functional part of the community and all that other bullshit, but I also have an obligation to myself. At the present time I'm obligated to gettin' high, and that's what I think would be my choice—that I could con-tinue to do this. The only thing that has any connotations that are bad about it for me, is that people would say something about it. If you find a man on narcotics and heroin gives him the kind of confidence and stuff to function in his society, how can you tell him not to use it, if that's the only way that he is able to be a functional part of the community. Stop downgradin' it. Each in-dividual has a choice of what he is gonna do and what he ain't gonna do, but when you're involved and that's all that's in your environment, the chances are that you might tend to get into it greater. Just don't downgrade him, just because he is a drug addict. Don't fuck with him because of that. Try to understand. (Nathan, age 28, Washington, D.C.)

In short, heroin provides users with an organizing principle for everyday life and offers the reward of feeling normal. Thus, most of the HLS men see little reason to trade for the methadone-maintenance lifestyle. They see it as self-defeating, a view that may help explain (along with methadone's re-ported ill effects) why methadone clients appear less healthy than heroin users. In fact, methadone clients were found to be more passive, less highly motivated and less inclined to undertake adult responsibilities than matched clients in drug-free programs (Brown et al. 1975).

It is significant that none of the HLS men had ever tried methadone-maintenance treatment and that, despite their criticisms, more than 75,000 addicts were enrolled in methadone treatment on December 31, 1982. In fact, 14,984 new clients, who were never treated in a methadone modality, were admitted to treatment between January 1 and December 31, 1982 (Food and Drug Administration 1983).

Rationale for Methadone Maintenance

Ironically, methadone maintenance both aims to free users from drug de-pendence and creates a drug dependence. What is the justification for treat-ing people with an addictive drug? Supporters argue that by providing a legal and closely monitored opiate, methadone maintenance treatment defuses users, reducing their criminal activities. Also, because of its pharmacological properties, methadone can be taken in one daily dose, making it easy to administer (compared with other drugs) and making the patient's life less hectic, often to the point where gainful employment can be obtained. Rosenbaum (1982) found that methadone offers heroin users a reprieve, "a chance to coast for a while—either to get it together to start a new life or at least to stop running for a while." These factors together, some argue, allow methadone clients to lead near-normal and constructive lives.

Indeed, this view is supported by 13 percent of the HLS men who had some positive things to say about methadone treatment:

> I think they doing some good, 'specially for a lot of older people. Yes, I think they do a lot of good. They need them, man, because there are more drug addicts out there than I have ever seen. (Chuck, age 33, New York)

> Methadone is useful for people that ain't got nowhere to go. I think the programs help people if they have some therapy along with the methadone. (Slim, age 38, New York)

> I got nothing against them programs except for the maintenance, but then again, they might be holding down something. I don't know if it's the crime or whatever. I do know it's keeping somebody working, you know, somebody Black. Most of them got Blacks working there. But still, I would like to see a better goal, to help you live like you would like to live—one-third of what you thought you could do as far as getting ahead. (Rick, age 27, Philadelphia)

Given these conflicting views, we were interested in finding out what might induce heroin users to enter and stay in treatment.

Entering and Staying in Treatment

Motivation to Enter Treatment

Little is known about what motivates heroin users to volunteer for treatment, especially when they have never been in treatment before. Despite the fact that street addicts and methadone treatment clients bad-mouth methadone, there is significant demand for it as a legal therapeutic drug and as an illicit street drug. Clearly, heroin addicts need strong motivation to give up heroin and the associated lifestyles (Preble and Casey 1969; Harford et al. 1976), both of which provide powerful reinforcing rewards.

The lifestyle can also become self-defeating. "Taking care of business" requires an enormous investment of emotional energy, time, and money. To succeed, addicts must engage in an absorbing and rigorous daily routine of hustling and copping. Each day is structured by the needs to make money, to maintain contacts, and to purchase drugs, and beyond that, to find time to get high (Looney and Metcalf 1974; Willis 1973; Hunter et al. 1978).

Indeed, 60 percent of the HLS sample said they could be persuaded to enter treatment under certain circumstances. Pressure from family members and the legal system were cited most frequently; other possible motivators were opportunity for job or skill development, peer pressure, inability to get heroin, illness, and fear of becoming an aging dope fiend.

Forty-two percent of those who saw treatment as a possibility said that pressure from the courts might motivate them to enter treatment; they would rather be in treatment than in jail, although they would prefer facing neither alternative:

> I don't particularly care for a drug treatment program myself. The only way I would go into one is if the court referred me. Like I say, if I were to get into trouble and the courts referred me I would do it. But other than that, I wouldn't consider using any methadone or any other program. (Larry, age 32, Washington, D.C.)

In fact, court pressure has been the primary avenue for getting heroin users into treatment; most clients enter drug treatment under legal pressure: being arrested, standing trial, or trying to qualify for parole or probation.

Forty-eight percent of those who indicated that they could be persuaded to enter treatment cited family pressure as the motivation. Such pressure could come from the wife or woman, mother, children, grandmother, or family as a whole. Not one respondent mentioned his father as a specific motivating influence. Sentiments such as these were typical:

> When your loved ones don't love you no more and all they are talking to you about is getting help, going into treatment becomes something to consider. Family, that's who you really listen to, you know. The niggers in the street, they only gonna tell you what they wanna tell you. They ain't gonna say what you really need to hear. (Anthony, age 30, Washington, D.C.)

> I look at my daughter, man, and I want off of them mothers. I got a baby, five, and I wanna offer her more than I done had, man. I look at myself and I can't offer her nothin' in this present condition that I'm in, man. You know, here I am a nice-lookin' man, got a nice-lookin' woman and a pretty baby, you know, and I'm runnin' around here doin' everything I ain't supposed to do. Family, yeah, that's what make me straighten up, man. (Quinn, age 27, Philadelphia)

Over time, hustling becomes harder; day after day, heroin users must outmaneuver others and avoid arrest and imprisonment. Maintaining the heroin lifestyle and the necessary relationships with associates and suppliers can create a set of overwhelming problems that eventually may outweigh the benefits of the lifestyle and make treatment acceptable.

Clearly, debates on this issue must take into account the fact that 40 percent of the HLS men said they would not seek drug treatment under any circumstances. Let us leave this discussion with these emphatic words:

> There's no way that someone could persuade me to enter treatment. That's something that I would never care to do—never care to get on. No way. I don't like programs, especially drug-treatment programs. If anything, I'm gonna kick cold turkey, my way you know. That's the only way that I know. No, I don't like programs. No, I never have and I never will. No. (Roscoe, age 27, Chicago)

Motivation to Stay in Treatment

A strong commitment is needed to enter treatment, and a different kind of commitment is needed to stay there. Most (72 percent) of the HLS men believed that rehabilitation would not work unless one was strongly self-motivated to change his lifestyle. Their views, expressed below, are consistent with reports in the literature:

> I don't think that you can really stop a person from usin' drugs unless they really want to stop. You can go into a program—I seen guys do it that I don't think they [programs] got the key to stop nobody from usin' drugs. They can talk to somebody about stop usin' drugs—it can't be done that way. You got to want to do it yourself. Nobody can do it for you. That's the only answer right there—it's you, man. (Ike, age 35, Philadelphia)
>
> It's up to the individual to say, "hey, I don't feel like messin' with this stuff no more." Once you take that initiative then you can go through the process of detoxin' your system from drug usin'—from heroin. A person has got to look at himself—just stand in front of a mirror and look at himself—see how your body and you are deteriorating. It's up to the individual himself. (Kevin, age 20, New York)

Twenty-seven percent of the HLS men who said they could be motivated to enter treatment cited the importance of a good counselor as a factor to staying in treatment. They described a good counselor as a caring person who understood their problems and lifestyle, who could be trusted, and who would serve as their advocate:

> It would have to be someone you're not scared of—somebody that you would just open up to, somebody that you trust. When you feel you can open up like that with somebody who is your friend or a man who is for you,

then you're gonna let your hair down and that's gonna bring about the help you need. (Dawson, age 28, Washington, D.C.)

A program is just words. It's the people that you get involved with that make me make up my mind. It's the relationships or whoever's counseling you that counts—that's a reflection on you too. The person who has jurisdiction to say so over you, on how good they are. It's like a coach or manager, it's a reflection of his works. He's got to have consideration and respect for the person, you know, without putting any stigma towards him—just deal with him as one human being to another, dig in deep enough to find out what it is about him that makes him that way. (Frank, age 33, Chicago)

In many respects, HLS men are outside the mainstream of normal society and of the urban poor community. They pay a price for their heroin use in physiological and social losses, and are not blind to the fact that many factors besides their drug use—especially racism and unemployment—work against them.

Yet, compulsory (involuntary) treatment mandated by courts in lieu of prison or as a condition of parole or probation is controversial; drug-treatment experts are divided on the appropriateness and effectiveness of mandatory treatment.

Strong advocates for mandatory treatment believe it does not make sense to wait until abusers hit bottom or become self-motivated, because that may be too late to provide the help needed (Bourne and Fox 1973; Schnoll 1981). Others view involuntary treatment as humanistic, providing heroin users, who otherwise lead destructive lives, with some opportunity for self-improvement (Glatt 1974). Some argue that because most users have favorable attitudes about using heroin, they cannot be expected to initiate or complete treatment voluntarily (Ausubel 1982), and still others point persuasively to studies of success achieved by heroin users who entered treatment because of court pressure (Looney and Metcalf 1974).

The school of disenchanted experts argues that clients coerced into treatment are not motivated, will avoid accepting responsibility for drug-related problems, will remain alienated from treatment activities, and will not benefit from treatment (Harford et al. 1976). One study, for instance, found that a majority of heroin users pressured into treatment lacked the necessary commitment and motivation, were not satisfied with the treatment experience, and, as a result, stayed in treatment for less than six months (Nurco and Shaffer 1982).

As John, a 31-year-old from Chicago, put it:

I don't want to just go someplace where they take me off heroin and nothing else is happening, you know. I might as well be using drugs. Don't get me off of drugs and keep me standing still in a holding pattern. To help me a program would have to put me in a position where I could better myself economically. That's the most important thing—to help me get a job where I don't have to limit myself. This is one of my prime considerations—not only psychology to make me drug free—not to entice me or trick me. Programs should approach treatment with some sort of compassion, respect, try to instill some motivation, treat you as a human being. If they realize you're successful with what you're doing they will be successful too.

Conclusions

This chapter has shown how the HLS men view methadone maintenance, the major drug treatment modality available to Black heroin users. Their perceptions of methadone maintenance treatment raise some important issues. What is the purpose of methadone maintenance? If the purpose is simply to reduce addiction to heroin, it may succeed. If the purpose is to reduce addiction, per se, it will not succeed. If the purpose is to render heroin users socially harmless by dispensing opiate-like drugs to them at little or no cost and keeping them off the street, methadone maintenance may benefit society. But does it really benefit the heroin user? Is it not hypocritical to treat heroin users with different, but highly potent, opiates to solve society's problems, while failing to provide significant resources to help the heroin users solve their problems?

This brings a number of other questions into focus:

To what degree are heroin users such as the HLS men actually physically addicted? Is methadone maintenance necessary or appropriate for heroin users who take one shot of heroin a day (combined with other drugs)?

How many HLS-type heroin users are being admitted to methadone clinics? On what basis? Does methadone maintenance induce people to become methadone addicts when they are not physically addicted to heroin?

If HLS-type heroin users do not need methadone maintenance (or, in any event, will not accept it) yet need help, what kind of help is available? Are traditional treatment modalities inappropriate for most contemporary heroin users?

These questions beg us to look at the heroin lifestyle and heroin treatment strategies from the heroin users' perspective. What does it mean that HLS men view methadone maintenance only as an avenue of last resort, an alternative of desperation? How can the treatment system compete with the perceived benefits of the heroin lifestyle? Can it offer these men a heroin-free lifestyle with dignity, feelings of self-worth, a sense of purpose? What kind of intervention will—as the heroin lifestyle often does—provide structure for daily activities, a reason to get up in the morning, goals to pursue, an opportunity for status and peer respect?

The problem is not simply that heroin is used to feel "normal"; it is the center of their lifestyles. Therefore, treatment must focus less on preventing regular heroin users from getting high and more on helping them build a new life. The medical model that views heroin users as sick people is too limiting and perhaps paternalistic. From their own perspective, heroin users are adapting quite rationally to their reality.

To be successful, those providing treatment must have an understanding of the meaning heroin users attach to their life patterns. This includes not just the heroin experience itself, but also the social and cultural patterns which evolve around, and become integrated with, the hustling, copping, and shooting of heroin. Their sexual behavior, social relationships, and ideas about themselves, as well as the communities they live in and the larger society, are all important intervention targets. This, of course, constitutes a considerable challenge. It will require sensitivity, careful planning, and the conviction that it is possible to help these men find alternatives and rewarding lifestyles.

Notes

1. The information in this chapter is based on content analysis of 124 tape recorded interviews. Most of these data came from an analysis of the responses to nine open-ended questions about treatment. These questions were designed to find out how HLS men view drug treatment. In addition to their opinions of treatment, the authors were interested in determining what would motivate them to enter and stay in treatment, as well as what they thought could be done to improve treatment. The quotes used in this chapter represent typical responses of the HLS men.

2. About two-thirds of all drug treatment clients enter a program to satisfy a requirement of the legal system (Weissman and Nash 1978).

3. For example, see Gearing et al. 1975; Dole and Herman 1977; Stimmel et al. 1977; Sells and Simpson 1980; Judson et al. 1980; Research Triangle Institute 1981.

4. Includes: Wilmarth and Goldstein 1974; Judson et al. 1980; McGlothlin and Anglin 1981; Edwards 1979; Sells and Simpson 1976; Jaffe et al. 1969; Newman et al. 1973; Cushman 1972.

5. Interviewers were trained to probe. After this question they attempted to get additional information, e.g., are programs useful? Do they get at the problems and needs of heroin addicts? Does the respondent like or dislike specific modalities? HLS men were responding to open-ended questions. Therefore, some percentages given in this chapter are not based on a 100 percent response rate.

References

Ausubel, David. 1982. Causes and types of narcotic addictions: A psychosocial view. In *Classic Contributions in the Addictions,* eds. Shaffer, H., and Burglass, M., New York: Brunner/Mazel. 301–309.

Ball, John C.; Rosen, Lawrence; Flueck, John A.; and Nurco, David N. 1982. Lifetime criminality of heroin addicts in the United States. *Journal of Drug Issues.* 12(3):225–239.

Bellis, David J. 1975. *Methadone Treatment Program Evaluation.* Ontario, California: West End Drug Abuse Control Coordinating Council, Inc.

Bihari, B. 1974. Alcoholism and methadone maintenance. *American Journal of Drug and Alcohol Abuse* 1:79–87.

Bourne, Peter G., and Fox, Ruth. 1973. Alcoholism: Progress in research and treatment. New York: Academic Press.

Brown, Barry, S.; Bass, Urbane F.; Garvey, Susan; and Kozel, Nicholas. 1972. Staff and client attitudes toward methadone maintenance. *International Journal of the Addictions.* 247–255.

Brown, Barry S.; Benn, Gloria J.; and Jensen, Donald R. 1975. Methadone maintenance: Some client opinions. *Journal of American Psychiatry* 132:623–626.

Bureau of Labor Statistics. 1983. *Employment Statistics, 3rd Quarter , 1983.* U.S. Department of Labor, Washington, D.C.

Chappel, John M. 1974. Methadone chemotherapy in drug addiction: Genocidal or lifesaving. *Journal of the American Medical Association* 228:725–728.

Cohen, Aaron; McKeever, William; Cohen, Murry; and Stimmel, Barry. 1977. The use of alcoholism screening test to identify the potential for alcoholism in persons on methadone maintenance. *American Journal of Drug and Alcohol Abuse* 4: 257–266.

Cushman, P. 1972. Arrests before and during methadone maintenance. *Proceedings of the Fourth National Conference on Methadone Treatment,* New York: NAPAN. National Association for the Prevention of Addiction to Narcotics.

DeLong, J.V. 1972. *Treatment and Rehabilitation in Dealing with Drug Abuse,* A Report to the Ford Foundation. New York: Praeger.

Dole, V.P., and Nyswander, M.E. 1967. Heroin addiction: A metabolic disease. *Archives of Internal Medicine* 120:19–24.

Dole, Vincent P., and Joseph, Herman. 1977. Methadone maintenance: Outcome after termination. New York State Journal of Medicine. 77(9):1409–1412.

Dumont, M.P. 1974. Drug treatment: Organization of programs at the state and local level. In Volume III, Revised Edition of *The American Handbook of Psychiatry.*

Edwards, Elizabeth. 1979. Arrest and conviction histories before, during, and after participation in a substance abuse treatment program. *Drug Forum* 7(3 and 4). 259–264.

Epstein, E.J. 1974. Methadone: The forlorn hope. *The Public Interest* 3–24.

Food and Drug Administration. 1983. Annual report for treatment programs using methadone: National summary. Rockville, Maryland: Department of Health and Human Services, FDA 1639.

Gearing, F.R.; D'Amico, D.A.; and Thompson, F. 1975. What's good about methadone maintenance after ten years? *Drug Abuse—Modern Trends, Issues, and Perspectives,* Proceedings of 2nd National Drug Abuse Conference, Inc., New Orleans, La. 546–666.

Glasscote, R.; Sussex, J.; Jaffe, J.; Ball, J.; and Brill, L. 1972. *The Treatment of Drug Abuse: Programs, Problems, Prospects.* Washington, D.C.: Joint Information Service of the American Psychiatric Association and the National Association for Mental Health.

Glatt, M.M. 1974. *A Guide to Addiction and Its Treatment.* New York: John Wiley and Sons.

Harford, Robert J.; Ungerer, James C.; and Kinsella, Kevin. 1976. Effects of legal pressure in prognosis for treatment of drug dependence. *American Journal of Psychiatry* 133:1399–1404.

Heyman, Florence. 1972. Methadone maintenance as law and order. *Society* (8): 15–25.

Holahan, James F. 1972. The economics of heroin. In *Dealing with Drug Abuse: A Report to the Ford Foundation.* New York: Praeger.

Hunt, Dana E.; Lipton, Douglas S.; Goldsmith, Douglas S.; and Strug, David L. 1982. *Problems in Methadone Treatment: The Influence of Reference Groups.* Report submitted to NIDA. Grant No. H81DA02300, Rockville, Md.

Hunter, Kathleen; Linn, Margaret; and Harris, Rachel. 1978. Self-concept and completion of treatment for heroin and non-heroin drug abusers. *American Journal of Drug and Alcohol Abuse* 5(4):463–475.

Isbell, H., and Vogel, V.J. 1948. The addiction liability of methadone and its use in the treatment of the morphine abstinence syndrome. *American Journal of Psychiatry* 105:909–914.

Jaffe, J.; Zaks, M.; and Washington, E. 1969. Experience with the use of methadone in a multi-modality program for the treatment of narcotic users. *International Journal of the Addictions* 4. 481–490.

Judson, Barbara; Ortiz, Serapio; Crouse, Linda; Carney, Thomas; and Goldstein, Avram. 1980. A followup study of heroin addicts five years after first admission to a methadone treatment program. *Drug and Alcohol Dependence* 6(5):295–313.

Kaul, Balkrishena, and Davidow, Bernard. 1981. Drug abuse patterns of patients on methadone treatment in New York City. *American Journal of Drug and Alcohol Abuse* 8:17–25.

Kreek, Mary J. 1978. Medical complications in methadone patients. In *Recent Developments in Chemotherapy of Narcotic Addiction,* eds. Kissin, Benjamin; Lowinson, Joyce, H.; and Millman, Robert B. New York: Academy of Sciences. 311:110–134.

Looney, Maryanne, and Metcalf, Suzanne. 1974. The fatigue factor in drug addiction: Insufficient motivation for treatment. *Hospital and Community Psychiatry* 25:528–530.

Maddux, James F., and McDonald, Linda Kay. 1972. Status of 100 San Antonio addicts one year after admission to methadone maintenance. *Report of The Thirty-Fourth Annual Scientific Meeting Committee on Problems of Drug Dependence.* Washington, D.C.: National Academy of Science.

McGlothlin, William, and Anglin, Douglas. 1981. Shutting off methadone. Archives of General Psychiatry 38: August. 885–892.

National Institute on Drug Abuse. 1981a. *Statistical Series: Data from the Client Oriented Data Acquisition Process, NIDA.* Rockville, Maryland: DHHS Pub. No. (ADM) 81–1143.

National Institute on Drug Abuse. 1981b. *Treatment Research Monograph Series: Drug and Alcohol Abuse, Implications for Treatment.* Stephen E. Gardner, ed. Rockville, Maryland: DHHS Pub. No (ADM) 80–958.

Nelkin, Dorothy. 1973. *Methadone Maintenance: A Technological Fix.* New York: George Braziller.

Newman, R.G.; Bashkow, S.; and Cates, M. 1973. Arrest histories before and after admission to a methadone maintenance treatment program. *Contemporary Drug Problems* 2:417–430.

Nurco, David, and Shaffer, John. 1982. Types and characteristics of addicts in the community. *Drug and Alcohol Dependence* 9:43–78.

Preble, E., and Casey, J.H. 1969. Taking care of business—The heroin user's life on the street, *International Journal of the Addictions* 4:1–24.

Preble, E., and Miller, Thomas. 1977. Methadone, wine and welfare. In *Street Ethnography,* ed. Robert S. Weppner. Beverly Hills: Sage Publications. 229–248.

Research Triangle Institute. 1979. *Summary and Implications: Client Characteristics, Behaviors, and Treatment Outcomes.* TOPS Admission Cohort, Report submitted to NIDA, August 1981 (Contract No. 271–77–1205).

Rosenbaum, M. 1982. Getting on methadone: The experience of the woman addict, *Contemporary Drug Problems.* 11(1):113–143.

Schnoll, Sidney. 1981. Patient Motivation. *Maryland State Medical Journal.* January. 30(1):40–43.

Sells, S.B., and Simpson, D.D. 1980. The case for drug abuse treatment effectiveness, based in the DARP research program. *British Journal of the Addictions* 75: 117–133.

Sells, S.B., and Simpson, D.D., eds. 1976. *Effectiveness of Drug Abuse Treatment,* 3–5. Cambridge, Mass.: Ballinger Publishing Company.

Siassi, Iradj, and Alston, Dominick C. 1976. Methadone Maintenance and the Problem with Alcohol. *American Journal of Drug and Alcohol Abuse* 3:267–277.

Siegler, Miriam, and Osmond, Humphrey. 1974. *Models of Madness, Models of Medicine.* New York: Macmillan.

Simpson, D.D. 1980. Followup Outcomes and Length of Time in Retirement. For Drug Abuse Institute of Behavioral Research Report, Report 90-9, Forth Worth: Texas Christian University.

Stimmel, Barry; Goldberg, Judith; Rotkopf, Edith; and Cohen Murry. 1977. Ability to remain abstinent after methadone detoxification: A six-year study. *Journal of the American Medical Association* 237(12):1216–1220.

Tims, Frank. 1981. *Effectiveness of Drug Abuse Treatment Programs.* Rockville, Maryland: NIDA: DHHS Pub. No. (ADM) 81–1143.

Tims, Frank. 1982. *Evaluation of Drug Abuse Treatment Effectiveness: Summary of the DARP Followup Research.* Rockville, Maryland: NIDA: DHHS Pub. No. (ADM) 82–1209.

Weissman, J.C., and Nash, G. 1978. A guide to the treatment of drug addict criminality. *Journal of Drug Issues* 8(1):123–137.

Willis, James. 1973. *Addicts: Drugs and Alcohol Re-examined.* Toronto, Canada: Pitman Publishing.

Wilmarth, S.S., and Goldstein, A. 1974. *The Therapeutic Effectiveness of Methadone Maintenance Programs in the USA.* Geneva: World Health Organization.

9
Conclusions and Implications

Elliott I. Bovelle
Andress Taylor

I n the preceeding chapters we have tried to set forth a holistic view of the contemporary lifestyles of inner-city Black men who use heroin regularly and who have never been in treatment. This has been a view from the inside, from men who live and function in the inner cities of four large urban areas. We sought first to listen to the HLS men's accounts of their lifestyles as told from their viewpoint and in their own often graphic and vivid language. Open-ended interviews were conducted by trained indigenous former heroin users. Then, using an ethnographic perspective, we analyzed this large body of material searching for emergent patterns and themes. This book is a report of that effort.

The HLS men speak out with such simplicity and conviction that their voice is far more powerful than mere statistics. In collecting these frank, first hand accounts of an underground culture, the HLS has produced unique and revealing data about the complex interaction of social environment, patterns of use, values, attitudes toward treatment and expectations for the future among people who live within the heroin lifestyle. The HLS provides insight into how these heroin users spend their time and progress through a typical day, their techniques for meeting the economic demands to support their habits and other daily needs, their perceptions of themselves and their relationships with their immediate world and the larger social world beyond, their social interactions, and their heroin experiences. In this concluding chapter we briefly draw together the main findings in this book and comment on their implications with respect to the public image of heroin users, the treatment available to them, and future research.

Findings

An unexpected finding is that the HLS men live rather structured lives in which successive daily time periods are spent engaging in a variety of fairly predictable and even conventional activities. Like men in straight society, they arise early in order to spend many of their waking hours "on the job"—

but in their case, this usually means hustling in pursuit of the wherewithal to maintain their once-a-day, relatively controlled heroin habits. Like most men in straight society they go about their business (legitimate work and/or hustling) during the day and pursue private pleasures in the evening.

Many of the men report having regular family responsibilities which must be taken care of along with their daily hustling and copping. For most HLS men hustling is a way to organize the day, to give it routine and meaning, and to provide stimulation and social life. The actual hustle is often preceded by social interactions involving exchange of small talk, as well as information relevant to obtaining money and heroin. Hustling is a central part of users' daily activities. Not surprisingly, the most frequently cited main hustle is theft, but the second most frequently reported source of income is more surprising: legitimate work. Other common hustles involve obtaining funds from family and friends through borrowing, but also often through manipulation, and dealing. Further, while this study found a wide diversity of most-common hustling activities, the analysis also suggested that four basic types of hustlers can be identified in the inner city: the opportunistic hustler, the legitimate hustler, the skilled hustler, and the dope hustler. This typology illuminates the social organization of hustlers and enables us to more carefully assess hustling's economic and social impact on inner city communities.

No matter what type of hustle HLS men prefer and no matter how difficult they say theft is becoming, most still claim to resist criminal activity involving violence. In fact, of the three most commonly mentioned sources of income, stealing, legitimate work, and borrowing, only the first is illegal and potentially violent. While some borrowing techniques are rather manipulative, they are rarely violent or illegal.

This knowledge, combined with the fact that the HLS men appear to be able to control their heroin use, suggests that economic considerations may be at least as important as physiologically or psychologically driven escalating drug habits in determining how much heroin one takes and therefore how much money must be hustled.

Most of the HLS men were familiar with heroin before their initial use because of its common presence in their communities. They were curious about it but also feared to use it, particularly intravenously; they recognized the peer pressure and status associated with its use, and considered their own ultimate use inevitable. Indeed, the HLS data show that the initiation into a career as a committed heroin user is more complex than simply being "hooked" after an initial, perhaps unpredicted, first use. Because of the regular availability of heroin and the structure of the relationship of inner-city residents to society, the heroin lifestyle has become firmly established as an alternative lifestyle for Black youngsters. This being the case, it is perhaps remarkable that the heroin-dependent segment of the population in these communities is no larger than it is.

Most HLS men were initiated into heroin use by a close friend. Although many experienced nausea, the first rush was usually so positive an experience as to outweigh any negatives. But the first unforgettable exhilaration is rarely duplicated, although by subsequent use they hope to recapture that experience. So regular users tend no longer to aspire even to euphoria; rather, they seek only a temporary calm and serenity, feelings of normalcy, relaxation, and capability to provide them with a respite from the bleak harshness of their lives. It is the pursuit of normalcy rather than of euphoria which propels these heroin users to continue to use the substance. In a society which has relegated them to a lowly status which they reject, the achievement of normalcy is an accomplishment that these men value.

Another striking finding from the HLS study is that the drug habits of this population of dedicated heroin users are flexible and that, on the average, most shoot up only once each day. They can adjust their use to changing external factors (such as price and availability) and they do not permit their heroin use to escalate unmanageably. This finding is significant for a number of reasons.

First, the fact that the HLS men are using heroin at all reflects the influence of the larger political and social structure on their lives. As Nathan, the 28-year-old heroin user from Washington, D.C., explained: "No Black man could have brought that kind of shit (heroin) into this country, they just don't allow that, they don't allow that." He points to the fact that: "There would be no problem if there was no drugs in this country." This perception reflects the reality that availability is the first prerequisite of drug use (Zinberg 1982). Larger social forces, controlled from outside the community, provided these men with an opportunity to self-select into the fraternity of heroin users. While many of the HLS men may share Nathan's perception, this, nevertheless, does not empower them nor supply them with the resources to change their lives.

Second, the flexible one-shot-a-day habit challenges the popular image that regular heroin users have an insatiable and uncontrollable appetite for heroin and that they therefore shoot up as many times as possible each day. Third, this type of habit makes evident their ability to adjust to the effect of larger social forces on such factors as the quality, availability and price of heroin, which are largely dependent on social and political processes controlled outside the ghetto community.

Fourth, as long as they can maintain this precarious, flexible balance, they can project an image of themselves as in control, and therefore not "down-and-out dope fiends." These men have made extraordinary adaptations in order to continue using heroin on a daily basis and to regulate their use. These adaptations allow many of them to sustain the belief that they are not heroin "addicts," but rather only "visitors" to the heroin scene.

Nevertheless, the data indicate that, while approximately one-third of the HLS men are usually employed in legitimate jobs, they are still very much a part of the heroin scene. Most of them hustle, cop, and even inject heroin socially, revealing a high level of cooperation in all phases of their heroin use. The specialized ingroup language of the heroin user is one primary indication of the men's involvement in the life. As is true of most vernaculars, it sets the ingroup off from the outgroup, in this case, straight society. However, while the HLS men continually and easily used heroin argot, many illustrated their connection with mainstream culture by their ability to shift easily in and out of standard English when expediency demanded, as, for example, when they were in fine stores for a shoplifting hustle.

Skillful and creative use of the special heroin argot conveys status to the user. It is also a major aspect of the manipulation which characterizes much of the users' hustling activity as well as some of their more recreational social interactions. Their colorful language helps these men share and clarify their experiences, bonding them and giving them a sense of identity in a community stigmatized by society. It also facilitates copping by demonstrating their mastery of the terminology of the distribution system.

While skillful use of language conveys status and contributes to the building of self-image, typical HLS respondents reveal a self-image which is characterized by conflict and ambiguity. They see themselves as neither down-and-out nodding, dehumanized junkies nor as the glamorous elite "cool cats" of the drug world. A basic aspect of their self-perception is their refusal to consider themselves as true denizens of the drug world, but rather as individuals who move confidently in and between both the drug and straight worlds. Indeed, much of their reported behavior lends support to their rejection of the addict stereotype as applied to themselves.

At the heart of their self-picture is the expressed belief of most HLS men that they are in control of their lives. Fundamental to this control, and functioning possibly as both antecedent and consequence, are their controlled habits. That they are able to control their heroin needs means that their habits are not likely to escalate, that they do not develop intense physiological and psychological dependence on the drug, and that the habit does not place an impossible financial burden on them. Associated with this control is their relative success at meeting economic needs, which may involve an artful balancing of legitimate and illicit pursuits, and the resourceful manipulation of hustles, which also are kept within controlled limits so that users are able, for the most part, to avoid being caught or resorting to violence.

Another aspect of control is manifested by their care with personal appearance. This is important to their self-image in several ways: it is evidence that they are not down-and-out junkies; it permits them to continue to say that they have one foot in the straight world and are able to function there, and it provides them with camouflage for certain of their hustles. Their semi-straight appearance also provides protection against police harassment.

Additionally, a highly significant aspect of their control is avoidance of treatment. This allows them to view themselves as being in charge of their own lives as independent persons. Being in treatment would make them feel that they had lost their freedom of action, that they could no longer take care of themselves, and it would damage their self-esteem by identifying them as junkies.

In addition to their feelings of control, the HLS respondents' value systems play an important role in what they think about themselves. They aspire to those conventional trappings of the straight world which they consider symbols of success, primarily by means of legitimate employment which will ensure financial security. Along with this goes the hope (and tentative expectation) of giving up heroin use and becoming drug free.

Not surprisingly, some of the men express ambivalence toward treatment, but for the most part their attitudes are negative. Since most of the HLS men have avoided treatment, it is not personal experience which has shaped their opposition to treatment. Their disapproval and rejection of methadone maintenance (in their minds virtually synonymous with treatment) stems from several beliefs: that methadone maintenance is just another drug habit, possibly even more addictive than heroin (particularly as the latter is used by them); that it has serious physiological side-effects; that it is ineffective in curbing heroin use; and that it fails to meet the real needs of users adequately. Also, since most of these men see themselves as nonjunkies or people who "use" rather than "abuse" heroin they consider treatment to be irrelevant because their heroin use is under control. But it can be surmised that there is another significant basis for their resistance to submitting to treatment: the fact that it would entail giving up the complex lifestyle attendant to their heroin use. By so doing, they would of necessity abandon the many activities and conditions which make their lives meaningful. While many recognize that they could be persuaded to seek treatment, they see this as an essentially involuntary decision stemming from legal coercion, pressures from loved ones, from illness or aging, or from inability to get heroin.

This composite picture of Black, inner-city, male regular heroin users who have never been in treatment reveals the existence of a unique and culturally complex group of heroin users. Their functioning in contemporary U.S. inner cities has major implications for at least three interrelated areas: the public image of Black inner-city heroin users and the policy implications of their lifestyles; policy decisions regarding how best to cope with, prevent, and treat heroin use; and future research on heroin use among inner-city residents.

Implications

The HLS study pierces the veil which has heretofore shrouded this world in mystery. If we listen, there is considerable agreement in what the HLS men have to say. Although their styles and many of their behaviors are unconventional, we find, upon closer inspection, that in many ways they are similar to those of us who do not use heroin. Their aspirations are similar: a desire for meaningful work, warm family relationships, and a quality of life which is not beyond what the middle class experiences.

Public Image and Public Policy

It is clear the HLS men do not fall into either of the generally accepted stereotypes of heroin addicts. On the one hand they do not resemble the stereotype of the down-and-out, nodding, dangerously crazed, unpredictable and dehumanized junkie. Nor, on the other hand, can they be considered part of the glamorous addict stereotype—the so-called aristocracy of the drug world (the stand-up cat)—whose presence helps elevate the status of the heroin habit. As we have seen, the HLS men, both in terms of what they say about their daily activities and their views of themselves, tend to fall in between these two types. Clearly their manageable heroin habits, their structured, daily routines, their identification with straight-world values, their social support from both the street and straight worlds, their desires to reject the junkie image and their ability to self-medicate and avoid treatment means they cannot be viewed as "righteous dope fiends."

This raises an obvious question: what is the dominant pattern of heroin dependency in U.S. inner cities? If the HLS men do represent a growing population of underclass Blacks who derive meaning from the heroin lifestyle and the "normalcy" obtained from a daily shot of heroin, then the assumptions upon which public images as well as public policies are formulated will have to be drastically changed.

Suppose that the patterns of heroin use and lifestyle found among the HLS men closely approximates the dominant pattern for inner-city Black male heroin users in the 1980s. Let us even speculate further that this lifestyle and pattern of heroin use has, or will, spread to other communities. The consequences would be profound.

In the first place, the public at large would be asked to accept a version of lives characterized by regular heroin use, where the nature and consequences of such use are perhaps considerably less dramatic and substantial than previously believed. In many ways this would be a message that the mainstream, non-heroin-using public would not want to hear, for it plays down the ugly, immoral, pathological side of heroin use. Instead it focuses more on the ways in which heroin use is an integral part of a lifestyle where it is used in a controlled manner as self-medication over long periods of time by men who are not filthy, crazed, or dehumanized. The logical extension of this line of thinking would require considerable adjustments in the beliefs of most middle- and upper-class White Americans regarding poor, inner-city Black male heroin users, about whom there currently exist rather well-defined, well-entrenched hostile feelings.

Further, if the HLS men represent the predominant pattern of heroin use today, it seems reasonable to argue that the addiction/tolerance spiral can be broken. The idea that continued use of heroin always leads to increased dosages and increased addiction would be disproven or, at least, would become the exception. Such evidence, as found in the HLS, would show that a combination of factors including personality, social and financial supports, drug preference and availability, and heroin quality and availability, have combined to empower the heroin user to use the drug in a controlled fashion that minimizes the likelihood of physical addiction and keeps heroin use within manageable limits. Once again this would challenge the predominant public image surrounding Black inner-city heroin users and would have implications for policy formulation.

Heroin Use and Crime

One highly controversial policy-related issue is the relationship between heroin use and crime. One of the most frightening consequences of drug use generally, and heroin use specifically, at least as perceived by the public, is its assumed relationship to crime, particularly violent, person-to-person crimes of acquisition. Yet only 18 percent of the HLS men reported involvement in armed robbery or stick-ups, despite the advantages such activities bring in the form of large amounts of ready cash and relief from daily hustling. Further, the majority of HLS men also report frequent begging and borrowing from family and friends. These and other HLS data suggest that the relationship is not causal, but correlative. Since the average dosage of heroin for the HLS men is both small and manageable, certain conclusions follow: (1) the volume of crime HLS men need to support their habits is lower than what has been previously attributed to inner-city heroin users; (2) their heroin intake adjusts to their economic circumstances, that is, they will use or not use heroin depending on their success at generating income; (3) their volume of crime is volitional rather than compulsive; and (4) the antidote for heroin-related volitional crime is probably not the administration of treatment but rather the administration of justice.

Drug Treatment Policy

Another area of importance is drug treatment policy. Both the HLS men's statements and the picture they provide of their lifestyles suggest that methadone maintenance would not be an effective treatment strategy. For one thing, the HLS men say they do not like methadone treatment for many reasons and would enter it only under very limited circumstances. In addition, the HLS exposes a user lifestyle where drug use, hustling, and socialization are valued and serve an organizing function in users' lives. They exist in a cybernetic rather than linear, causal relationship. Since no one dimension is the direct cause of the other, policy that predicates one on the other in a causal manner will be likely to fail. Methadone maintenance, in particular, would be ineffective since, in comparison with the HLS men's lifestyles and patterns of heroin use, it is more disruptive to their lifestyle than heroin, it is less subjectively satisfying, and it may be riskier physiologically. Most assuredly, any public policy and treatment strategies that are motivated by (and whose success is largely measured by) the assumption that sobriety will result in a significant drop in crime will probably fail.

For these reasons, now may well be the time to reexamine the wisdom of current treatment programs and strategies. Given what has been reported and the concerns raised by the HLS men about methadone, attention should be given to this form of chemotherapy and how it should be used. As Ausubel (1983) suggests, methadone treatment should only be used as adjunct to treatment "when it reasonably meets agreed upon and empirically based criteria. . . ."

Future Research

Clearly, further research on the use patterns and lifestyles of the nontreatment population of heroin users among the HLS population and among the nontreatment population of other groups is required in order to determine just how widespread the pattern of controlled heroin use is. Indeed, the HLS data and the discussion of the consequences of a predominant lifestyle pattern, such as that of the HLS men, only serves to point to the urgency of such research. It seems likely that public knowledge and policy formulation are operating on outdated assumptions. While this, of course, can have dire consequences for existing heroin users, it is equally unfortunate for those young people who are currently (much like the HLS men were) being socialized into the heroin lifestyle. If, for instance, we knew more about the degree to which young people are learning to use heroin in a controlled way, we might be able to develop effective intervention methods which would take into account the importance and complexity of the heroin lifestyle and prevent the further development of its core aspects.[1] A positive interpretation is that both young and old heroin users who have flexible, manageable, self-medicating habits might be more amenable to innovative community or street-level intervention techniques than users whose habits are not as well controlled.

Many different intervention and early prevention methods need to be tested and evaluated. There is obviously a need for more holistic intervention programs for HLS-type men that take into account basic non-drug-related components of their lifestyles. However, based on what we have learned in this study, some approaches would be more appropriate than others. Employment programs are particularly apropos in view of the interests and desires expressed by the HLS men. Many of the men appeared genuinely interested in the possibility of finding a job and most saw employment as one of the possible ways out of the heroin lifestyle. Without employment opportunity, there is little hope for achieving self-satisfaction, improving one's self-image or escaping the cycle of illicit activity and drugs which provides an alternative source of self-esteem and prestige.

However, mere ritualistic job-counseling services, which are not coupled with a program of skills assessment, supportive services, and job development and placement, are not only likely to be unproductive, but may result in exacerbating cynical distrust of the system if they are seen as another "White man's game." What is needed, perhaps, are educational programs whose main focus is not drugs or drug use or drug counseling, but the entire person and his/her lifestyle as it intersects larger social, political, and economic structures. This kind of program would aim at reinforcing the strengths and sturdiness of character the HLS men display and would seek to provide, especially to young inner-city Black men (and women), alternative understandings of their social environment and alternative techniques for managing their social and cultural worlds.

After all, the HLS data support the argument that these men's lives and their roles in the community, while somewhat unconventional, are still intact. In theory this would mean that this type of heroin user has a greater possibility of limiting or stopping heroin use than men who have experienced a greater degree of social disintegration in their lives. An early-intervention program with this kind of orientation would provide the opportunity for policy makers and drug researchers to break significant new ground in dealing with the heroin subcultural system in poor, urban, Black communities. Early intervention would allow drug researchers to establish control and experimental groups among those in the at-risk population who are trying out heroin for the first time. Such studies could attempt to determine the correlation between profile characteristics and future involvement with heroin. Longitudinal studies of those who accept and those who reject heroin may provide some basis for predicting which individuals are more likely to become regular heroin users.

Further, development of effective early-prevention and early-intervention strategies would provide the opportunity for youthful heroin experimenters to discontinue drug use by stressing, among other things, their need to understand and manage their social and cultural system. Typically, teenagers have a limited knowledge of their social environment. Their firsthand knowledge is often restricted to family, school, and immediate neighborhood. In addition, poor inner-city Black teenagers frequently have a negative self-image and a negative image of their own ethnic group. Their firsthand knowledge of the world needs to be increased through experiences which improve these images of themselves and of their ethnic group. For the HLS men and young people first beginning to pick up on the controlled-heroin-use lifestyle, intervention programs oriented toward the nondrug aspects of users' lives may be more effective than traditional drug counseling per se in preventing further heroin use.

Some will argue that the HLS men represent the hard core of a larger social problem area, and that their chances would not be good even without heroin abuse. To that, we must respond that they deserve a fair chance. Given the resources to provide that chance, some will find their way out of this social and cultural trap. Perhaps more important, there is a need to provide the financial and human resources to intervene early with youngsters who are in the early stage of experimenting with drugs and alcohol, and to prevent their being drawn into the lifestyle.

Indeed, as just noted, more sensitivity to and research on basic nondrug components of the heroin users' lifestyles is needed. Enhancing potential users' opportunities for meaningful work, education, recreation, and other sources of self-esteem would perhaps be more beneficial than simply providing them with alternative drug treatment or even drug-free treatment. This suggestion is not new, although attempts to implement it have been infrequent. In keeping with this, a second important suggestion can be made. That is to say, more efforts should be made to inform those who do not use illegal drugs about the true nature of inner-city heroin use and heroin lifestyles. Although we have not explored it here, much could be made of the similarities between the controlled heroin use lifestyle explicated in this book and the controlled drinking or even legal drug taking of mainstream American society.

It is true, of course, that the opportunity structure will not be enhanced for inner-city Black heroin users or dispossessed people, generally, until decision makers and the public at large develop a more positive, balanced, and understanding view of these groups. Perhaps, such material as presented in this book can help lead to a fuller, more accurate, and more humanistic view of Black male inner-city heroin users and even heroin users generally. This in turn may contribute to forming a social basis upon which to begin to build a broad societal commitment to allocate funds and human energy not only to explore innovative, experimental, more appropriate, and more successful intervention efforts for heroin users such as the HLS men, but also to remove existing social and economic barriers to their full participation in mainstream life.

Note

1. For a recent detailed discussion of the impact of the "social setting variable" on controlled opiate users see Zinberg (1982).

References

Ausubel, D.P. 1983. Methadone maintenance treatment: The other side of the coin. *The International Journal of the Addictions* 18(6):851–862.

Zinberg, Norman E. 1982. Nonaddictive opiate use. In *Criminal Justice and Drugs: The Unresolved Connection*, ed. James C. Weissman and Robert L. Dupont, 5–21. Port Washington, New York: Kennikat Press.

Appendix:
The Heroin Lifestyle
Study Methodology

Bill Hanson

This chapter describes the research methodology, procedures, and techniques employed in the Heroin Lifestyle Study (HLS). More specifically, it:

1. sets forth the purpose of the study,
2. describes the research design and its application and use in the study,
3. discusses the various phases of the research process,
4. points out the main problems and difficulties encountered,
5. draws attention to some of the limitations of the data, and
6. indicates some of the advantages and disadvantages in conducting an ethnographic multicity study using indigenous interviewers.

Purpose of Study

The rationale for conducting this study is set forth in the introduction, which points out that, outside of the classic ethnographic studies, there is a relative dearth of research on heroin users who have never been in treatment. More recent work results from surveys and addresses the process of "natural recovery" from opiate addiction (cf. Robins and Murphy 1967; Robbins 1973; Robins et al. 1975; O'Donnell et al. 1976; Waldorf and Biernacki 1979, 1981; Nurco 1981). It was believed that greater understanding of this relatively unstudied group of users would prove a valuable supplement to the large body of existing research on heroin users in treatment. As Waldorf (1980) has pointed out, most of our present knowledge about drug use and drug users comes from research conducted in institutional settings, hospitals, prisons, and treatment programs; although, as noted by Waldorf (1980) and in the introduction to this book, there are exceptions to this. Yet it is true that much of our knowledge still comes from what Waldorf calls "extreme cases"—the user who is treated in an emergency room for a drug overdose, the addict apprehended by the police—or the drug abuser who seeks treatment in a methadone clinic. A major goal of this investigation was to go beyond these institutional settings to locate users who had never been in treatment and to interview them in their own communities. The study would focus on the lifestyles of untreated heroin users seen as much as possible from their own perspective, in order to learn how they maintain their habits and cope with pressures without ever entering treatment programs. A further concern was the reported heavy use of drugs among members of social and ethnic minorities (e.g., National Institute on Drug Abuse 1981) and the disproportionate impact of drug abuse on minority communities (e.g., Espada 1979).

After different study methodologies were considered, an ethnographic approach focusing on untreated Black inner-city heroin users seemed likely to best serve the purposes of the study. Ethnographic studies have the potential of reaching hard-to-locate population groups and can often lead to new paradigms and alternative understanding not provided through quantitative surveys and secondary data sources. Most important, ethnography has the potential of providing cultural description—a portrait of the people under study in their own words, from their own viewpoint, unfettered by any a priori research assumption. The result is almost always an "insider's" view, suggesting new insights into human behavior (Feldman et al. 1979).

Earlier experience (c.f. Beschner and Feldman 1979) suggested that it would be difficult to contact heroin users who had not received treatment through formal treatment agencies and organizations. It was necessary to find a way of locating heroin users in their natural setting, not just any heroin users "on the street," but those most typical of heroin users who have not been in treatment. After considering various alternatives, it was decided to have ethnographers train and supervise indigenous former addicts as interviewers. It was believed that this strategy would provide us with the best access to the study population, enabling the study team to locate and screen typical inner-city regular users not known to treatment personnel, as well as to capture an uninhibited view of their social worlds from the inside.

It was hoped that the study would help answer the following types of questions:

1. How do hardcore untreated Black, male, inner-city heroin users view their life situation?
2. How do users who have never been in treatment survive in the inner-city heroin world?
3. What are their daily activities?
4. What do they think and feel?
5. What meaning(s) do they attach to their drug use?
6. How do they cope with their own drug use without using formal treatment?
7. What are their images of and attitudes toward treatment programs and their effectiveness?

8. How and to what degree can treatment programs be designed and implemented to reach users who attach special meaning and status to the use of illicit drugs?
9. Should culturally oriented treatment programs be planned for some population groups?
10. What should the expectations be for treatment programs oriented toward hardcore drug users?

While these questions are certainly not new, they are still important and largely unanswered, especially with respect to users who have never been in treatment.

The HLS study then was designed with the following four purposes:

1. To learn more about the lifestyle(s) of hardcore, inner-city, Black male heroin users who had never been in treatment, by encouraging each user to describe his daily activities in detail and to give his own view of his social world as he experienced it.
2. To obtain a more holistic understanding of the contemporary inner-city Black male heroin user—how he spends his time and how he copes with his habit in the context of his immediate community and the larger society.
3. To determine the implications, if any, of data from addicts who have never been in treatment for guiding policy decisions regarding the future planning of treatment programs.
4. To evaluate the efficacy of carrying out an ethnographic field study coordinated from one central location, using indigenous interviewers in four different cities to locate and interview a population group that is hard to reach and sensitive to the presence of outsiders.

Organization of the Research Project

Before discussing the research process itself a brief description of the overall organizational structure of this project may be helpful. The project was designed and directed by the four editors of this volume, working very closely during all phases of the study. Each of the four maintained close contact with the field supervisors in each city throughout the project. Following the formulation of the research design and the development of the interview schedule, the main tasks were to coordinate the data gathering, analyze the data, and develop the plan for the book. In addition to these research tasks, two important organizational functions were field supervision and interviewing. A field supervisor and two indigenous Black male interviewers were assigned to each of the four study sites (Chicago, Philadelphia, New York, and Washington, D.C.). The supervisors (who included social scientists, drug researchers, and local drug clinic personnel) were in regular contact with the interviewers in the field in order to monitor the interviewing process and review progress made by each of the interviewers in meeting the sample quota goals. The supervisors were also responsible for providing interviewers with interview schedules and money for paying interviewees and for mailing completed interview schedules to the project coordinators. Project coordinators held weekly discussions with each supervisor regarding the entire interviewing process to make sure that the interviewing was proceeding smoothly and uniformly in each city, and often talked directly with the interviewers when problems arose or as a supplement to the initial training. All the interviewers were middle-aged Black male former addicts involved in some aspect of drug abuse work.

Most of the early ethnographic studies of heroin addiction in Black communities were conducted by White ethnographers (Lindesmith 1947; Sutter 1966; Feldman 1968; Preble and Casey 1969; Agar 1973). As noted earlier, it was felt that this study would be enhanced by use of indigenous Black male former heroin users trained in ethnographic interviewing and who had contact with the street (cf. Moore et al. 1980; Hughes et al. 1982).

Former addict interviewers who are trusted by the respondents and who are familiar with and can empathize with many features of the respondents lives are most likely to elicit frank, valid, authentic, unguarded information from a qualitative, ethnographic perspective (cf. Ball 1967; Yancy and Rainwater 1970; Stephens 1972; Agar 1976; Bonito et al. 1976; Bale 1979; Myers 1979; Zinn 1979). HLS coordinators were able to locate and select Black indigenous interviewers with the help of other researchers pursuing drug research in the four target cities. The individuals selected were, indeed, familiar with the "street scene" and were already known in the communities where they did the interviewing. They had access to many users, felt comfortable in most field situations, and were trusted by those being interviewed. These qualities, in addition to the interviewers' knowledge of the language and culture of the inner-city communities, provided quick access to the field and added much to the ethnographic dimension of the study.

Interviewers were carefully selected through contacts in each city and were interviewed by city field supervisors to determine their ability to carry out the type of interview planned. All had had at least some prior experience in conducting interviews. All received approximately two days of interviewer training from at least one of the coordinators as well as continuous supervisory sessions (by phone and in person) during the interviewing period. The interviewers, except for their regular contact with the field supervisors, functioned independently in making contacts, screening potential interviewees, conducting the interviews, and paying the respondents.

Although in many ways the three-level organizational structure functioned adequately, a number of coordination problems did emerge. These, combined

with the already difficult job of monitoring independent indigenous street interviewers, made coordination of the study more difficult and time-
consuming than anticipated. Some of the problems which arose will become
apparent in the subsequent discussion of the research process.

Methodology and Research Design

The underlying guiding methodology for this study was founded in the
philosophical traditions of qualitative research (e.g., Bruyn 1966; Glaser and
Strauss 1967; Berger and Luckman 1967) and ethnography (Preble and Casey
1969; Agar 1973; Weppner 1977; Feldman et al. 1979; Spradley 1979; Akins
and Beschner 1980). By means of uniform, open-ended questions, the goal was
to obtain knowledge of respondents' lifestyles in their own words, thus capturing the essence of their social worlds and realities as they see it. Therefore,
while respondents were questioned in detail regarding broad and diverse areas
of their lives, the indigenous interviewers refrained as much as possible from
suggesting potential answers, words, or content areas, but rather encouraged
respondents to reveal as many of the intricacies of their social worlds as possible in their own words and style.

The research plan called for interviewing a total of at least 130
respondents, 30–35 in each of the four study cities, during a period of approximately six months. Since the study focused on serious, dedicated heroin users
who had never been in treatment, in order to qualify for inclusion in the sample
respondents were required to be Black males who had injected heroin at least
once a day on at least eight days during the previous two weeks, and who had
never been enrolled in a drug treatment program. Finally, interviewers were to
select equal numbers of respondents from at least two different copping areas
and social networks.

To meet the above criteria, each interviewer screened a number of potential respondents; the field supervisors at each site were responsible for monitoring the screening process and reaching the sample quotas. The interviewers
functioned independently in making contact with respondents in the field. All
of the interviewers were familiar with the local drug scene and already knew
heroin users. The first task was to use existing contacts to establish enough
trust within the community. The predominant mode of making contacts was
either through one respondent referring other potential respondents to the interviewer, or using a contact person who sent potential respondents to the interviewer. The contact men were paid a nominal fee for referring individuals
who were ultimately interviewed. Making contact with untreated users proved
to be a time-consuming, laborious task for all interviewers in their function as
recruiters. The interviewers were trained to explore all means of contacting
potential respondents and screening them according to the criteria. In the event

that interviewers had difficulty locating heroin users who had never been in treatment, a priority system was established for classifying respondents who may have had some limited treatment experience. The majority of the respondents (80 percent) reported never having had treatment experience; of the 20 percent who had received some treatment, approximately 15 percent reported only short-term treatment, such as detoxification or emergency room visits. It proved more difficult to locate young (ages 15–19) heroin users and consequently the quota for respondents in the 15–19 age category was not met, since only 14.2 percent fell into this group.

In addition, it proved difficult and unnecessary to obtain equal numbers of respondents from the different social networks and copping areas. On-site monitoring of the sample selection process (including regular contact with the interviewers) indicated that, in general, respondents did not know each other and did not cop on the same corners. Occasionally, an interviewer would report that he was on a "run" wherein respondents were referring others to be interviewed. This kind of "snowball sampling," however, was not the predominant mode of recruiting respondents, and even when it occurred there was no evidence that people were coming from just one social group or copping area. Indeed, interviews were conducted over a six-month period and took place in many different locations in each of the cities. This is not to say that the sample is representative of all untreated heroin users, but that respondents came from a range of different age and social groups and copping areas and represent a diverse group.

Interview Schedule Construction

Each respondent (who was asked not to use any name by which he could be identified) was interviewed intensively for two to three hours, in accordance with an open-ended interview guide. Although the indigenous interviewers were close to the lifestyle of current Black male heroin users, they tended to be inexperienced at conducting open-ended, probing interviews lasting from two and one-half to three hours. The interview was therefore designed to provide more direction than would be required by most experienced ethnographers. However, in order to encourage the respondents to use the language of their social worlds and to convey the reality of their lives as they view it, unencumbered by researchers' preconceptions, much of the interviewer training focused on use of a three-stage probing process designed to facilitate natural responses from interviewees.

The final interview schedule comprised two parts. The first (section A) was composed of short-answer questions dealing with basic social, demographic, and drug-use information. The second and much longer part (section B) was made up of the open-ended questions designed to elicit detailed information about the lifestyles of heroin users and their everyday existence. These questions examine areas such as the user's typical day, his copping and hustling activities, drug use patterns, opinions about drug treatment, and his physical and mental health, as well as his perception of society, his family, himself, and his hopes for the future. These provided a picture of the respondents as holistic, integrated individuals rather than merely as heroin users. The interview material in section B was tape-recorded.

In developing both sections of the interview schedule, the coordinators drew upon the knowledge of current and former addicts (Black and White) as well as of experienced researchers. While the project coordinators knew the kind of information and the specific areas to be covered, the former addicts and the interviewers helped to make the schedule practical from the standpoint of the current inner-city heroin scene. They reviewed early drafts of the schedule and helped pretest it at different stages on current users, some with treatment experience and some with none. Revisions were made after each pretest and a few after the interview training sessions.

While section A of the schedule was rather straightforward in terms of traditional sociodemographic information and interviewing techniques, section B was designed so that interviewers could encourage respondents to talk on their own about general topics, or if this did not readily occur, interviewers could use the guide to help obtain specific details. The format for this deserves a brief comment.

Since we wanted to suggest as few answers as possible in our questions, we first identified general topical areas and related questions we wanted users to talk about. A fairly elaborate checklist of specific items and a three-stage probing process was developed as a guide for the interviewers (cf. Gordon 1975). First, they were to ask the general questions in a conversational manner, keeping to the specific wording in the schedule as closely as possible. The interviewers were taught techniques to encourage respondents to freely associate and freely express ideas not included on the interview schedule. During the responses, the interviewer referred to the checklist items for each question to make sure the subject area was being covered. The interviewer was trained to probe (without suggesting specific responses) on any of the responses if he felt more useful information could be obtained. Only when the respondent stopped speaking was the interviewer to proceed to the second stage, which was simply to ask if there was anything else the respondent wanted to talk about. Still at this stage, the interviewer was trained to avoid suggesting specific response categories. However, if a respondent said nothing or very little, the interviewer was not to resort quickly to the check list, but was rather instructed to use various techniques to encourage the respondent to speak freely. In the third stage, if the interviewer believed that more useful information could be obtained, he probed on any of the questions. His training emphasized the importance of and techniques for avoiding suggesting specific response categories, even as examples. When the respondent finished talking after a second probe, the interviewer asked about specific items on the check list which had not been covered or about which more information was desired. In this way respondents were encouraged to think in their own terms and to raise matters and topics of importance to them in the context of the general question. This made it possible to determine the salience of given material in the life of any individual. This questioning procedure was followed in all situations.

The training sessions were structured to accomplish three goals. First, they were to provide guidance to interviewers inexperienced in conducting focused, open-ended, in-depth interviews. Second, each interviewer was trained, by referring to the checklist, to keep track of topics mentioned by respondents during a long discourse. Third, after first allowing for spontaneous, free, unfettered responses, interviewers were trained to probe for more information. To a large extent these goals were achieved, but as indicated in discussion of the interview process below, some problems did arise with this kind of interviewing.

The Interviewing Process

The purpose of the study and the particular interview methodology were explained to each interviewer during the course of intensive training prior to going into the field. Each question on the proposed schedule was reviewed to make sure the interviewers understood its purpose and felt comfortable with it. Trainees had an opportunity to conduct practice interviews with one another and/or heroin users. These recorded interviews were then criticized by the project coordinators and the interviewers themselves. Various techniques were discussed to enhance the quality of the interview and the Interviewer's Guide was studied in preparation for entering the field.

Once interviewers were established in the community, and had located typical heroin users who had never been in treatment, and had convinced them to take an anonymous three-hour tape-recorded interview, interviewers had to arrange interview schedules and find places in the community where the respondents felt comfortable being interviewed. The interviews were conducted at all hours of the day and night. Except for a very few cases in which users either came to or agreed to be taken to the interviewer's neighborhood, all interviews were conducted on the users' turf. They took place in apartments, barber shops, fast-food places, restaurants, local public parks, playgrounds and recreation centers, and in cars. Occasionally, interviews were rushed or disrupted or even terminated before being finished, and some interviewees did not show at all. However, these situations were kept to a minimum, and the overall quality of the interviews was not adversely affected.

Once recorded, the interview schedule and tapes were sent immediately in preaddressed envelopes to Philadelphia to be transcribed, put on cards, and coded.

The field supervisors and the interviewers agree that the majority of the respondents were relaxed, willing to talk, and interested in participating in the interview. This is supported by the interviewers who concurred that the respondents did not consider the twenty dollars they received for an interview a significant amount of money for about three hours of interviewing. Respondents seemed to enjoy the interview and many thanked the interviewers at the end of the interview. Some even indicated that this chance to talk to someone about their heroin use was helpful.

The fact that respondents were willing to be interviewed did not of course preclude problems with the interviewing process. In addition to having to deal with common problems, such as background noises and interruptions (car motors, horns, telephones), tape-recorder malfunctions, safety considerations, and either excessively talkative or occasional "closed" respondents, at least four other problems emerged.

In some ways, the indigenous interviewers were too familiar with many aspects of the users' surroundings and lifestyles which the project was designed to investigate in more depth. As a result, despite the precautions given during the training and subsequent supervision sessions, interviewers sometimes neglected to probe more deeply or ask the meaning of some comments, events, or phraseology. This problem was not related to the amount of time allowed for the interview or to interviewers' probing skills, but rather stemmed from interviewers' assumptions that the project directors knew more than they did or, more likely, that they simply would not be interested in much of what the interviewers considered the trivia of everyday life.

A second, closely related problem, perhaps a more common one in open-ended, unstructured interviewing, does have to do with some inconsistency in probing skills. Monitoring and analysis of the tapes and transcripts show that the probing was uneven and sometimes incomplete, despite sufficient evidence that all the interviewers could probe skillfully. The fact that they did not always probe when it was appropriate to do so may be related to several factors: their rapport with specific types of respondents, their own lack of interest in the subject, their lack of awareness of the need to probe, their sensitivity to the respondents' concerns about being identified and revealing secrets, and time constraints. Whatever the reasons for the uneven probing, it does not follow that the probing was not effective. Indeed, it was. It is probably more accurate to say that too much was expected of the indigenous interviewers in their attempts to probe areas which most nonindigenous interviewers would hesitate to even broach.

The third problem relates to interview procedure and style. One of the first aspects requiring modification in the early weeks of monitoring the interviewers' completed tapes was the formal bureaucratic style and procedure-bound approach which characterized some interviewers. In their concern to do what they thought was expected of them, they were at times too formal in their interviewing style. The natural flow of communication, interest, and trust in the conversation was sometimes lost in the formal style of the initial interviews. The extent of this difficulty varied among interviewers, but all exhibited some tendency toward this style. Since considerable change in this style of interviewing was accomplished, it may be that the original stiffness was a means of coping with insecurity during the initial interviews.

This matter of style contributed to one last problem concerning the item checklists mentioned earlier. At times the interviewers used the checklist before they had exhausted their attempts to encourage the respondent to speak freely, without imposing any structure on him. This problem arose primarily in a few of the questions with long checklists (for example, the health questions, treatment entry questions) when, either after some attempt to encourage respondents to talk or occasionally before any such attempt, the interviewer would simply read through the list sequentially and accept a brief one- or two-word answer. Of all the problems encountered, this proved the most difficult one to alter. The interviewers' desire to cover everything, coupled with the presence of the long checklists, sometimes resulted in using a checklist too literally and too soon. Also, use of checklists increased when the interview got tough or simply when time was growing short.

Once again, as with the other problems mentioned above, this one applied to rather few questions and interviews and was less of a problem for some interviewers than others. Indeed, it may have contributed significantly to or even resulted from the probing difficulties described earlier.

Conclusions

In closing, it seems appropriate to raise one nagging question for the future: in a study attempting to use an ethnographic perspective, but not limiting itself to traditional ethnographic techniques and resources, should indigenous former participants or professionally trained ethnographers be used as interviewers? Of course, the advantages and disadvantages of each type of interviewer need to be weighed against the purposes of any study. This matter will not be explored here. However, experience in this project indicates that indigenous interviewers can be an invaluable resource.

But if they are to be used, considerable time must be devoted to training indigenous interviewers. It is extremely important that they have a genuine understanding of the purpose and nature of the overall plan to be used in carrying out ethnographic research. Particular attention should be given to the difficulty of getting indigenous interviewers to recognize and ask questions regarding the indigenous features of their interviewees' responses. This is not meant to be a criticism of indigenous interviewers, since it is well known that trained participant observers often experience similar problems when they become immersed in their study settings. Nevertheless, our experience in conducting the Heroin Lifestyle Study suggests that, in terms of time, energy, funding, and data quality, it is important to consider the costs involved in training indigenous interviewers versus nonindigenous but perhaps more experienced ethnographers. Resolution of this question has important implications for the planning and implementing of future, larger ethnographic research projects where the focus is on less accessible and unstudied subpopulation groups.

It is difficult to assess the full impact of the problems that were encountered on the entire body of data. Certainly, it would have been preferable to obtain far more information in some of the areas pursued. Also, in retrospect, we would have worded some questions differently, eliminated some questions, and added others. Finally, it would have been preferable to increase the length of interviewer training sessions and to give more attention in the training program to the purpose of the study and to interview techniques.

However, the monitoring procedures, internal validity checks, and the examination and analysis of the data clearly indicate that within the boundaries of the research design, the study successfully uncovered rich, in-depth, valid and accurate information on a range of topics in the life experiences of Black, inner-city heroin users, a hard-to-reach, infrequently studied population whose life experiences are customarily clouded in secrecy and mystery. Indeed, it may be that this research has been successful in identifying and obtaining information about a group of heroin users whose actual numbers are considerably underestimated and growing, and about whose attitudes and behavior rather little is known.

References

Agar, M. 1973. *Ripping and Running: A Formal Ethnography of Urban Heroin Addiction*. New York: Seminar Press.

Agar, Michael. 1976. One up, one down, even up: Some features of an ethnographic approach. *Addictive Disease: An International Journal* (4):619–626.

Akins, C., and Beschner, G. 1980. *Ethnography: A Research Tool for Policymakers in the Drug and Alcohol Fields*. Rockville, Maryland: National Institute on Drug Abuse, DHHS Publication No. (ADM) 80-946.

Bale, Richard N. 1979. The validity and reliability of self-reported data from heroin addicts: Mailed questionnaires compared with face-to-face interviews. *International Journal of the Addictions* 14 (7).

Ball, J.C. 1967. The reliability and validity of interview data obtained from 59 narcotic drug addicts. *American Journal of Sociology* 72(6):650–654.

Berger, Peter L., and Luckman, Thomas. 1967. *The Social Construction of Reality.* Garden City, New York: Doubleday.

Beschner, G.M., and Feldman, H.W. 1979. Angel Dust. Introduction in: *Angel Dust: An Ethnographic Study of PCP Users*, eds. Feldman, H.W.; Agar, M.H.; and Beschner, G.M. Lexington, Massachusetts: Lexington Books.

Bonito, M.S.; Nurco, David N.; and Shaffer, John W. 1976. The veridicality of addicts' self reports in social research. *International Journal of the Addictions* 11(5):719–724.

Bruyn, Seweryn T. 1966. *The Human Perspective in Sociology: The Methodology of Participant Observations.* Englewood Cliffs, New Jersey: Prentice Hall.

Espada, Frank. 1979. The drug abuse industry and the "minority" communities: Time for change. In *Handbook on Drug Abuse*, eds. Robert L. Dupont, Avram Goldstein, and John O'Donnel. Rockville, Maryland: National Institute on Drug Abuse.

Feldman, H.W. 1968. Ideological supports to becoming and remaining a heroin addict. *Journal of Health and Social Behavior* 9:131–139.

Feldman, Harvey W.; Agar, Michael H.; and Beschner, George M. 1979. *Angel Dust: An Ethnographic Study of PCP Users.* Lexington, Massachusetts: Lexington Books.

Glaser, Barry G. and Strauss, Onselm. 1967. *Discovery of Grounded Theory.* Garden City, New York: Doubleday.

Gordon, Raymond L. 1975. *Interviewing: Strategy, Techniques and Tactics.* Homewood, Illinois: The Dorsey Press.

Hughes, P.H.; Jarvis, G.R.; Khart, U.; Media-Mora, M.E.; Navaratnam, V.; Pshyachinda, V.; and Wadud, K.A. 1982. A rationale for identification of cases of drug abuse. *Bulletin on Narcotics* 34(2):1–15.

Lindesmith, A. 1947. *Opiate Addiction.* Bloomington, Indiana: Principia Press.

Moore, Joan; Garcia, Robert; and Salcido, Ramon. 1980. Research in minority communities: Collaborative and street ethnography models compared. In *Ethnography: A Research Tool for Policymakers in the Drug and Alcohol Fields*, eds. Akins, C. and Beschner, G. Rockville, Maryland: National Institute on Drug Abuse, DHHS Publication No. 46–63 (ADM) 80-946.

Myers, Vincent. 1979. Interaction in the research interview and drug related disclosures among respondents. *Journal of Drug Education* (2):105–117.

National Institute on Drug Abuse. 1981. *Statistical Series: Data from the Client Oriented Data Acquisition Process.* Rockville, Maryland: National Institute on Drug Abuse. DHHS Pub. No. (ADM) 81-1143.

Nurco, David N. 1981. Lifestyles of narcotic addicts and their pathways to treatment. Unpublished report. Rockville, Maryland: National Institute on Drug Abuse, Treatment Research and Assessment Branch.

O'Donnell, John A.; Voss, Harwin L.; Clayton, Richard R.; Slatin, Gerald T.; and Room, Robin G.W. 1976. *Young Men and Drugs—A Nationwide Survey*, Research Monograph No. 5. Rockville, Maryland: National Institute on Drug Abuse.

Preble, E., and Casey, J.H., Jr. 1969. Taking care of business—The heroin user's life on the street. *International Journal of the Addictions* 4:1–24.

Robins, L.N., and Murphy, George E., M.D. 1967. Drug use in a normal population of young negro men. *American Journal of Public Health* 57(9):1580–1596.

Robins, L.N. 1973. *The Vietnam Drug User Returns*. Washington, D.C.: U.S. Government Printing Office.

Robins, L.N.; Helzer, J.E.; and Davis, D.H. 1975. Narcotic use in Southeast Asia and afterwards: Interview study of 898 Vietnam returnees. *Archives of General Psychiatry* 32.

Spradley, James. 1979. *The Ethnographic Interview*. New York: Holt, Rinehart and Winston.

Stephens, R. 1972. The truthfulness of addict respondents in research projects. *International Journal of the Addictions* 7(3):549–558.

Sutter, A.G. 1966. The world of the righteous dope fiend. *Issues in Criminology* 2:177–222.

Waldorf, D., and Biernacki, P.L. 1979. Natural recovery from heroin addiction: A review of the incidence literature. *Journal of Drug Issues* 9(2):281–288.

Waldorf, D., and Biernacki, P.L. 1981. The natural recovery from opiate addiction: Some preliminary findings. *Journal of Drug Issues*, Winter, 11(1):61–74.

Waldorf, D. A brief history of illicit-drug ethnographers. 1980. In *Ethnography: A Research Tool for Policymakers in the Drug and Alcohol Fields*, eds. Akins, C. and Beschner, G. 21–35. Rockville, Maryland: National Institute on Drug Abuse, DHHS Publication No. (ADM) 80-946.

Weppner, Robert S. ed. 1977. *Street Ethnography: Selected Studies of Crime and Drug Use in Natural Settings*. Beverly Hills: Sage Publications.

Yancy, W.L. and Rainwater, L. 1970. Problems in the ethnography of the urban underclasses. In *Pathways to Data: Field Methods for Studying Ongoing Social Organizations*, ed. R.W. Haberstein. Chicago: Aldine.

Zinn, Maxine Baca. 1979. Field research in minority communities: Ethical, methodological, and political observations by an outsider. *Social Problems* 27(2): 209–219.

Index

About the Contributors

W.A. Brower, a graduate of Antioch College, conducts research in three areas—social issues, popular music and Afro-American culture. He has studied employment practices and discrimination in the public sector, public housing tenants, crime in public housing, and drug and alcohol programs in the District of Columbia. In the cultural sphere he has done extensive research and has published widely on popular music, with a particular emphasis on jazz.

Allen Fields, who holds a Ph.D. in sociology, is currently student affairs officer at the University of California, Santa Cruz. He was previously a senior research associate for Youth Environment Study, Inc. He completed an independent ethnographic study of young marijuana dealers in 1983 and has published the results.

Austin S. Iglehart is a public health scientist in the Treatment Research Branch of the National Institute on Drug Abuse. He has previously published on topics related to behavior disorders and drug abuse among foster care adolescents and the relationship between methadone maintenance dosage levels and program outcomes. He recently completed a study and published results on the impact of current policymaking decisions on clients and communities served by methadone clinics. Additionally, he has been evaluating the efficacy of both traditional and innovative therapies in the treatment of cocaine abusers.

Richard W. Morris, Ph.D., is a senior associate at University City Science Center, a research and development facility in downtown Philadelphia. He directs the Health Systems Planning and Research Division, specializing in the utilization of health care services by special populations (for example, drug users, minorities, older adults, and refugees) and in management consulting to alternative health care providers. Dr. Morris is also responsible for new program development in biomedicine, having recently managed a project to establish a regional facility providing specialized services in bioprocessing and pharmaceutical research. Dr. Morris maintains applied or research interests in biomedical entrepreneurship, health service management, cultural aspects of learning and literacy, social psychiatry, and technology management.

Andress Taylor holds a Ph.D. from the University of Pennsylvania. He established the School of Continuing Education at the University of the District of Columbia, the nation's first urban land-grant institution. A significant part of his work included the development of drug treatment and drug rehabilitation programs for inmates and ex-inmates of the District of Columbia Department of Corrections.

About the Editors

Bill Hanson holds a Ph.D. in sociology from Brown University and is currently an assistant professor of sociology at Mary Washington College in Fredericksburg, Va. Prior to this, he spent eight years teaching at California State College in Bakersfield. Before going to Mary Washington College in 1981, he spent a year at the National Institute on Drug Abuse as a public health analyst in the Treatment Research Branch. His responsibilities there included carrying out and monitoring research projects in the area of race and ethnicity and drug use, primarily heroin use. Since that time, he has continued to carry out research and consulting activities with NIDA. Much of this work and his publications have revolved around teaching and research interests in ethnographic research in the health and drug abuse fields.

George M. Beschner is the chief of the Treatment Research Branch, National Institute on Drug Abuse (NIDA). An official of NIDA since 1971, he has designed, implemented, and coordinated numerous research studies. Previously, he was on the faculty of the University of Maryland for three years. He directed community action programs in Washington, D.C. and Maryland from 1964 to 1967. Mr. Beschner began his career in the delinquency field with the New York City Youth Board, starting as gang worker in 1958 and ending as a borough director in 1964. He has received a BS degree in business administration (New York University) and completed his graduate studies in social work at Columbia University.

James M. Walters has degrees in anthropology from the University of Pennsylvania and social psychiatry from the Medical College of Pennsylvania where, in 1979, he also earned his doctorate in social science. He first encountered the world of heroin users while a police officer in Philadelphia. Since then he has served as director of social science research at the University City Science Center (a Philadelphia-based research institute) and as director of programs for the Citizens Crime Commission of Delaware Valley (also based in Philadelphia). A member of many professional organizations, he is a co-founder of the National Association for Ethnography and Social Policy and of the Pennsylvania Drug and Alcohol Abuse Prevention Consortium. A contributor to varied journals and edited volumes, he has written on the sociology and psychodynamics of police and their families, on the procedures and ethics of field work among deviant populations, and on substance abuse, especially among adolescents.

Elliott I. Bovelle is a professor of social work at the University of the District of Columbia. He is also the director of program development for Family and Medical Counseling Service, Inc., Washington, D.C., and is co-principal investigator of an adolescent heroin use study in the District of Colubmia. He received Bachelor of Science and Masters degrees at Columbia University. In addition, Dr. Bovelle obtained a doctorate from the Heller School for Advanced Studies in Social Welfare in 1980. He has had a distinguished career with the government, serving as the deputy director of the Peace Corps programs in Sierra Leone and West Africa, and as the chief of volunteer support in Washington, D.C. His professional career began in the delinquency field with the New York Youth Board from 1958 to 1965. Dr. Bovelle directed a national study on the utilization of former addicts employed in addiction programs for the Center of Human Services in Washington, D.C. He also conducted an ethnographic study of substance abuse and treatment programs. More recently, he undertook a study of the funding policies and practices of the National Institute on Alcohol and Alcohol Abuse.